THE UNIVERSITY OF KANSAS
Franklin D. Murphy Lecture Series

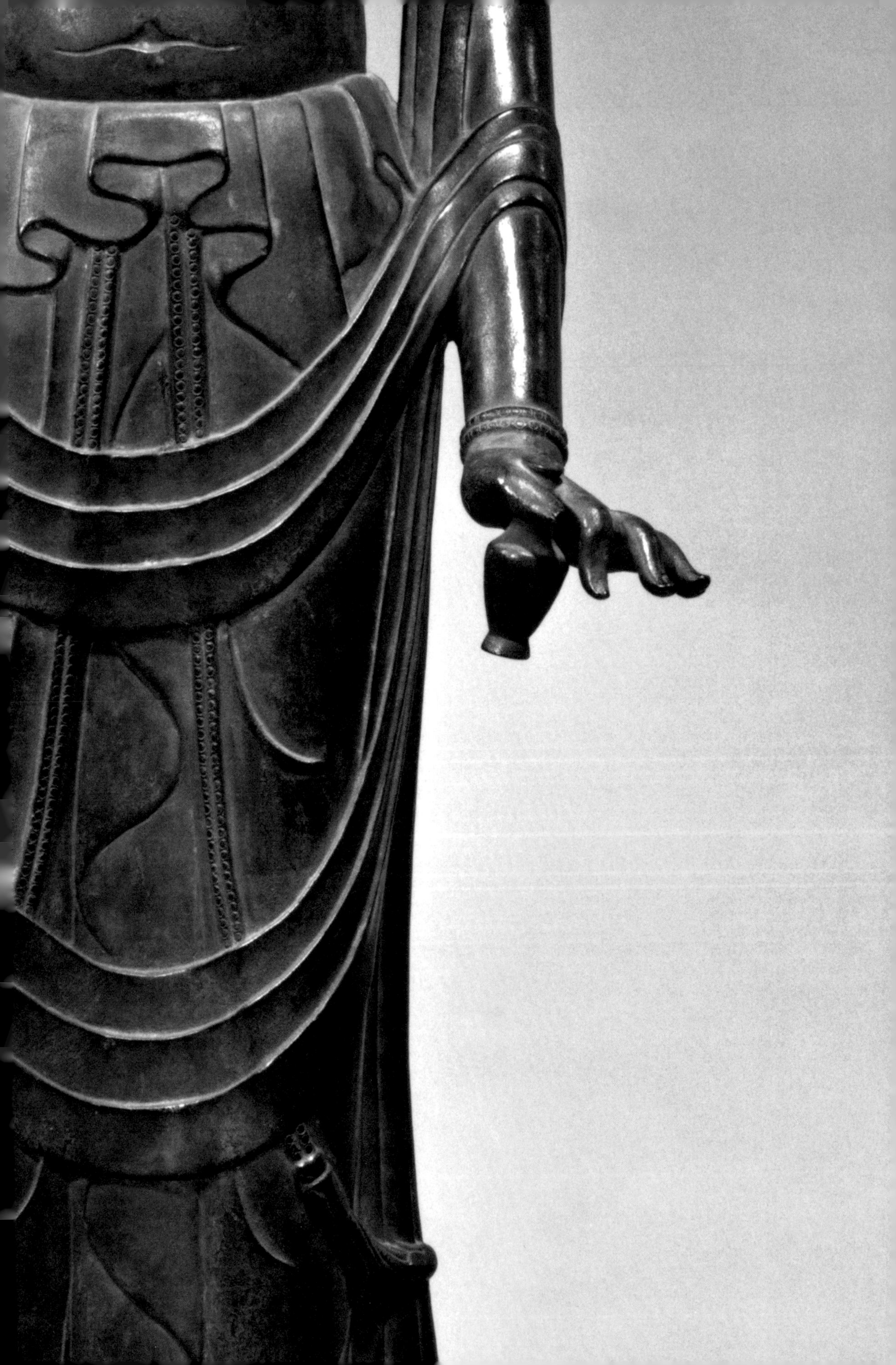

Hakuhō Sculpture

DONALD F. McCALLUM

SPENCER MUSEUM OF ART
The University of Kansas, Lawrence

in association with

UNIVERSITY OF WASHINGTON PRESS
Seattle and London

The Murphy Lecture Series is sponsored by the Spencer Museum of Art, the Kress Foundation Department of Art History at the University of Kansas, and the Nelson-Atkins Museum of Art. The lectureship was established in 1979 through the Kansas University Endowment Association in honor of former chancellor Dr. Franklin D. Murphy.

Published by the University of Washington Press
  for the University of Kansas Franklin D.
  Murphy Fund
Printed in the United States of America
Design by Thomas Eykemans
16 15 14 13 12   5 4 3 2 1

SPENCER MUSEUM OF ART
The University of Kansas
1301 Mississippi Street
Lawrence, KS 66045–7500 USA
www.spencerart.ku.edu

UNIVERSITY OF WASHINGTON PRESS
P.O. Box 50096
Seattle, WA 98145 USA
www.washington.edu/uwpress

LIBRARY OF CONGRESS
CATALOGING-IN-PUBLICATION DATA
McCallum, Donald F. (Donald Fredrick), 1939–
Hakuhō sculpture / Donald F. McCallum. — 1st ed.
    p. cm. — (The Franklin D. Murphy lecture series)
Includes bibliographical references and index.
ISBN 978-0-295-99130-6 (cloth : alk. paper)
1. Buddhist gilt bronzes—Japan.
2. Gilt bronzes, Japanese—to 794.
I. Title.
NK7984.A1M39 2012
730.952—dc23   2011030670

For Sumako, James, Sachiko, and Jackson

CONTENTS

PREFACE

To the best of my knowledge, this book is the first in any language devoted entirely to Hakuhō sculpture.[1] Even in the well-known Shibundō series, *Nihon no bijutsu* (Art of Japan), which at this writing has passed five hundred titles and which seems a likely venue for such a study, no such volume exists. True, in 1968 Uehara Shōichi published *Asuka-Hakuhō chōkoku* (The Sculpture of the Asuka and Hakuhō Periods), and nearly forty years later (2004) Matsuura Masaaki published *Asuka-Hakuhō no butsuzō* (Buddhist Sculpture of the Asuka and Hakuhō Periods),[2] but both of these distinguished scholars, like many others, consider the Hakuhō period only in conjunction with the Asuka period. This is the common view, in which Asuka and Hakuhō form a discrete unit preceding the magnificent accomplishments of the Nara period, often conceived as the "classic" phase of sculpture in Japan. I find the two periods to be so distinct in character that joint presentation risks a distortion of our understanding of the development of Buddhist sculpture during the seventh century in Japan. My purpose in this book is to assess the significance of the years circa 650–710 within the broader framework of Japanese art, not just as one component of its first couple of centuries.

Perhaps a word about the term "Hakuhō" would be appropriate here. Hakuhō ("White Phoenix") is beautiful in calligraphic form and in sound, as well as evocative of a majestic imaginary bird of good omen. The term first appears in the text of *Shoku nihongi* in an edict referring to the reign periods from Hakuhō to Suzaku.[3] Texts of the Heian (794–1185) and Kamakura (1185–1336) periods apply it as an era name (*nengō*) associated with the reign of Tenmu *tennō* (r. 672–686); however, there is no contemporaneous evidence for its use, making these later textual references unreliable. *Nihon shoki* (720) records a purported earlier era name, Hakuchi ("White Pheasant"), for the years 650–654, so some scholars have suggested an association between Hakuhō and Hakuchi. This might be so, but I doubt that era names were used that early.[4] When exactly era names did first appear in Japan is uncertain, but since this question is not directly relevant to the present study, we need not consider it. In essence, Hakuhō is a largely mythical term, having no specific historical correlative as far as can be determined; nevertheless, Hakuhō is so firmly embedded in the terminology of Japanese art history that it seems unlikely it could be eliminated. In any case, the appealing qualities of the term may argue for its retention.[5]

Most Hakuhō images are gilt-bronze, therefore I shall concentrate on sculpture in that material. I have somewhat reluctantly decided not to consider the few images in wood and clay at any length, but only to comment briefly on them here. By far the most important wood image is the Chūgūji Miroku, formerly considered to belong to the Asuka period, although now most scholars recognize it as Hakuhō. Two images at Hōrinji (Nara Prefecture, near Hōryūji), a Buddha and a bodhisattva, also are dated from the Hakuhō period.

The preceding three images all have many characteristics in common with Asuka sculpture, so excluding them from our discussion does not significantly modify our conclusions. On the other hand, there are a few wood images, such as the "Six Kannon" in the Hōryūji Museum, that clearly belong with Hakuhō sculpture, although they share so many traits with images of the "boyish" group of the early Hakuhō period that discussing them would not lead us to substantially different conclusions. A very large-scale clay representation of Miroku at Taimadera is often dated to 685, but I have strong doubts about this date, and so will not include it in this study. Of course, the most important group of clay images of the Hakuhō period is the *senbutsu* category, small plaques showing Buddhist deities in relief. In general they are quite different in character from the three-dimensional icons with which we are concerned.[6] Based on the preceding, a reader might legitimately suggest a modified title, such as "Gilt-bronze Sculpture of the Hakuhō Period," yet I propose to stick with my broader version, as I believe this study does characterize Hakuhō sculpture as a whole.

Another matter should be broached at the outset, since to a considerable extent it determines the nature of this study. I am speaking here of the search for prototypes and influences from China and the Korean peninsula for the sculpture of the Hakuhō period. Such searches to a high degree have dominated the study of seventh-century sculpture in the Japanese islands for the last few decades and have frequently achieved important results. Nevertheless, a too intense focus on continental and peninsular prototypes has somewhat skewed our understanding of Hakuhō sculpture by often ending the discussion of specific pieces or groups when it is thought that the "source" has been located. I should like carefully to consider specific pieces as individual efforts, not merely as the progeny of sculptures across the sea. To that end, I shall direct this study to the activities of artists active in the Japanese archipelago during the Hakuhō period.

In a recent essay Gregory Levine examines the epistemological status of Zen visual culture, laying out a spectrum ranging from the viewpoint that only a fully enlightened adept could possibly comprehend the true significance of, for example, a Zen figure painting, to a basically secular perspective in which such a painting is seen primarily in aesthetic terms.[7] Fierce battles have raged among advocates of these and other perspectives primarily because of, on the one hand, the importance of Zen practice and thought, and on the other, the general attractiveness and appeal of Zen art to large numbers of art lovers. Levine's brilliant analysis addresses a variety of important issues, as he traces many of the historiographical, theological, and aesthetic considerations underlying the interpretative strategies applied to Zen art.

Does this sort of analysis have any relevance for our study? Needless to say, Hakuhō sculpture has never been subjected to the intense debates associated with Zen art, and in fact the entire field of Japanese Buddhist sculpture has tended to avoid such controversy in most respects. That being acknowledged, we should still question the term "Hakuhō sculpture," striving to make clear from the start what we mean; perhaps enough has already been said about the word "Hakuhō," allowing us now to focus on "sculpture." Obviously, an ancient worshiper would in some sense recognize a three-dimensional image as a "sculpture," but just as obviously he or she would conceptualize it as an icon, imbued with the power of the deity to inspire and respond to devotion. Such icons range from the crude and ungainly to pieces of sublime beauty. The latter type is what interests me most here, although I shall also comment on lesser examples.

There is, of course, a direct relationship between sculpture/icon and viewer/worshiper, and this relationship, in my view, differs somewhat between "Hakuhō sculpture" and "Zen art" because the latter is built on very complex theological and cultural foundations, whereas Hakuhō sculpture would seem to evoke a simpler, more immediate devotional response. In contrast to the rather broad range of subjects in Zen figure painting, Hakuhō sculpture presents a pantheon that is limited to just a few deities. In the present study the most common icon is a standing representation of the bodhisattva Kannon. Although we may assume that most lay worshipers had a strong sense of Kannon's benevolence and beneficence, it is unlikely that this sense was grounded in deep theological or aesthetic reflections. How different from all the complexities mediating our various responses to a Zen painting![8]

A frequently discussed aspect of Kannon devotion is the believer's desire for the granting of wishes, extending from crass material benefits to hope for rebirth in paradise. To a person unaffiliated with Buddhism, such desires are certainly understandable. There is, however, an additional dimension in the encounter, religious or secular, with Kannon that should be considered; one that I assert is fundamental to the present book. As noted above, many Kannon images of the Hakuhō period are of great beauty, and beyond that aesthetic quality they generally manifest a profound sense of serenity, something that a sensitive viewer might recognize and perhaps even respond to empathetically. These qualities are partly the result of the diligent efforts of sculptors drawing on a long tradition of icon-making that extended back centuries into the past. Of course, the representational characteristics of an icon-type have a theological basis, but too exclusive a focus on theology inevitably minimizes the contribution of the sculptor.

The icon maker as artist is the central theme of this study. Clearly the Hakuhō images considered here were made as objects of religious devotion, but just as clearly most resulted from the intense efforts of individuals whom I see as artists. To call these men "artisans" or "craftsmen" is unobjectionable as long as no pejorative implications of inferior or lesser talent are implied. Their sculptures must have been expensive "luxury products" and as such would repay their consideration within an economic framework.

Some people may respond enthusiastically to Hakuhō sculptures because these images display qualities resulting from superior skills, adequate time for production, costly materials, and knowledge of prototypes. Additionally, Hakuhō sculpture is characterized by a freedom of expression and imaginative vitality that situates the finest pieces within the highest level of Japanese Buddhist sculpture. Yes, they are objects of pious religious devotion, but also and at the same time they potentially serve as objects of profound aesthetic contemplation.

ACKNOWLEDGMENTS

THIS BOOK IS A RESULT OF MANY YEARS of deep interest in the small gilt-bronze images of the Hakuhō period. The approach taken here may be seen by some as rather old-fashioned, but since my previous two books dealt primarily with religious, historical, and archaeological matters, I indulge myself here with aesthetics and style. Over the years, I have been able to see almost all of the images discussed, sometimes in museums, other times at temples. The culmination of this looking was the great exhibition at the Tokyo National Museum in 1987, where over two hundred sculptures were available at once, offering a unique opportunity to survey virtually the entire corpus.

To be nostalgic for a moment, those of us of a certain age will remember the old "Hōryūji Treasure Hall" on the grounds of the museum: it was somewhat primitive, open only on Thursdays—if it wasn't raining—and the "Forty-eight Buddhist Deities" that make up a substantial portion of this study were displayed with their backs to the wall, greatly limiting what one could see. In 1999 a lavish new treasure hall was erected, directly reflecting the boom years of the Japanese economy, now with the images displayed in a much more satisfactory manner and available for study and appreciation any day the museum is open.

While investigating various aspects of the sculpture of Japan I have had the opportunity to meet with most of the scholars in Japan specializing in this area, all of whom have been unfailingly helpful in facilitating my research. It is impossible to thank all of these scholars individually, but I would like to name a few who particularly assisted my studies: Asai Kazuharu, Ikawa Kazuko, Iwasa Mitsuhara, Kaneko Hiroaki, Kurata Bunsaku, Kuno Takeshi, Machida Kōichi, Matsuura Masaaki, Murata Seiko, Mōri Hisashi, Nishikawa Kyōtarō, Nishikawa Shinji, Shimizu Zenzō, Tanaka Yoshiyasu, and Uehara Shōichi.

The present book results largely from the Franklin Murphy seminar and lecture series presented at the University of Kansas in Spring 2003. This program offers an extraordinary opportunity to pursue a specific art historical topic with a group of interested graduate students and faculty. The enthusiastic student participants, Hillary Pedersen, Halle O'Neal, Amanda Wright, Matthew Scanlon, Chang Qing, Kyungwon Choe, Youmi Efurd, Derek Freeman, Eric McNeal, Soo Kim, Alison Miller, and Veronica de Jong, were lively in their comments and questions, teaching me more than I taught them. Professor Sherry Fowler invited me to come to Lawrence and made sure that my time there was both enjoyable and productive, for which kindness I offer my greatest appreciation. Professor Marsha Weidner was a constant presence in the seminar and, together with Professor Fowler, helped to lead the meetings in a stimulating and exciting manner. Members of the seminar will fondly recall our quasi-legal meeting when the twelve participants were divided into two groups of six, charged with the task of arguing the pros and cons concerning the authenticity of a well-known gilt-bronze sculpture recently purchased by a major museum. Each team was so effective in its presentation that one emerged totally convinced by the two presentations despite the fact that they both couldn't be correct! Other faculty and staff at the University of Kansas, as well as individuals at the Nelson-Atkins Museum of Art, contributed greatly to a most enjoyable stay.

Closer to home, colleagues at UCLA, as always, were most supportive, beginning with members of my own department, of other departments, and especially of the Terasaki Center for Japanese Study which funded most of the field work in Japan. A special word of appreciation to Professor Fred Notehelfer who for more than forty years has offered encouragement and who directed our Center in an exemplary manner for many years; his leadership is greatly missed. Mariko Bird, the assistant director, also was invariably helpful.

Several people read the manuscript at various stages including Sherry Fowler, Chari Pradel, Yoko Shirai, and Yui Suzuki— I have taken their comments and criticisms into account and I am responsible for any remaining errors. In the mid 1970s I carried on a long-distance debate with Mimi Yiengpruksawan about Hakuhō sculpture while she was in Sendai; this exchange did much to sharpen my ideas about the topic and although she may not agree with much in this book I would still like to thank her for engaging in this dialogue.

At an early stage Naomi Noble Richard edited the text with her usual tact and diligence, and I join others in the field in thanking her for her wonderful efforts. At the University of Washington Press I was assisted by Pat Soden, Jacqueline Ettinger, Marilyn Trueblood, Judith Singsen, and Kathleen Pike Jones. Without any coaching from me, the designer, Thomas Eykemans, came up with the striking jacket design.

My wife, Toshiko, was ever ready with a smile, even when there wasn't that much to

smile about; my son, Kenneth, and daugh-
ter-in-law, Takayo, frequently welcomed me
to their home in Tokyo and made my stays
there particularly memorable; and finally
the dedicatees of this volume, my daughter,
Sumako, son-in-law, James, and our two
wonderful grandchildren, Ella Sachiko and
Jackson James Turner, have added much
joy and pleasure to my life. To my whole
family and to my many friends I would like
to express my deepest appreciation for their
love and support over the years.

HAKUHŌ SCULPTURE

Introduction

THIS STUDY DIRECTS THE READER'S ATTENTION TO A VERY SUB-
stantial number of superb Buddhist images, most of which may confidently be placed within the Hakuhō period, here defined as the years
circa 650–710. Even within the extraordinary riches found in the
broader tradition of sculpture in Japan, the corpus from this brief sixty-
year span, especially the small gilt-bronze icons, is impressive. I believe
that a study limited to a single medium such as sculpture and carried out from a stylistic perspective is viable today. I hope to convince skeptical readers that this may be a fruitful methodology *if* applied to a carefully defined, discrete category of objects.[1] Consequently, technical matters and iconography are of only limited relevance here. I shall focus instead on stylistic expression in particular and larger aesthetic questions in general. I am taking this approach fully aware that I tread an unpopular path, one avoided by many art historians today. Nevertheless, it is undoubtedly best to be explicit about my approach at the outset in order to avoid subsequent misunderstanding.

We should perhaps first ask ourselves why so many gilt-bronze images survive from the Hakuhō period, particularly in comparison with the preceding and follow-ing eras. Earlier, during the Asuka period (circa 590–650), the Buddhist religion clearly had not yet developed in Japan to the degree that large-scale production of icons was necessary. From the following Nara period (710–784/94) a few small gilt-bronze images survive, but substantially fewer than larger images made in clay, lacquer, wood, or bronze, most of them intended for important temples. The concentrated production of small gilt-bronze icons is unique to the Hakuhō period.

Early bronze sculptures were made using the lost-wax technique, allowing no possibility of multiple copies of the same image emerging from a single mold. Each image is a unique object, and even those closely similar must be understood as freehand copies rather than mechanical reproductions.[2]

In an earlier study I considered the determinants associated with the commissioning and production of icons, including selection of iconography and questions of size and cost.[3] The process remains obscure, but one can assume that studios possessed models or sketches from which the patron could make a choice. Certainly, the great variety observable within the corpus of Hakuhō gilt-bronze images indicates considerable freedom in production, suggesting that the sculptors were free to innovate, at least within certain parameters.

One exceedingly vexing problem lurking in the background of this study must be addressed at the outset: the question of what can be known about the iconographical and stylistic decisions of individual sculptors working in a time and culture far removed from our own, especially when little or no documentary evidence is available. Although many scholars quite reasonably eschew this topic, seeing it as basically unknowable, I work on the assumption that certain images or groups of images do seem to reveal signs of their makers' individual design decisions.[4]

PROTOTYPES: CHINA AND KOREA

Prerequisite to an understanding of the origins of Buddhist sculpture in Japan, and especially of its development during the earlier phases, is a grasp of the contemporary conditions in China and on the Korean peninsula. The popularity of small gilt-bronze icons in China from the Six Dynasties period through the Sui and Tang dynasties must have been a determinant of the prominence of such icons in sixth- and seventh-century Korea and Japan. Being easily transportable, Chinese icons would have greatly influenced the initial stages of Buddhist worship and the production of icons both on the Korean peninsula and in Japan. The Hakuhō-period predilection for bronze images significantly echoes that of contemporary China, where a distinguished metallurgical tradition dating from the Shang and Zhou periods was already available for the making of icons when Buddhism appeared on the scene.[5]

Although I do not intend to devote space to the search for prototypes in China and Korea, one topic must at least be broached: the impact of Sui-dynasty styles on Hakuhō sculpture. Traditionally, the study of Asuka and Hakuhō art and, to a lesser degree, the art of the Nara period, has been plagued by what I refer to as the "gap theory." Thus, it is asserted that the sculpture of the Asuka period was based on the styles of Northern and Eastern Wei and Liang of almost one hundred years earlier, and, similarly, that early Hakuhō was derived from Northern Qi and Northern Zhou, also of approximately a century before.[6] As precursors of Hakuhō images, both the Sui and early Tang styles also are usually mentioned, but what is not fully analyzed is just exactly how Northern Qi and Northern Zhou could have impacted the Japanese islands from the chronologically unlikely remove of about seventy or a hundred years. In my view, Northern Qi, Northern Zhou, and Chen styles probably never had any direct effect on Hakuhō; rather, the sculptors of the Sui dynasty combined features of the prior sixth-century modes, melding these into synthetic styles that were probably dominant in China from the end of the sixth until the middle of the seventh centuries. These styles were transmitted to the Three Kingdoms and early Unified Silla stylistic complexes, there to be modified to some extent by sculptors on the Korean peninsula. This transmission would have occurred during much of the seventh century and certainly during its middle decades.[7]

The early phases of Buddhism on the Korean peninsula, in the kingdoms of Koguryo, Paekche, and Silla, were characterized by quite modest religious establishments and equipment, especially when contrasted with what already existed in China. Small gilt-bronze icons were ideally suited for the environment they entered in sixth-century Korea and later in Japan, for, as noted, such icons were easily portable and could serve as models for replication. Only later were many large temples established, these holding life- or over-life-size icons to serve as impressive centers for state-sponsored worship. In much scholarship devoted to Three Kingdoms' sculpture, especially by Korean specialists, a major concern is determining which of the kingdoms produced a specific monument. This question need not trouble us here, but it is important to note that for sculptors of the Asuka period, Paekche was the likeliest source of prototypes, whereas the new styles developed by Hakuhō sculptors circa 650–700 were profoundly influenced by the later phases of Paekche and Silla, as well as by the first decades of Unified Silla. If this scenario is correct, there was no "gap," but rather the smooth transmission of Chinese styles to the Korean peninsula and thence to the Japanese islands.[8]

ASUKA SCULPTURE

Although the beginning of Buddhism and Buddhist sculpture in the Japanese islands is obscure, some documentary and material evidence exists that allows us to sketch out a basic picture.[9] Travelers to the Korean peninsula and to China must have seen Buddhist temples and activities by the fifth century at the latest, but not until the sixth century do traces of the new religion appear on the islands. A number of entries in *Nihon shoki* (720) provide information as to the early stages of Buddhism, some of it reliable, some legendary. Of the more reliable, the famous story of King Song of Paekche offering a Buddhist icon and ritual implements to "emperor" Kinmei has long served as a marker for the initial stage of the religion in Japan, at least from an official perspective.[10] In this scheme, the Asuka period is dated 538/552–645, the terminal date marked by the so-called Taika Reform; but because this book does not focus on the Asuka period, its exact years are not especially relevant. Even so, I prefer a beginning at circa 590 (with the founding of Asukadera by Soga no Umako, d. 626) and an end at circa 650 (the approximate year when the Soga clan fell from power).

Buddhism was practiced and icons were used in worship prior to circa 590, but primarily by individuals from the Korean peninsula. These people, typically referred to as "immigrants" (*kikajin* or *tōraijin*), would have brought the religion from their homelands on the peninsula and with it, undoubtedly, portable Buddhist icons.[11] In my essay "Earliest Buddhist Statues in Japan," I provided a detailed analysis of what I take to be the most significant early icons in Japan, concluding that they were probably made on the Korean peninsula and in that respect are best conceptualized as "pre-Asuka."

The true beginnings of Japanese production of Buddhist monuments might best be associated with the activities of the Soga clan, particularly their erection of a clan temple, Asukadera.[12] From this date onward the Buddhist religion with its accompanying temples and icons very gradually spread out among the aristocracy and other elite groups; I make this point here since there has been a tendency to assume that Buddhism was more widely diffused during the early periods than I think likely.

Important Buddhist icons of the Asuka period that are more or less closely related stylistically are invariably referred to as the "Tori group" or the "Tori style." Some of the crucial monuments of that style are the "Great Buddha" of Asukadera; several images at Hōryūji, including the Shaka triad in the Golden Hall, the Yumedono Kannon, and a Buddha triad, dated to 628, in the Hōryūji Museum; as well as a few images in the "Forty-eight Buddhist Deities group," now housed in a special building at the Tokyo National Museum.[13] Although this may not seem a large corpus, it does, in fact, account for the majority of extant Asuka icons and certainly must be considered the mainstream of early Japanese sculpture. Most important is the generally uniform style observable in these monuments, attesting their derivation from one specific current, even though significant variations can be seen within the group. Although most scholars maintain that this evident stylistic consistency results from the work of one sculptor, "Tori-busshi," and his assistants, I believe that Tori, as the leader of the important "saddle-makers guild" (*kuratsukuri be*), was most likely a supervisor rather than a hands-on sculptor.[14] Consequently, one of his major tasks must have been to recruit sculptors from the Korean peninsula to make icons as required, thus explaining much of the variety seen within the corpus.

In studying the monuments cited above, several distinct patterns become apparent. A triad consisting of a seated Buddha flanked by standing bodhisattvas appears to have been the basic iconographical type. Although this triad format is based on Korean prototypes, among extant triads of the Three Kingdoms period the most common type has all three figures in standing pose.[15] I would suggest that the Soga clan received a Shaka triad of the "seated Buddha/standing bodhisattvas" type, which became the standard model for Asuka triads. In addition, I think it likely that the Soga also received an independent standing bodhisattva, which came to serve as a model for similar icons during the Asuka period. All of the Buddha figures in this group wear heavy drapery with precisely articulated folds: especially characteristic is the drapery overhang. The emphasis is on frontality, and the images possess a dignified, rather remote demeanor. The bodhisattvas, both in a triad and as independent icons, are closely related to each other in style and motif. All wear prominent mountain-shaped crowns and very similar drapery arrangements. As with the Buddha figures, their robes permit only a limited sense of bodily forms.

Apparently because the Soga leaders wielded great political power, the specific icon types they favored seem to have become canonical, so that when other images were needed they were usually made in this mode. The Soga, as the dominant patronage group, strongly influenced the early stages of the production of Buddhist sculpture in Japan. That there were several studios during this early phase seems unlikely, and I believe the available data are best interpreted by postulating only *one* important studio, that headed by Tori. I propose to label this studio's output the "Soga-Tori" style, thereby acknowledging the contributions of patronage group as well as supervisor.

Two icons in the Hōryūji Museum characterize the overall category in general terms.[16] A Shaka triad (fig. 1), dated to 628 and apparently made to enhance the postmortem prospects of Soga no Umako, displays the common stylistic traits mentioned above, especially the strongly frontal, rather hieratic appearance. At the same time, it manifests its own particularity: for example, the Buddha figure is taller and more slender than in other triads, such as those in Asukadera or the Hōryūji Golden Hall.[17] Additionally, certain details in the handling of the drapery folds are in some respects dissimilar to other members of the group. A standing bodhisattva in the Hōryūji Museum (figs. 2a, b) serves as a typical Asuka bodhisattva, and apart from the difference in iconography it also shares many traits with the Buddha figures: relatively squat proportions, heavy drapery, and a masklike face. Its large crown, necklace and other jewelry, and costume format of skirt (*dhoti*), undergarment visible at the chest (*sōgishi*), and a very long and prominent scarf are characteristic iconographical features of all bodhisattva images.[18] More specifically Asuka elements in the present sculpture include the arrangement of the scarf as it crosses over in front of the legs in an X pattern with the two ends that loop over the arms and descend in fish-tail folds. The icon clasps a large "wish-granting jewel" held chest-high. This element will be discussed in detail later, while here it

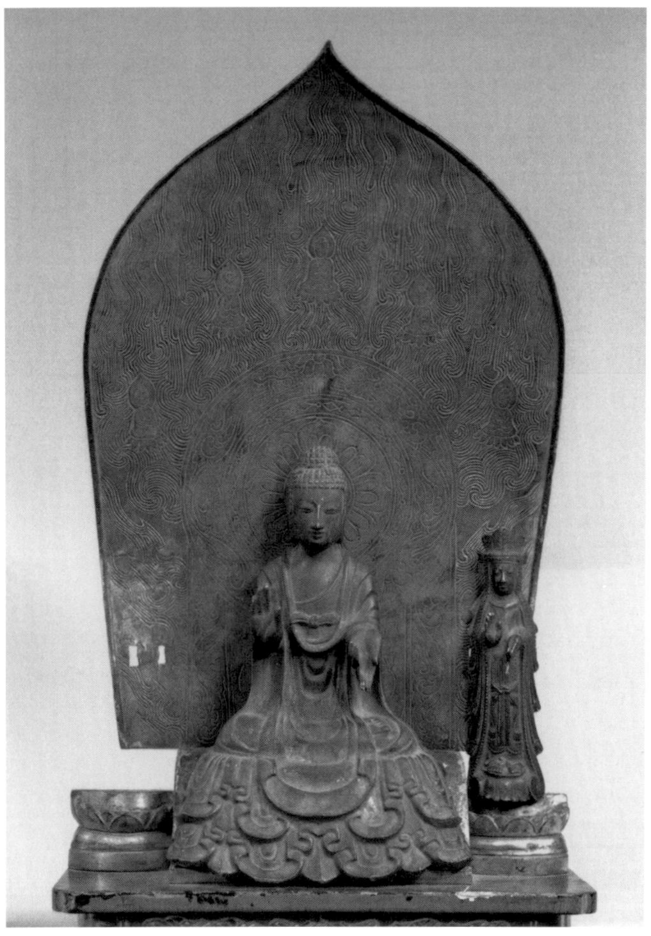

1   Shaka Triad (628 CE), H: Buddha 16.7 cm. Hōryūji Museum
     Photo courtesy of Tokyo National Museum (hereafter TNM)

is noted only that the arrangement of the scarf in back is normally quite unusual in standing bodhisattvas.

Along with the dominant Soga-Tori style, other currents were present during the Asuka period. Among the latter are two especially important monuments that perhaps reflect the styles of south China: the Kudara Kannon housed in the Hōryūji Museum and the Four Heavenly Guardians (Shitennō) of the Hōryūji Golden Hall.[19] Another image in a non-Soga-Tori style is a meditating bodhisattva, presumably Miroku (Sks. Maitreya), at Kōryūji in Kyoto.[20] Like the Kudara Kannon and the Shitennō, Kōryūji's Miroku is not made of bronze but of wood; unlike them, it is apparently not polychromed. Needless to say, its most salient characteristic is its remarkable similarity to the great meditating bodhisattva now housed in the National Museum of Korea, Seoul.[21]

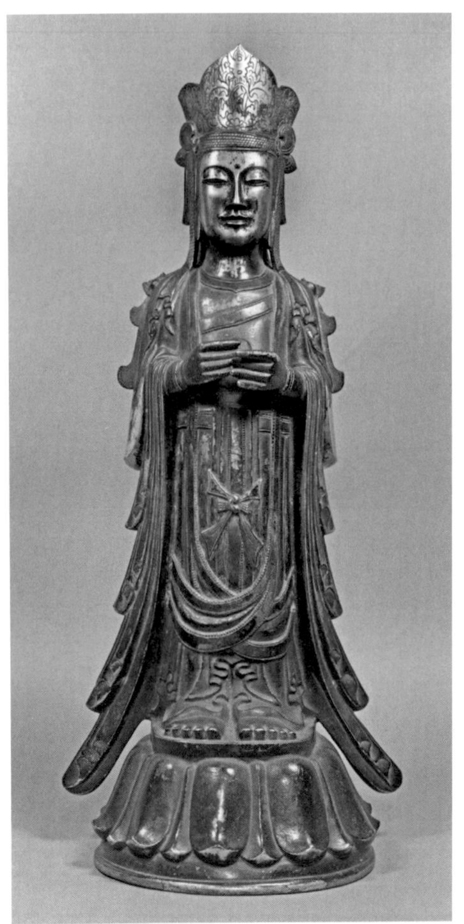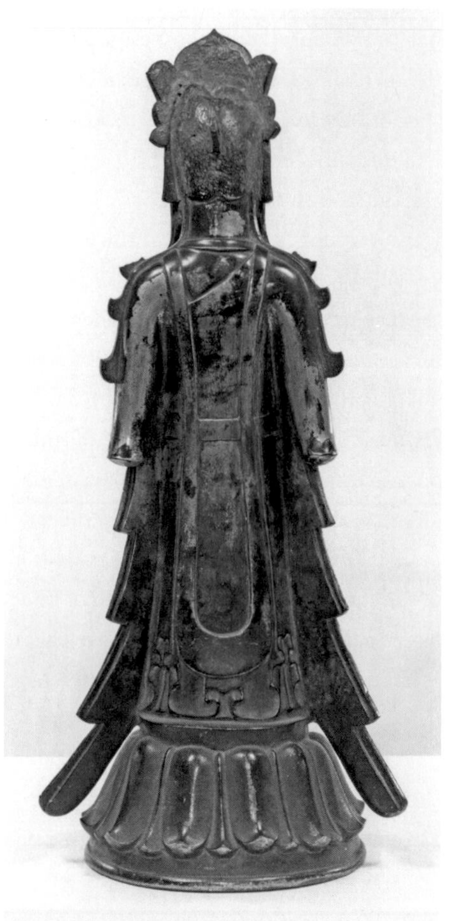

2   Standing Bosatsu, H: 56.7 cm. Hōryūji Museum   a. front   b. back
Photo courtesy of Nara National Museum (hereafter NNM)

Although brief, this discussion of Asuka sculpture does provide certain prerequisites to a consideration of Hakuhō sculpture: first, familiarity with the deity types that will be most common in Hakuhō sculpture—a Buddha triad, an independent standing bodhisattva, and a meditating bodhisattva; and second, a summary of Asuka styles that forms the basis for analyzing developments in Hakuhō sculpture.

HISTORICAL AND RELIGIOUS CONTEXTS OF HAKUHŌ SCULPTURE

A general characterization has been presented of the Asuka period, the time of the the Soga clan's greatest power, marked in visual culture by the building of Asukadera and by the development of what I call the Soga-Tori style in sculpture. The fourth decade of the seventh century saw the reign of Jomei (r. 629-641), a notably uneventful period with the exception of the vowing by Jomei (and presumably the start of construction) of Kudara Ōdera, the first Buddhist temple that can be directly associated with the royal family.[22] Jomei was succeeded by his widow, Princess Takara, who first ruled as Kōgyoku. As was the case several decades earlier, when Suiko succeeded at the death of Sushun, Princess Takara probably took the throne because the most likely heir, Prince Naka, was then only sixteen. Her first reign (642–645), although short, was filled with significant political events, especially the assassination of the entire family of Prince Shōtoku by a leader of the Soga clan in 643. Revenge was essential, and Prince Naka in turn murdered the assassin, Soga no Iruka, in 645. The day after this event Kōgyoku abdicated and was succeeded by her brother, Prince Karu, who reigned as Kōtoku (r. 645–654).[23]

What was clearly a coup is characterized in traditional historiography as the "Taika Reform" (*Taika no kaishin*), which was seen to place the Yamato state among the more developed polities of East Asia. Evidently, a significant transition in politics occurred toward the end of the second quarter of the seventh century, when the main line of the Soga clan, dominant for at least one hundred years, fell from power. Although innovative in their ascendance, the Soga seem to have become increasingly conservative, certainly out of touch with important developments taking place in China during the first decades of the Tang dynasty.[24]

Kōtoku transferred the capital to Naniwa (present-day Osaka), where he built what is believed to be the first full-scale palace in Japan. In recounting the beginning of Kōtoku's reign, *Nihon shoki* offers a full account of the development of Buddhism. Importantly, this is related entirely in the context of Soga activities, particularly those of Soga no Iname (d. 570) and Soga no Umako. In conformity with imperialist ideology, *Nihon shoki* portrays the Soga leaders as always responding to the "commands" of the monarchs.[25]

Upon Kōtoku's death in 654, Princess Takara began her second reign (r. 654–661), taking the name Saimei. One of her first acts was to move the capital back to Asuka, where she commissioned many construction projects.[26] From the middle of the seventh century the Korean peninsula was in turmoil. The Three Kingdoms—Koguryo, Paekche, and Silla—existed in a state of shifting alliances and chronic war with one another, and on five separate occasions Tang emperors sent armies into the peninsula, nominally in aid of one or another contending state but actually to impose Chinese control. At the point when a Tang-Silla alliance (which had already destroyed Koguryo) threatened Paekche, the Yamato government sent troops to assist its ally on the peninsula, but in the end Saimei's forces were defeated and Paekche fell. Many of the leaders of Paekche fled to Japan,[27] which may have contributed to the arrival of new forms of Buddhist art in the islands during the 660s.

Saimei died in 661, and although it might be expected that Prince Naka would thereupon have ascended the throne, in fact it was some years before he did so. Many theories have been presented to explain this. The most likely suggests that he was building up Yamato's defenses, such as by constructing forts, something that might have been harder to supervise if he was actually the monarch. These efforts culminated in another transfer of the capital, this time to Ōtsu on the shore of Lake Biwa, an area presumably more easily defended than either Naniwa or Asuka. Finally, in 668, Prince Naka became monarch, reigning as Tenji. Although he wished his son Prince Ōtomo to succeed, Tenji's brother Prince Ōama defeated Ōtomo in a civil war called the Jinshin Disturbance (*Jinshin no ran*), and reigned as Emperor Tenmu (672–686). One of Tenmu's first acts was to transfer the capital back to Asuka.[28]

The Jinshin Disturbance was a crucial event in Japan's later seventh-century history, since the accession of Tenmu led to far-reaching changes in the political world, most importantly an increasingly centralized government. In addition to the documentary evidence, important material remains point to that ambitious project. From the Buddhist perspective the last of the Four Great Temples, Yakushiji, was vowed by Tenmu in 680 as a prayer for the recovery from illness of his consort, Princess Uno.[29] The most significant architectural campaign, however, was the construction of a vast new capital, Fujiwarakyō. Although only occupied from 694 to 710, I believe that planning for it began soon after Tenmu returned to Asuka in a major effort to bring Yamato up to par with its rivals on the continent.[30]

Buddhism made great strides during Tenmu's reign. For example, in 673 came an imperial order accompanied by an imperial donation to copy the entire Buddhist canon at Kawaradera, the temple generally believed to have been dedicated to the memory of Tenmu's mother, Saimei.[31] Also in that year the second of the Four Great Temples, Kudara Ōdera, was moved by imperial order from its original site to a place nearer the court and renamed first Takechi Ōdera and then, in 676, Daikandaiji.[32] This is not the entire story for 673, however, since in addition to supporting Buddhist institutions, Tenmu and his court also took action to control them, particularly the clergy, by appointing various supervisors.[33]

Considerable political activity regarding Buddhism is also recorded for 679: the regulation of temples and the assigning of proper Buddhist names to them; stipulation of the appropriate garb and attendants for monks and nuns; and rules for the care of sick clergy.[34] An important edict of 680 was related to the court supervision of temples, especially the great national temples.[35] By the early 680s the court, now organized more efficiently, was exercising broad authority over Buddhist individuals and institutions.

For the present study, by far the most important edict is one of 685, toward the end of Tenmu's reign, which reads:

Orders were sent to all the provinces (*kuniguni*) that in every House (*ie goto*) a Buddhist shrine (*bussha*) should be provided and an image of Buddha with Buddhist scriptures be placed therein. Worship was to be paid and offerings of food made at these shrines.[36]

Various theories, extending back to medieval times, have been advanced concerning the exact meaning of this edict. There is general agreement that although the term *kuniguni* is inclusive, it was most particularly directed to provinces outside the capital region. The terms *ie goto* and *bussha*, however, continue to be debated. With regard to the former, the variety of interpretations includes "everybody's house," "provincial headquarters," and "the houses of the provincial elite." The first alternative was advocated by Kokan Shiren (1278–1346), by Motoori Norinaga (1730–1801), and more recently by Ienaga Saburō,[37] but it seems very unlikely, given the social and economic status of ordinary people during the Hakuhō period. That the term referred to "provincial headquarters" is more plausible; Joan Piggott renders *ie goto* as "government office," and some Japanese scholars have offered variations of this interpretation.[38] At present, though, few scholars accept this possibility. In the generally accepted interpretation, *ie goto* referred primarily to the residences of the great provincial families (*chihō gōzoku*). Subsequently, most provincial and county headquarters were placed at or in the immediate vicinity of the *gōzoku*; nevertheless, it is probably best to avoid the term "provincial headquarters," inasmuch as it suggests a strong central government presence at a very early date.

Much of Japanese literature maintains that the term *bussha* means "temple," which would imply icons larger than the small gilt-bronzes to be discussed in this book. I submit that *bussha* can more reasonably be seen as referring to the type of shrine box (*zushi*) that held small icons.

Central to discussions of the 685 edict is the large number of temple sites that can be dated to the Hakuhō period. The medieval text *Fusō ryakki* states in an entry of 692 that there were 545 temples in the country at that time; initial skepticism about the veracity of this entry must give way before recent archaeological research, which has located between 550 and 600 temples of Asuka and Hakuhō date, the vast majority of which fall within the Hakuhō period.[39] On the basis of these discoveries, some scholars have argued that the 685 edict motivated this extensive construction of temples. For example, the distinguished authority on early Buddhism Tamura Enchō conceptualizes the transition from Asuka to Hakuhō as a movement from "Clan Buddhism" (*shizoku bukkyō*) to "State Buddhism" (*kokka bukkyō*), and he asserts that under "State Buddhism" the central government assisted the great provincial families in the building of temples.[40] In his explanation, Tamura refers back to the 594 edict of the monarch Suiko, which states that nobles competed with one another to build *bussha*. Significant to his argument is the following statement, "*bussha* are called temples (*tera*)."[41] I remain skeptical about the participation of Suiko in Buddhist activities, but in any case it seems unlikely that there were many nobles competing to build temples in 594, when work was just commencing on Asukadera. Consequently, I place little weight on the equation *bussha=tera*.

Yoshida Kazuhiko argues vigorously—and convincingly, in my view—against Tamura's hypothesis.[42] Yoshida recognizes the early formation of "State Buddhism" in the capital at about this time and the concomitant erection of temples, but he also demonstrates that the situation in the provinces was far more complex than Tamura allows. In particular, Yoshida points out that the central government had neither the power nor the authority to order the building of temples throughout the country; he further indicates that many of the provincial temples were constructed prior to 685 and thus could not have been built in response to the edict. As he shows, the great provincial families themselves were responsible for the enormous number of temples constructed during the Hakuhō period. Yoshida cites examples of this from *Nihon reiiki* and *Izumo fudōki* and further points out that there is absolutely no documentary evidence that the central government supported or guided this temple-building activity.[43]

Kuno Takeshi is convinced that the term *bussha* does not denote a large structure, such as a clan temple (*uji dera*), but rather refers to a Buddha shrine within a private residence, presumably similar to those seen in Japanese homes today.[44] This sort of shrine could not contain a large-scale icon, so Kuno also argues that such shrines originally held the very numerous small, gilt-bronze icons extant today. In addition to the distribution of small icons in the provinces, Kuno has noted that most Hakuhō images from the central region are clustered in Asuka and Fujiwara temples and at Hōryūji,[45] while very few are found in the great eighth-century Nara temples, suggesting that by this time small images were not popular.

This somewhat lengthy digression is, in fact, essential in establishing a context for the icons to be discussed in the present study. We need not doubt that Buddhist practice became widely diffused during the Hakuhō period, at least among the elite, but, as Yoshida has indicated, some counties held many temples and others none, certainly suggesting that there was no one-to-one correspondence of temples and county offices. This being the case, I suggest that the small gilt-bronze images so ubiquitous during the Hakuhō period were intended primarily for private worship within the households of the great provincial families and the capital aristocracy

On balance, I tend toward the hypotheses that "*ie goto*" refers to the residences of the provincial elite and that "*bussha*" is best understood as indicating household shrines. Two critical inferences support these hypotheses: first, by 685 the central government was extending its influence out to the provinces, and Buddhist icons and practice would have seemed an effective means to unify the state; and second, as mentioned above, the numerous small gilt-bronze statues spread throughout Japan, mostly of Hakuhō date, are best understood as having been used in private shrines, not in temples, which would normally require a larger icon.

Kuno and many other scholars believe that an edict of 691 promulgated by Jitō *tennō* directly relates to the 685 edict already discussed.[46] Princess Uno, consort of Tenmu, seems to have enthusiastically shared her husband's plans, and at his death, since there was no suitable male heir, she succeeded to the monarchy as Empress Jitō (r. 686–697). Tenmu and Jitō had planned to have their son, Prince Kusakabe, succeed Tenmu as monarch, but the prince's early death only two years after his father necessitated a change of plans. Although Jitō abdicated in 697, evidently she was a power behind the throne until her own death in 702.

Jitō's edict of 691 asserted her very strong support of Buddhism:

The Empress addressed a decree to the Ministers (*maetsukimi*) saying: "In the reigns of the former Emperor you erected Buddhist Halls (*butsuden*)[47] and Scripture Treasuries, and practised the six monthly fasts. The Emperor from time to time sent officials (*ōtoneri*) to inquire about circumstances, and the same has also been done in Our own reign. Let us therefore with zealous hearts continue to uphold the Buddhist faith."[48]

Although earlier sections of *Nihon shoki* must be read with caution, by the time of this entry the text is quite reliable, so there is no particular reason to doubt Jitō's support of Buddhism expressed here. Moreover, the edict indicates a quite well-developed system of institutional support of the religion. I assume that "former Emperor" and the "Emperor" in the next sentence are both singular, believing that the title does not refer to a group of Jitō's predecessors, but only to her own husband, Tenmu, although conceivably the references to "Emperor" could be plural. Jitō, unlike her husband, was cremated and her remains placed in an urn next to the coffin of Tenmu, which may give a clue to her personal faith.[49]

Jitō's successor, Prince Karu, who ruled as Emperor Monmu (r. 697–707), was the son of Kusakabe and Princess Abe, a daughter of Tenji by a Soga consort, Mei no Iratsume. Only fourteen years old when he acceded, one assumes he was primarily a figurehead until the death of his grandmother in 702. Upon Monmu's early death a familiar situation arose. Who should be the next monarch? Again a well-established practice was evoked, and Princess Abe now ascended the throne in place of her deceased son, ruling as Genmei (r. 707–715). During her reign the court abandoned the Fujiwara capital and in 710 moved to a new capital, Heijōkyō (present-day Nara City). This development takes place at a time beyond the scope of this book.

Early Hakuhō Sculpture

INITIALLY, THE MAIN QUESTIONS ARE WHEN, WHY, AND HOW THE previously dominant Asuka style disappeared and totally new stylistic currents came into fashion. A fundamental postulate of art-historical study asserts that there is practically never a one-to-one correspondence between sociopolitical changes and those in art. A new "period" does not imply a new "style." Notwithstanding, profound transfers of power and changes in government occurring at the middle of the seventh century clearly appear to have had a strong impact on the production of sculptural icons after about 650. The fall of the main line of the Soga clan and the rise of a new elite significantly altered the political, religious, and cultural environment within which Buddhist images were made and employed. The style that I have labeled "Soga-Tori" was intimately related to the patronage of the Soga clan and its allies and supporters, so that with their loss of power their tastes no longer dominated the production of icons. That is not to say that Soga-Tori elements do not appear after 650, only that the earlier style was no longer dominant. Certainly there was no active reaction against the Asuka monuments, which continued to be respected and cherished; rather, one perceives a gradual exploration of new styles and, to a lesser extent, new iconographies, by artists who now had the opportunity to work in modes reflecting later developments in China and Korea.

HISTORIOGRAPHY

Before turning to the monuments, a consideration of the historiography of Hakuhō

sculpture is essential. Periodization is a
constant problem in any historical investigation and certainly for the early Buddhist
sculpture of Japan. Generic terms such as
"ancient" or "medieval'" are of little use,
especially as they were initially formulated
for the Western tradition. In Japan, as in
other countries, specific chronological
schemes and corresponding nomencla-
tures are employed, and those devised for
Japan are often based on the successive
capitals, yielding "Asuka," "Nara," "Heian,"
"Kamakura," etc. Generally speaking, this
system is useful and has many advantages
for art historians; unfortunately, for our
subject it is problematic, since Hakuhō does
not refer to a capital.[1]

Apparently the term "Hakuhō" first
appeared in the art-historical literature in
a 1901 article by the well-known scholar
Sekino Tadashi.[2] Subsequently, scholars
contended over the dates to which the term
was most meaningfully applicable. The
three basic hypotheses were as follows.

Standard Hakuhō (645–710)

A precise explanation of this dating was
given by Mizuno Seiichi, who saw the
beginning as 645 (Taika Reform) and the
end as 710 (transfer of capital to Heijōkyō).[3]
As a specialist in Chinese Buddhist sculpture, Mizuno carefully linked the Japanese
stylistic phases with those of China: Asuka
with late Wei; Hakuhō with Northern Qi,
Northern Zhou, and Sui; and Nara with
Tang.

Modified Hakuhō (various dates)

This is more complicated than the preceding but generally sees the development thusly: "Asuka," 538/552–645; "Late
Asuka," 645–670; and "Hakuhō," 670–710.
A number of scholars have advocated this
approach, arguing that the years circa
645–670 are best seen as a continuation
of Asuka proper, and only the years circa
670–710 display stylistic differences significant enough to necessitate the distinguishing label "Hakuhō."[4]

The Hakuhō Period Did Not Exist

There are two versions of this third theory.
The first argues that the span 645–710 is
best considered as a forerunner of the Nara
period and is designated "Early Nara."[5] The
second divides the period roughly in half
and calls the earlier part a continuation of
Asuka, while subsuming the later within
the Nara period.[6] Although it is evident
that significant historical developments
occurred in the 670s, to break Hakuhō
into two subperiods seems unreasonable,
because the stylistic evolution seems gradual throughout the period, suggesting that
no particular historical events produced
a fundamental reorientation of sculptural
production.

Since I think the standard periodization of Hakuhō is most reasonable with
only a slight modification of the beginning year (circa 650 rather than 645), my
discussion will begin at the middle of the
seventh century. As mentioned earlier, I do

not conceive a hard-and-fast line dividing Asuka from Hakuhō; rather, I prefer to see a transitional phase in which older modes give way to newer ones.

TRANSITIONAL SCULPTURES

Of the very few dated Hakuhō images, two of the "Forty-eight Buddhist Deities" group in the Tokyo National Museum are central to a consideration of the Asuka-Hakuhō transition: a meditating bodhisattva (no. 156; figs. 3a,b) and a standing Kannon (no. 165; figs. 4a,b).[7] Both bear cyclical characters yielding possible dates: the latter's corresponds to 591 or 651, the former's to 606 or 666. For both, I accept the later alternative, thereby placing the two images at the early stages of Hakuhō, roughly the 650s and 660s.[8]

Meditating bodhisattva no. 156 has long been the subject of controversy over its date.[9] Some writers have adopted the earlier date of 606, prompted by the feeling that earlier is better; but this is not reasoning, merely predilection. Others support their preference for 606 by citing stylistic dissimilarities between no. 156 and a meditating bodhisattva at Yachūji (fig. 27), which bears the same cyclical characters, in this case interpreted as referring to 666. This is a genuine argument, but it proceeds from the supposition that the Yachūji image's fleshy face, modeled body, and treatment of jewelry is characteristic of Hakuhō, whereas the slender, less articulated body of no. 156 is more typical of earlier sculpture. Not much need be said about the first hypoth-

esis. The second, based on a specific stylistic comparison, is more interesting. I do find appropriate the Hakuhō attribution for the Yachūji image, even though I have doubts about the specific date of 666. In my view, the stylistic argument for dating no. 156 to 606 is premised on a failure to recognize that two or more styles can coexist simultaneously. Close inspection of no. 156 reveals a number of traits characteristic of Hakuhō but not seen in Asuka sculpture, including the three-plaque crown, a full face, heavy jewelry, and complex drapery folds.[10]

Kannon no. 165 has some stylistic features that can be associated with such Soga-Tori images as the Hōryūji Museum bodhisattva (fig. 2), discussed in the preceding chapter. These include fish-tail folds, long scarf looped in an X pattern in front of the legs, an unarticulated pectoral, emphasis on frontality, and the like.[11] Of course, its defining iconographical features are the representation of Amida in the crown (*kebutsu*)[12] and the jewel-clasping gesture. Concerning the latter, one notes the U loop of the scarf at back, also seen in Asuka images such as the Yumedono Kannon and the Hōryūji Museum bodhisattva (fig. 2). Lena Kim was the first to point out that, both in Korea and in Japan, many icons shown clasping a jewel also show the scarf in a large U loop at the back.[13]

The jewel-clasping motif evidentally carries iconographical meaning, but what can be said about the U loop? The following is a guess: perhaps in experimenting with various arrangements, and not necessarily while working on a jewel-clasper,

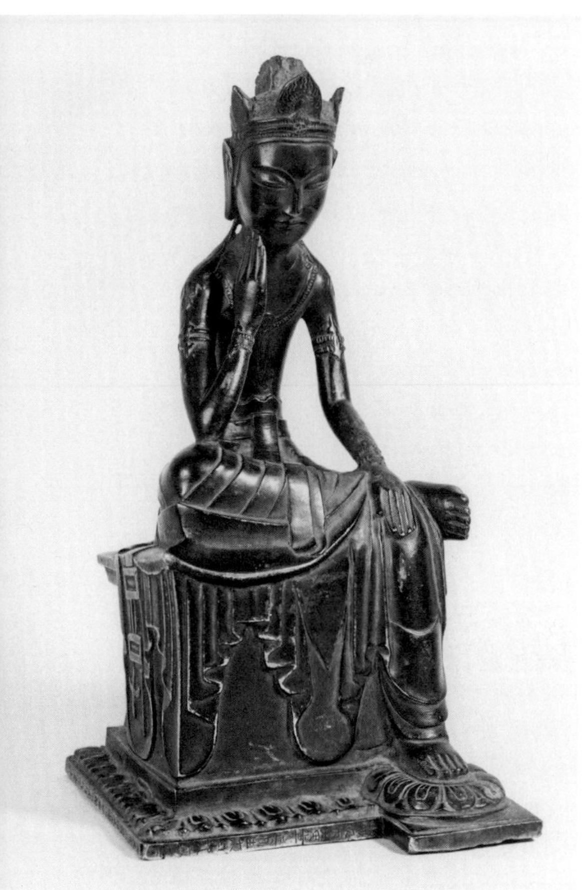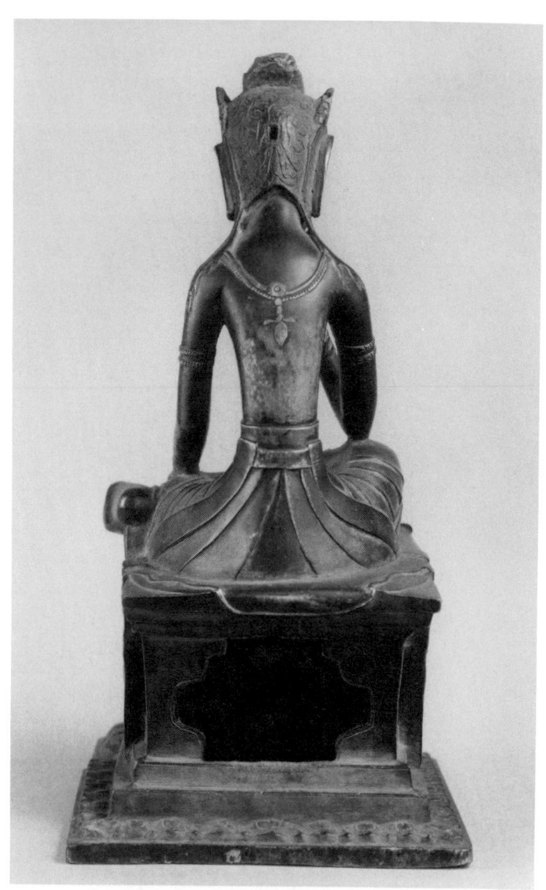

3   TNM Meditating Bosatsu no.156, H: 28.6 cm.   a. front   b. back
Photo courtesy of TNM

an enterprising sculptor hit upon the U loop.[14] At some time the two elements came together and subsequently often appeared together on icons. At a certain point some specific "jewel-clasper/U-loop" bodhisattva may have been perceived as particularly efficacious, perhaps in healing or in granting other wishes, thereby motivating the replication of icons with this combination of elements. There would have been no need to include other standard elements of the prototype in later versions, since it was the

jewel/U loop that was seen as important.

Despite the above-mentioned traits related to the Soga-Tori style of the Asuka period, that Kannon no. 165 could date from 591 is unlikely for two reasons. The Soga-Tori style is not documented for such an early year; and Kannon no. 165 is in numerous ways subtly different from Asuka manifestations of the Soga-Tori category, those differences being indicative of an early Hakuhō date. That being said, there can be no doubt that the sculptor had the

CHAPTER 2

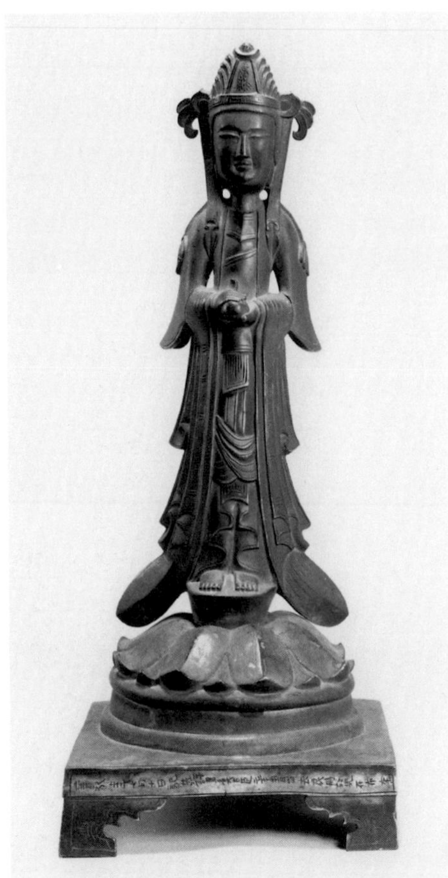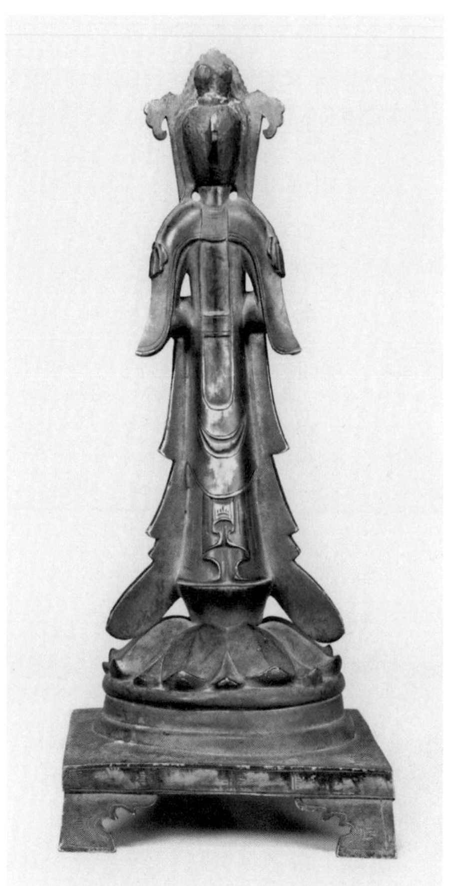

4　TNM Standing Bosatsu no.165, H: 23.5 cm.　a. front　b. back
Photo courtesy of TNM

Soga-Tori style in mind when designing this image, especially those traits mentioned above; but crowns of this shape are not seen in Asuka sculpture, nor can the facial expression be readily associated with Soga-Tori images. Additionally, an element of schematization in the drapery details is also suggestive of a post-Asuka date, as is the relatively slender build of the body, especially noticeable in the upper torso.[15]

A key transitional standing bodhisattva is no. 166 (figs. 5a,b), which, unlike Kannon no. 165, is uninscribed and thus must be dated on stylistic grounds. Both icons are jewel-claspers with the associated U loop at back and with the scarf ends falling in fish-tail folds. Evidently, no. 166 was designed at least in part with the mainstream Asuka style and iconography in mind, but in various features it can be differentiated from Asuka and appears to have been made early in the Hakuhō period by a sculptor willing to combine old and new traits. Thus, the crown of no. 166 has

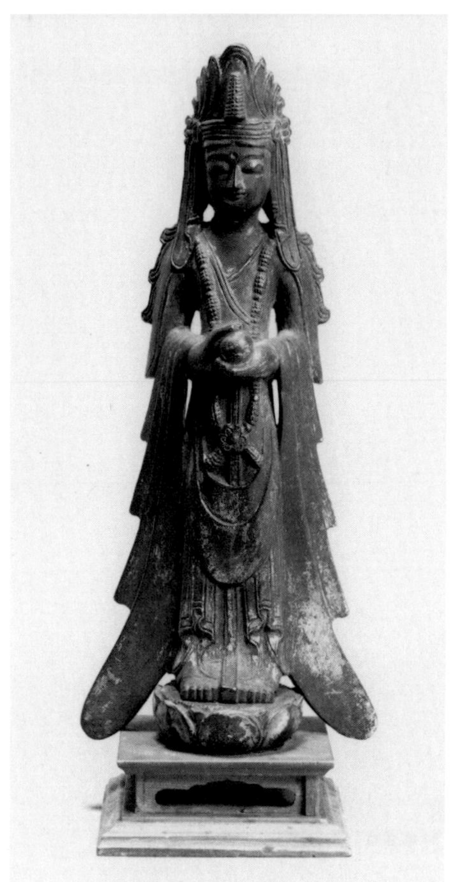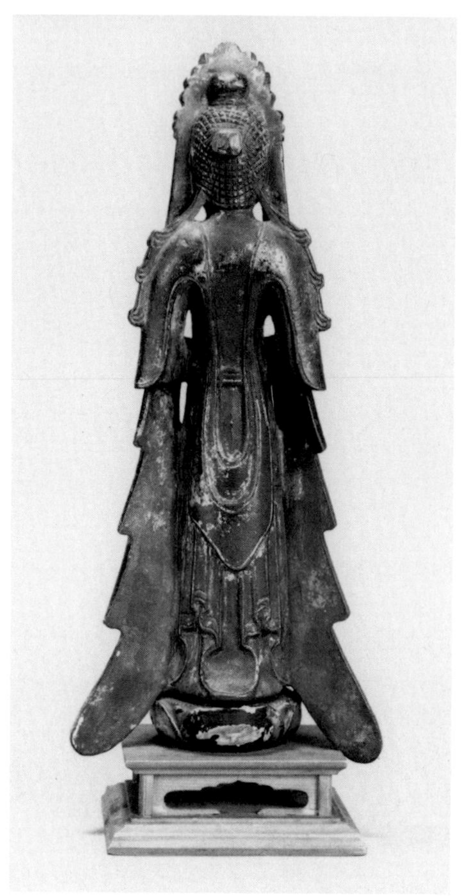

5   TNM Standing Bosatsu no.166, H: 24.4 cm.   a. front   b. back
     Photo courtesy of TNM

a tassel at center, a motif not seen among the Soga-Tori group.[16] More importantly, one notes immediately the very sweet facial expression, quite remote from the typical face of earlier icons. The image is taller, and its greater slenderness is articulated by the spaces between the arms and chest and between the scarf and the hips; yet the effect of slenderness is vitiated by the planar surfaces of the scarf ends, which have absolutely no internal detailing to indicate folds. Since fold-lines paralleling the overall contours are present else-where on the clothing, the absence of such internal detailing on the scarf ends seems deliberate. In other aspects the drapery is unusual. For example, there are two hems crossing the chest obliquely, but there is no indication of these hems continuing to the back.[17] The two ends of the jewel strings cross in front at the level of the knees with a rosette at the point of crossing. The lower strings disappear under the cross-over of the scarf and do not reappear at back. These

CHAPTER 2

jewel strings are very heavy, even clunky, although careful inspection reveals considerable variety in design.

How might such an image have come about? I conjecture that the artist had in mind a gentle, sweet face combined with a relatively tall, slender figure; the tendency to emulate certain Soga-Tori traits produced the quite ungainly scarf; but the somewhat peculiar, very heavy jewelry must have come from some other source, since this type is not found among Asuka images.[18] Although bodhisattva no. 166 can be placed confidently in the transition leading from Asuka to early Hakuhō, it really stands more at the end of a tradition than at the commencement of something new; nevertheless, the facial expression and bodily proportions strongly hint at what is to come in the next few years, even though our artist was still constrained by old-fashioned traits.

BEGINNINGS OF A MATURE HAKUHŌ STYLE

The Kanshinji Kannon (figs. 6a,b) is a representative example of the initial development of the standing bodhisattva in the Hakuhō style. Although at first glance it may seem quite different from standing bodhisattva no. 166, actually the two images share some highly important characteristics, especially in the newly conceived proportions and facial expression. The Kanshinji Kannon retains some transitional characteristics, such as the X crossing of the scarf, but this motif appears occasionally in typically Hakuhō pieces, perhaps as an archaistic element. A distinguishing component of the Hakuhō bodhisattva—the three-plaque crown— appears in an early version in the Kanshinji Kannon with a large central plaque and two smaller side plaques, a feature that becomes canonical in Hakuhō imagery. This is a Sui trait and appears together with other Sui elements, presumably transmitted via the Korean peninsula.[19]

As a jewel-clasper, the Kanshinji Kannon follows the iconography discussed in the two preceding images. It displays, however, one significant variation: the scarf does not descend at the back in the U loop seen in most other examples, but rather wraps around the shoulders and upper back. This difference is hard to explain. Perhaps the artist did not feel it necessary to adhere to a trait presumably without specific meaning, or perhaps he was unaware that the standard design of jewel-clasping icons usually included the U loop.

Generally speaking, the drapery and jewelry elements are standard, although a new feature is the very long jewelry string that follows the arrangement of the scarf over the front of the body and falls from the arms to the pedestal. The pedestal consists of two joined lotus blossoms: the smaller, upper one with up-turning lotus petals and the larger, lower one with down-pointing petals. As no attachment fixture for a halo is present either at the back of the head or on the pedestal, it is hard to tell how one would have been attached. A halo in the Nezu Museum, Tokyo, with an inscription

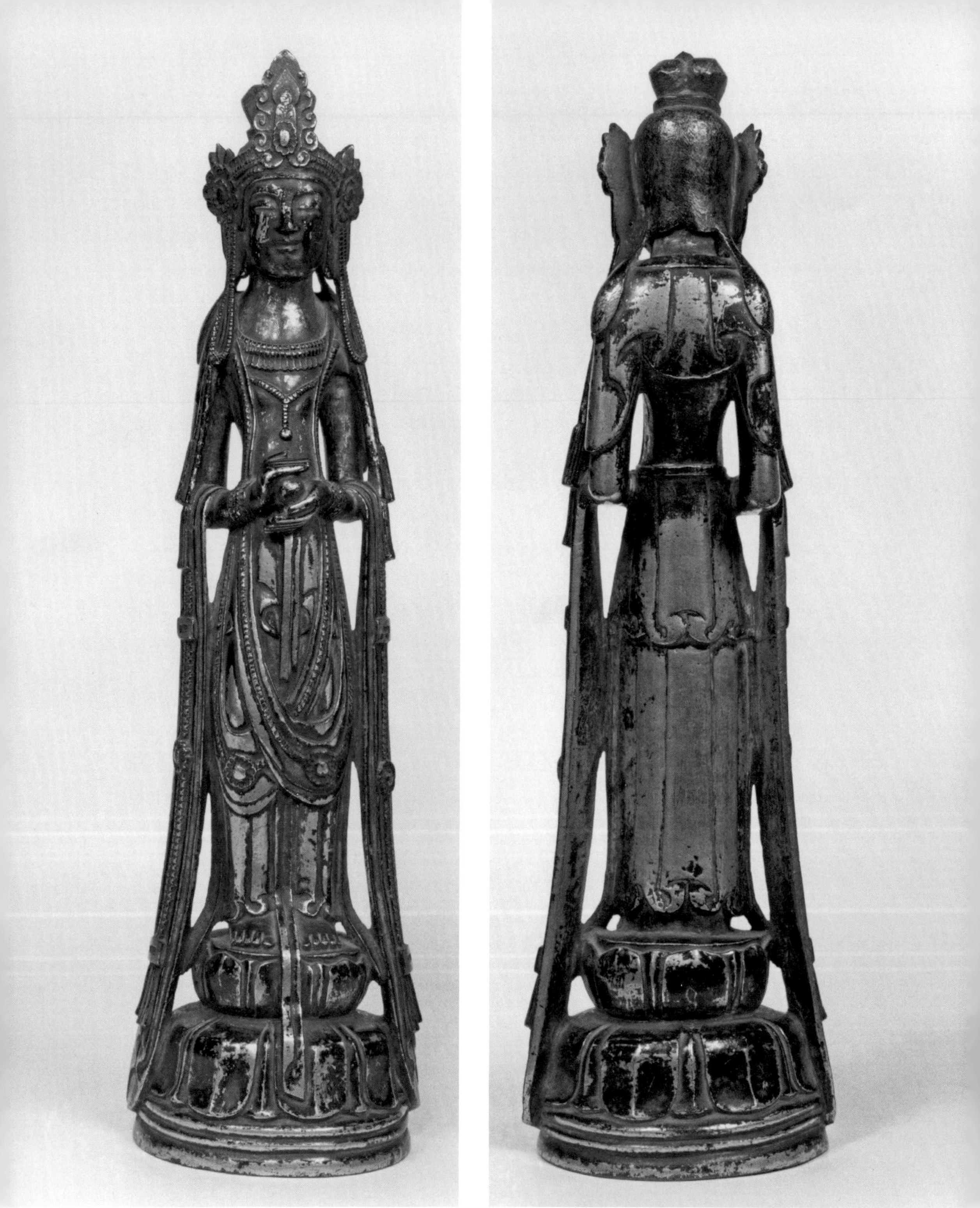

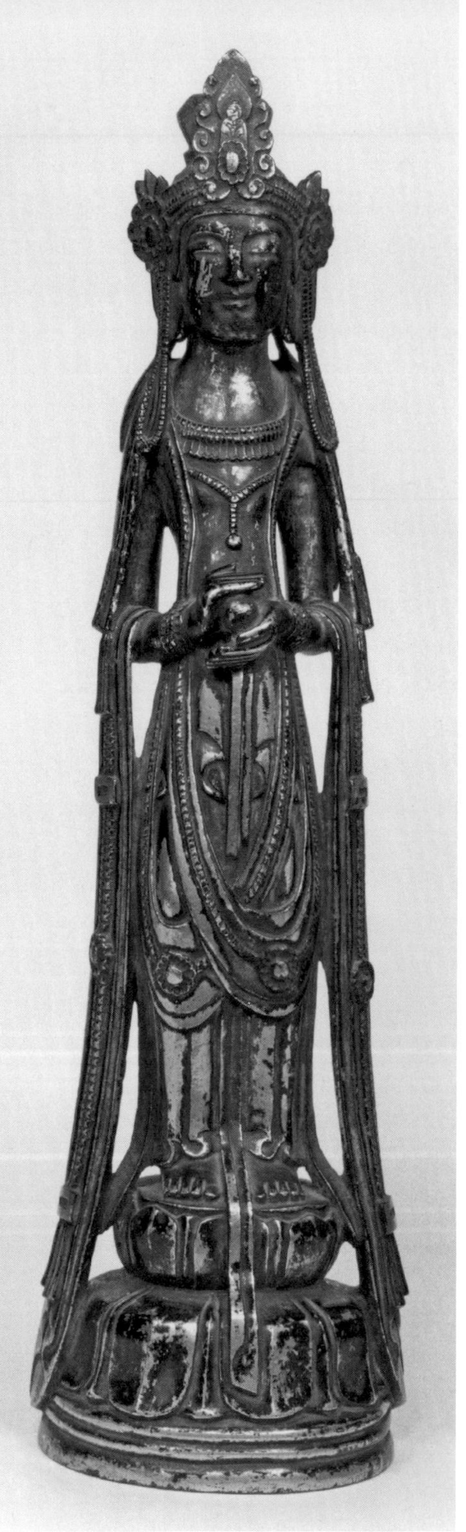

6   Standing Kannon, H: 33.3 cm. Kanshinji, Osaka   a. front   b. back
     Photo courtesy of NNM

                                                          CHAPTER 2

equivalent to 658 has been associated with the present image, but I find that doubtful.[20]

The Kanshinji Kannon repays careful study on account of its key location on a cusp between two important stylistic trends. Although it reveals a number of new features in only tentative form—for example, the just barely perceptible modeling of the chest—its overall configuration has moved beyond the Asuka style, even if it has not yet achieved a fuller expression of the Hakuhō style. Clearly, the artist had seen a new style of icon and was confident enough to attempt his own version of it. The Kanshinji Kannon manifests this fresh spirit more fully than does no. 166, in which residual Soga-Tori elements are not well integrated into the composition.

Within the "Forty-eight Deities" group few icons are as fascinating as the one to which we turn next, the Amida triad no. 144 (fig. 7), bearing an inscription identifying it as the Yamadaden zō (hereafter referred to as the "Yamadaden triad," the icon of Yamada Hall). Virtually all scholars of early Japanese art believe that "Yamadaden" refers to the important seventh-century temple Yamadadera, located in Asuka, quite close to Asukadera. We shall have occasion to discuss this temple further in chapter 3, when the Kōfukuji Buddha head (fig. 34) is considered, but it would be helpful here to provide some historical background for Yamadadera.

Yamadadera was established in 641 by Kura Yamada Ishikawa Maro (d. 649), a grandson of Soga no Umako and a leading figure in a secondary branch of this powerful Soga clan. He sided with the Ōkimi (royal) faction during the Taika Reform, against the main line of his own clan, then headed by Emishi and Iruka, and as a reward was appointed to the second highest post in the bureaucracy, Minister of the Right. Ironically, after aiding in the destruction of his own clan's main line, he, too, suffered. First he was slandered by a younger brother, Soga no Himuka, and then he was forced to commit suicide along with members of his family in 649, four years after the Taika Reform.[21] Subsequently—and rather conveniently—those in power recognized that the forced death of Ishikawa Maro had been a "mistake," and they are said to have "regretted" compelling the suicide.[22]

Considerable progress was made on Yamadadera in the 640s, with the Golden Hall begun in 643 and the first monks moving into the temple in 648. After the suicides of 649, work ceased, and only in 663 was the decision taken to build a pagoda. Work began in 673, but the pagoda was not completed until 676. Where does the Yamadaden Amida triad fit into this chronology? Evidently, the temple did not cease to function after 649, and if my chronology for the temple is accurate, I would suggest that it was between 649 and 663, or possibly slightly later, that the triad was made. In any case, this small triad is unrelated to the sixteen-foot triad started in 678 and finally completed in 685, which we shall turn to in chapter 3.

The triad consists of a central Amida figure seated on a large pedestal, flanked

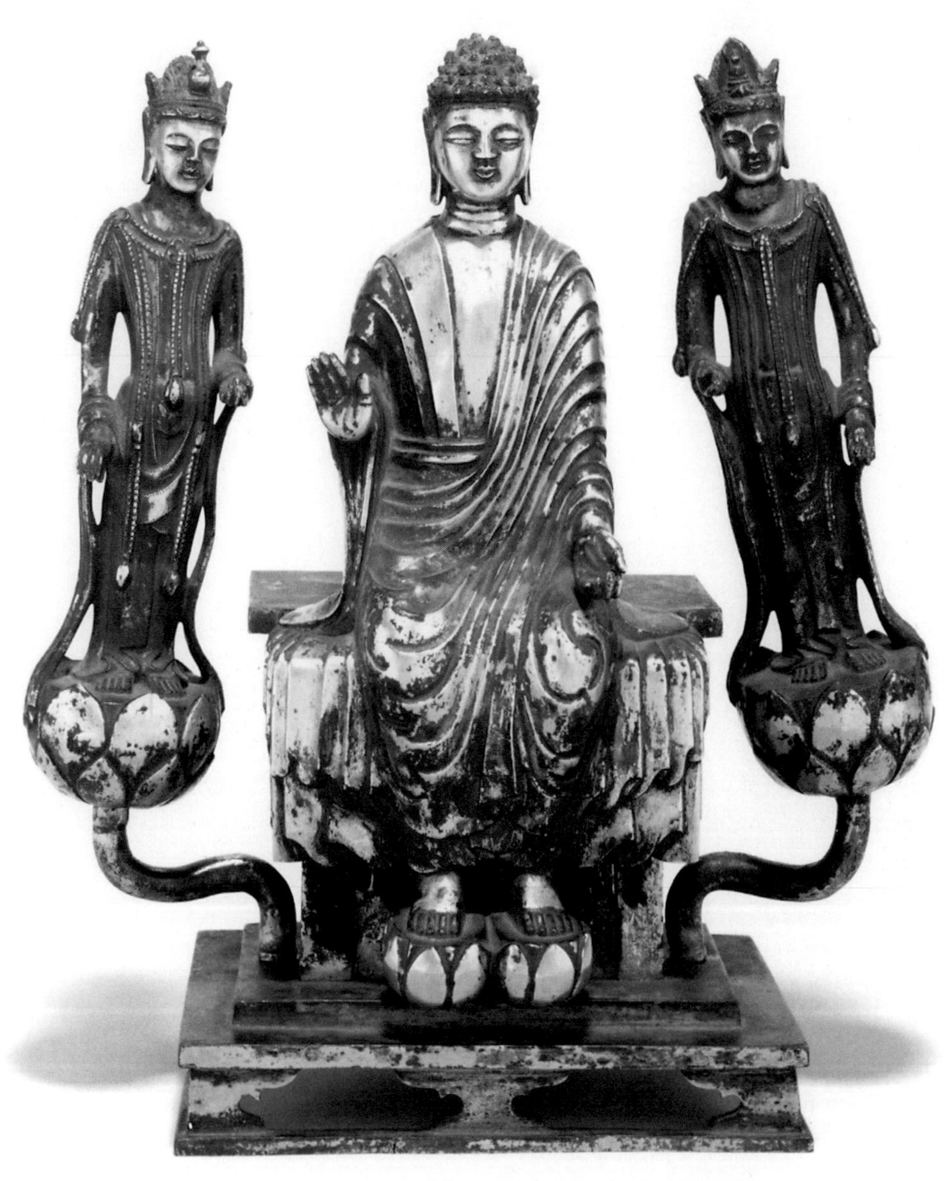

7   TNM Yamadaden Amida Triad no.144, H: Buddha, 28.4 cm.

Photo courtesy of TNM

by two bodhisattvas standing on lotus pedestals; to Amida's left is Kannon, to his right Seishi. Certainly, the most striking characteristic of the Yamadaden triad is the pose of the central Buddha, seated "Western style" with legs pendent.[23] Scholars have investigated the origins and development of the Western-style posture in Indian Buddha figures, and traced its movement to China and Korea.[24] Normally the seated Amida is shown in cross-legged posture, but there are somewhat later Japanese images that do represent the central Amida Buddha seated in this pose. Particularly impressive is a tile plaque (*senbutsu*) kept at Hōryūji.[25]

Moving from iconography to style, the Amida has somewhat awkward proportions, the head being rather small in relation to the total height of the figure, especially if one pictures the deity standing rather than seated. Moreover, the sculptor evidently had little experience with the "Western" pose, for there is a distinctly unnatural feeling about the way Amida sits. Since this always was an unusual posture in East Asian Buddhist art, and perhaps unprecedented in Japanese sculpture at the time the Yamadaden triad was executed, the slightly ungainly appearance is not surprising. Amida's robes display a complex treatment, including a *henzan*: a piece of fabric, separate from the robe, which covers the right shoulder both front and back.[26]

The two standing bodhisattvas, Kannon and Seishi, complete the triad iconography. As attendant figures to the principal deity, they were made only about one half of Amida's size. Each holds the inner hand at hip level, the outer arm pendent, thus symmetrically bracketing the central deity. Kannon has the usual three-plaque crown with a *kebutsu* in the central plaque; Seishi's crown has the two side plaques, but in place of the central plaque is a large water vase, Seishi's attribute. By comparison with Amida, the bodhisattvas' proportions are a little more natural: their heads are somewhat larger in relation to their bodies and their upper torsos are shorter than their legs.[27]

I should like to compare the drapery and jewelry systems of these bodhisattvas with those of Kannon no. 167 (figs. 8a,b).[28] The latter figure, an independent icon rather than part of a triad, is a jewel-clasper and so holds its arms differently from the Yamadaden bodhisattvas, who do not hold jewels, but excepting that and some minor details in execution, facial expression, and proportions, Kannon no. 167 is very similar to the other two. In all three the scarf crosses at knee level in the familiar X pattern and is arranged at the back in the U-loop variation.[29]

The artist(s) placed a great deal of emphasis on the jewelry, and although the figures lacks armlets, the necklaces with pendent elements are elaborate. The Yamadaden bodhisattvas and Kannon no. 167 wear similar necklaces, and the elements are elaborate, although that of no. 167 does not continue around the back. In both, long jewel strings hang from the side rosettes of the necklace at front. The Yamadaden

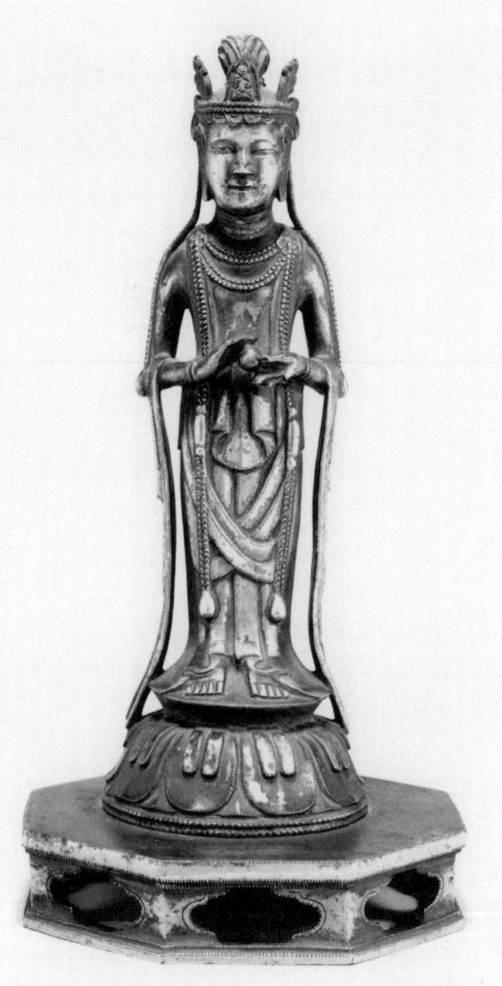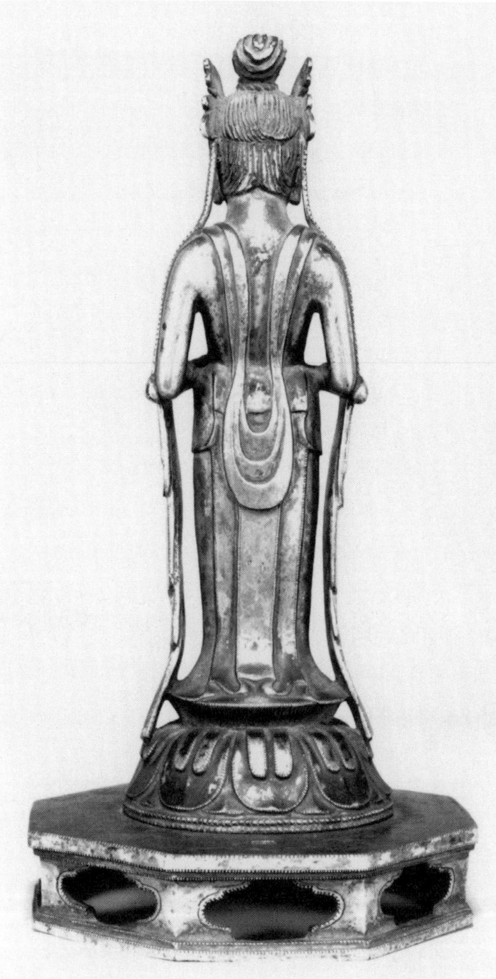

8   TNM Standing Kannon no.167, H: 22.9 cm.   a. front   b. back
Photo courtesy of TNM

bodhisattvas have an additional string hanging at center front; this Kannon no. 167 lacks, presumably because it holds a jewel at center front instead.

Although the complicated pedestal of the Yamadaden Amida triad merits detailed analysis, only a few comments can be presented here. Of course, the triad format necessitates separate supporting elements for the three figures, and since the central figure is seated while the flanking bodhisattvas stand, further complications arise. The pedestal of the Hōryūji Golden Hall Shaka triad may be taken as a general precedent, even though that central Shaka sits cross-legged. In the Yamadaden triad the Buddha sits Western style on the boxy structure of the main pedestal, while the

CHAPTER 2

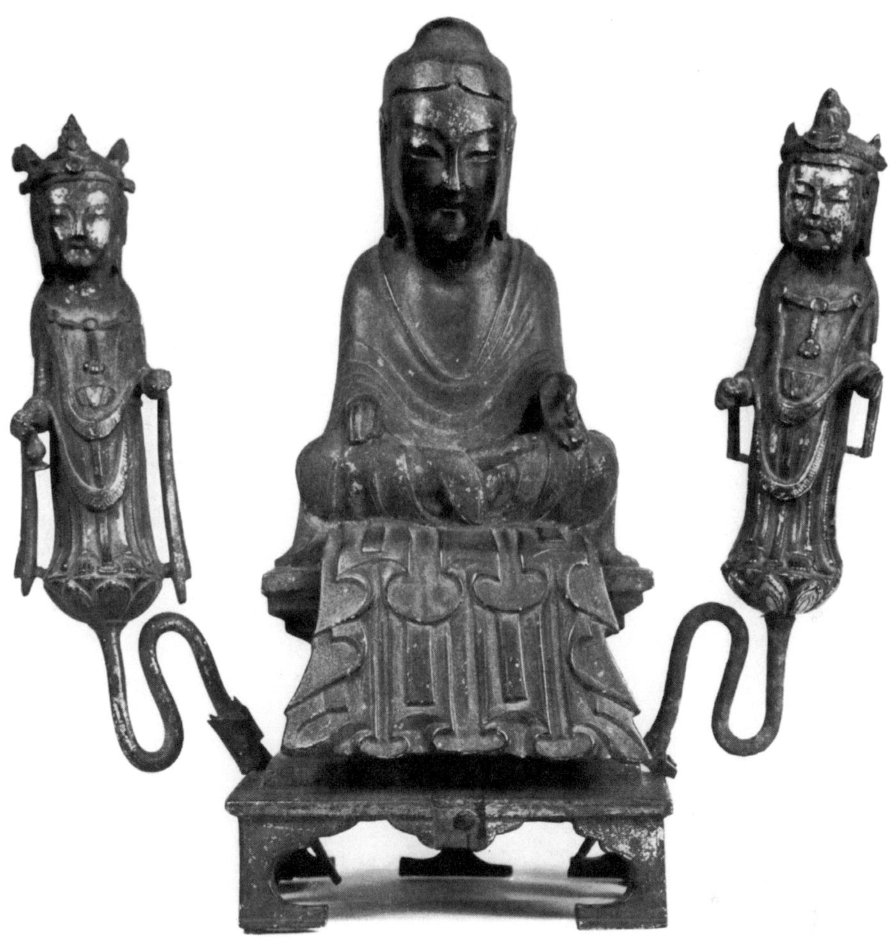

9   Yakushi Triad, H: Buddha, 19.0 cm. Yakushiji, Ishikawa
Photo courtesy of the temple

flanking bodhisattvas stand on lotus pedestals that grow out of the lower part of the
main pedestal.[30]

A second example of the triad format in
early Hakuhō sculpture is the Yakushi triad
of the Ishikawa Prefecture Yakushiji (fig.
9). In this triad, Yakushi sits cross-legged,
while the flanking bodhisattvas, like those
of the Yamadaden triad, stand on lotus

pedestals. Although archaic in flavor, the
figural style, and especially the full, fleshy
face, does not appear to be directly related
to Asuka predecessors. The drapery over-
hanging the Buddha's pedestal certainly
relates back to the Soga-Tori format, but
seems stylized in comparison with earlier
manifestations. Being short and squat with
very large heads, the flanking bodhisatt-

vas have the appealing quality of babies. A notable feature of their drapery is the manner in which the scarf passes in the front of the legs in two registers rather than in the X pattern seen on the bodhisattvas considered thus far.[31]

At the temple the icon is referred to as a Yakushi triad, but because the proper left flanking bodhisattva has an Amida in its crown, it seems more likely that this, like the Yamadaden triad, is an Amida triad. At present its identity remains an open question. Because Ishikawa Prefecture is remote from the central region of Japan, some scholars have suggested that the triad may display a provincial style, which of course could have been accompanied by confusion in iconography.[32]

A quite odd image from the early Hakuhō period is the standing Kannon (figs. 10a,b) at Ichijōji in Hyōgo Prefecture.[33] Unfortunately, a scorching fire not only darkened the surface but broke the image at about waist level. Although somewhat larger than the average small gilt-bronze image, it has the squat proportions and the odd posture just noted in the Ishikawa Yakushiji triad. Its large head and slightly smiling, full, fleshy face also relates it to the triad. The crown is atypical in form, including the *kebutsu*, in which Amida does not sit in the usual yoga position, but rather has the left foot resting in front of the right in the posture of royal ease.

The body is columnar, with little modeling. Drapery consists of the standard Hakuhō elements of scarf and skirt, with the scarf passing in a double register before the legs, as in the flanking bodhisattvas of the Yakushiji triad. Also typical of Hakuhō sculpture is the heavy jewelry, especially the jewel strings that follow the line of the scarf. Most unusually, ovoid forms decorate the belt end. The pedestal, also a little strange, is a prominent aspect of the composition, with very large inverted lotus petals much ornamented with striations.

THE "BOYISH" GROUP IN HAKUHŌ SCULPTURE

A distinctive category of Hakuhō sculpture consists of images that Japanese scholars refer to as the *Dōgan* (Boyish face) or *Dōgyō* (Boyish form).[34] It includes the following images: standing Buddha no. 153; Kannon no. 179 and bodhisattva no. 188; Hōryūji Museum Kannon no. 1 and no. 2;[35] Meditating bodhisattvas no. 159 and no. 160; Meditating bodhisattva in private collection; standing bodhisattva in wood.[36]

A number of other sculptures in both bronze and wood can also be associated with the "boyish" category, but those enumerated consititute, in my view, a significant group that probably emerged from a single studio. Since I have dealt with the "boyish" group in a separate study, a broader consideration is unnecessary here; rather, I shall concentrate on those details of design and execution suggestive of studio practice.[37]

Since standing Buddha no. 153 (figs. 11a,b) is treated in detail in my article, the account here will be brief. That should not be taken to mean that I consider this

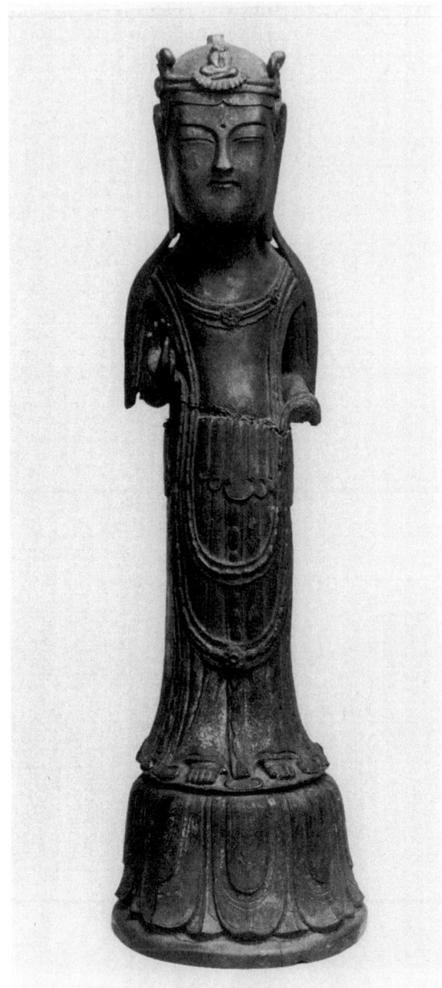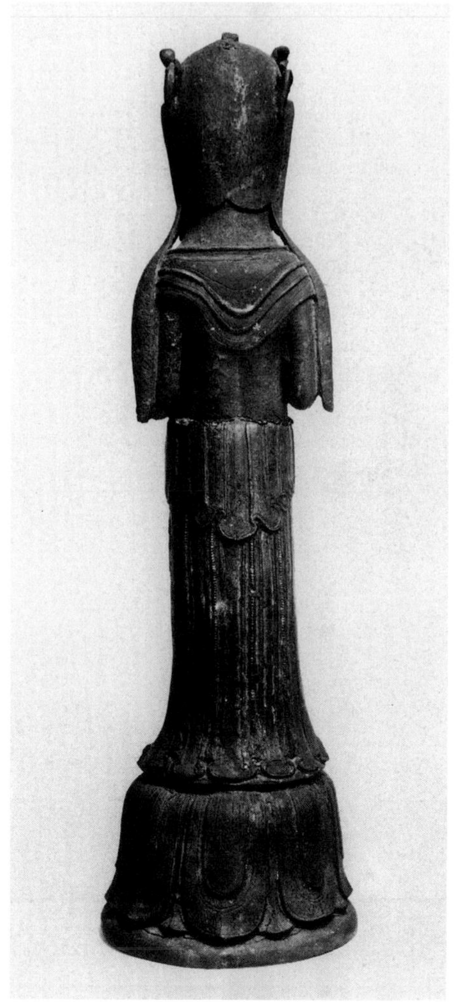

10   Standing Kannon, H: 48.0 cm. Ichijōji, Hyogo   a. front   b. back
Photo courtesy of NNM

sculpture unworthy of careful consideration; quite the opposite, in fact. Typical of the "boyish" group, the image has a rather large head in relation to its body with narrow shoulders and a rather understated torso. Certainly, the image gives no sense of monumentality; rather, one is conscious of a gentle, tender presence. As mentioned in the discussion of the Yamadaden Amida (fig. 7), theories differ regarding the nature of the robes worn by Buddha images. It is now generally recognized that the robes seen in icons directly reflect the garb of Buddhist priests. The question is just exactly which item of priestly apparel corresponded with which part of the robes seen in sculptural or pictorial representations. Yoshimura Rei, who has written two

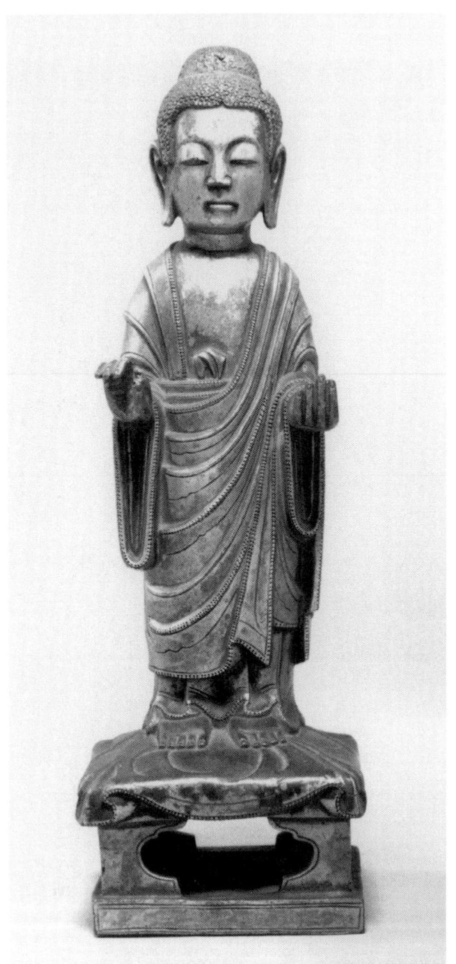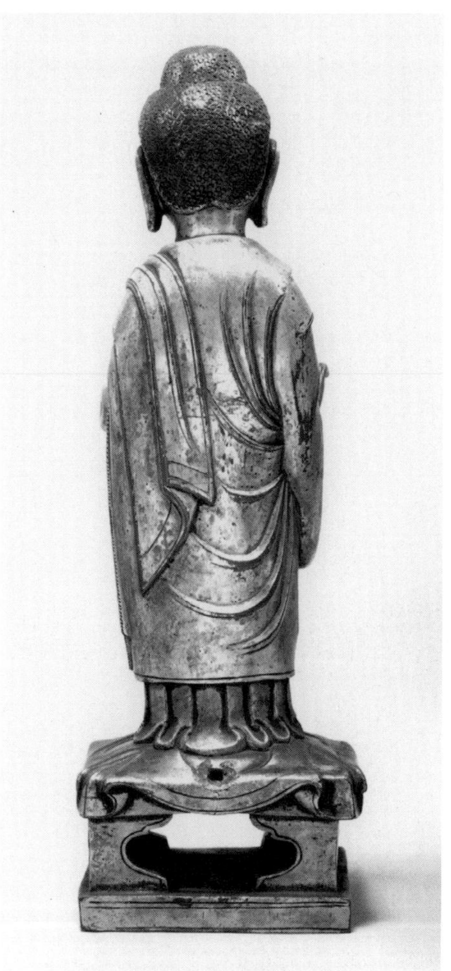

11   TNM Standing Buddha no.153, H: 29.5 cm.   a. front   b. back
      Photo courtesy of TNM

detailed articles on priestly garb, rejects Kuno's theory that a *henzan* is present on the Yamadaden Amida. He identifies the fabric that Kuno calls the *henzan* as the *sōgishi*,[38] but suggests that Buddha no. 153 is one of the very rare examples of a sculptural icon wearing a *henzan*. A square hole on the top surface of the pedestal, behind the figure, must have been made to accommodate the shaft of a halo, perhaps of the type clearly seen in the Kudara Kannon of Hōryūji.[39] A peculiar feature of the pedestal of no. 153 is the total lack of any lotus element.

Kannon no. 179 (fig. 12) and bodhisattva no. 188 (fig. 13) are also discussed in my earlier study, hence consideration of them will be abbreviated. Their exceedingly close resemblance has long been recognized, and it has been suggested that they might have

CHAPTER 2

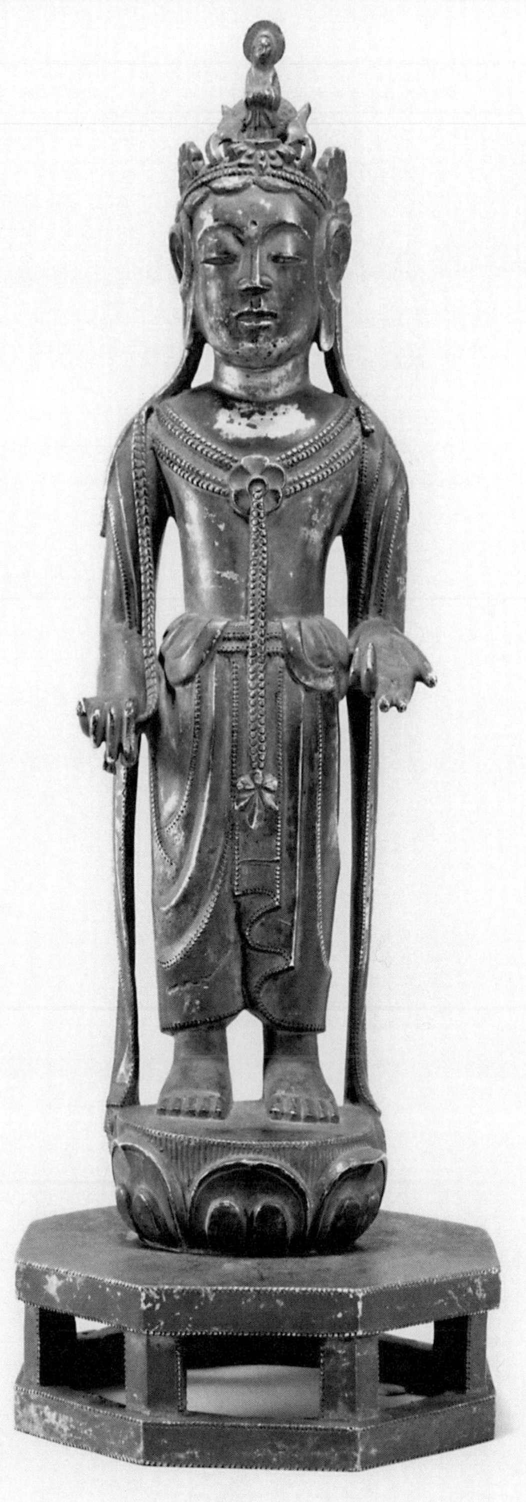

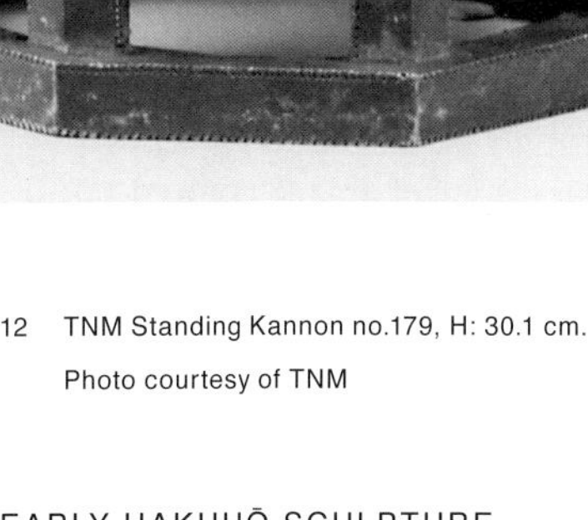

12   TNM Standing Kannon no.179, H: 30.1 cm.
Photo courtesy of TNM

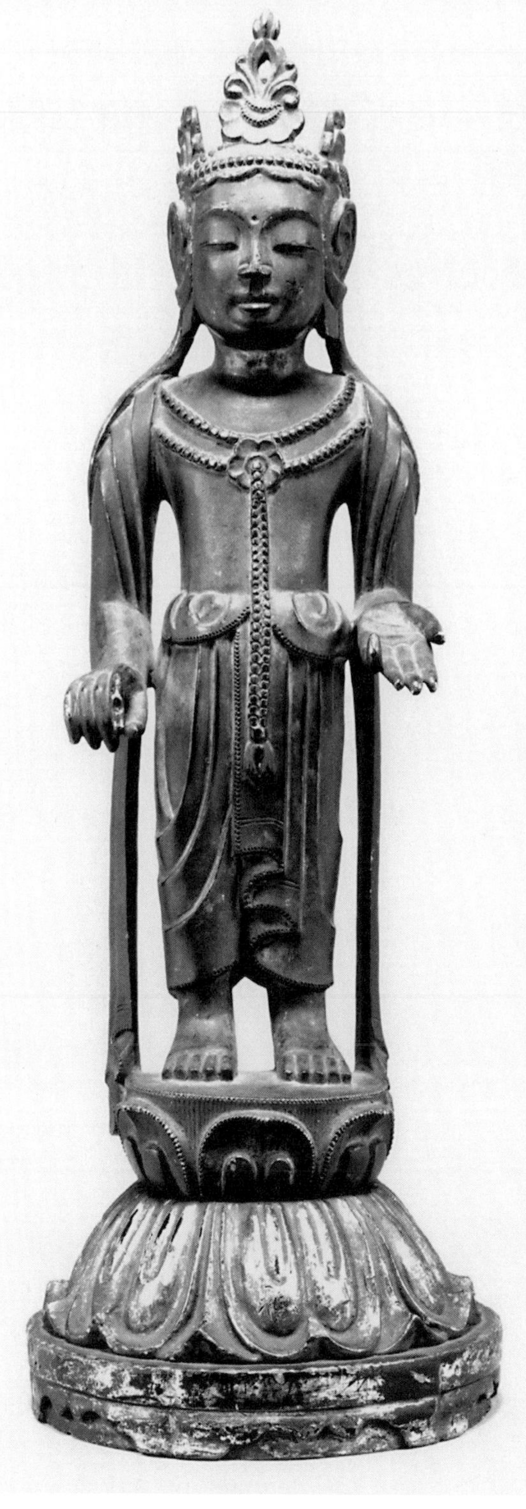

13   TNM Standing Bosatsu no.188, H: 30.0 cm.
Photo courtesy of TNM

EARLY HAKUHŌ SCULPTURE

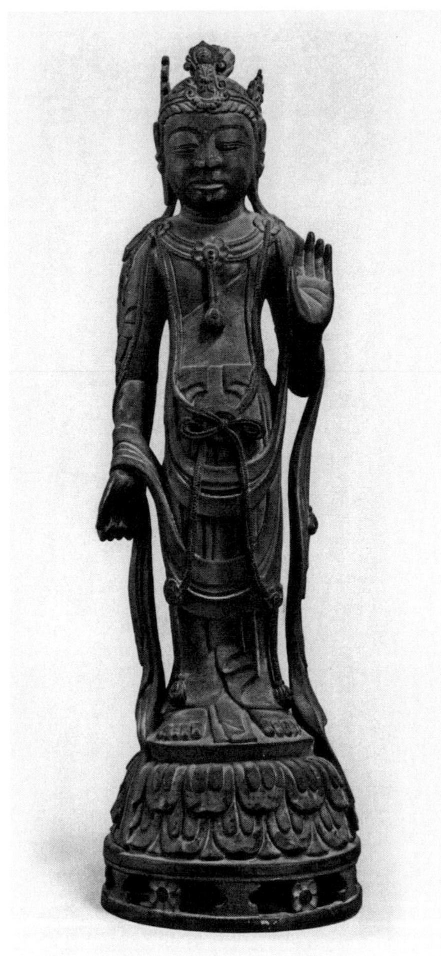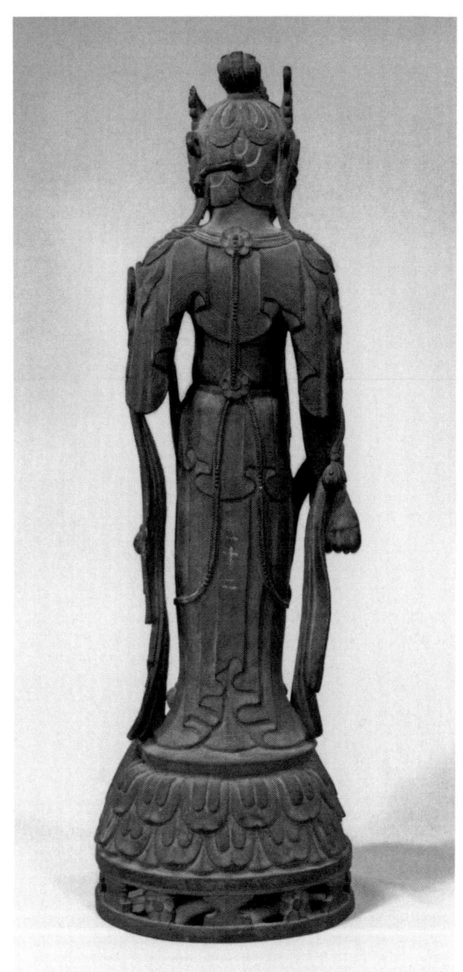

14   Standing Kannon No. 1, H: 54.5 cm. Hōryūji Museum   a. front   b. back
Photo courtesy of Hōryūji

been the flanking bodhisattvas of standing Buddha no. 153. This hypothesis seems to me unlikely. I find enough differences between them to suggest that, although they were undoubtedly made in one studio at about the same time, and perhaps by the same artist, they most likely are independent icons.

Of all the images in this category, these two bodhisattvas are the most "boyish" in appearance, as can be seen in their innocent, childlike facial expressions and in their bodily proportions, especially their short legs. They differ most obviously in the central plaques of their crowns: no. 179 has a *kebutsu* in the central plaque, whereas the central plaque of no. 188 is composed of a floral arrangement of uncertain iconographic significance. On both, the scarf is arranged so that the two ends fall down the

CHAPTER 2

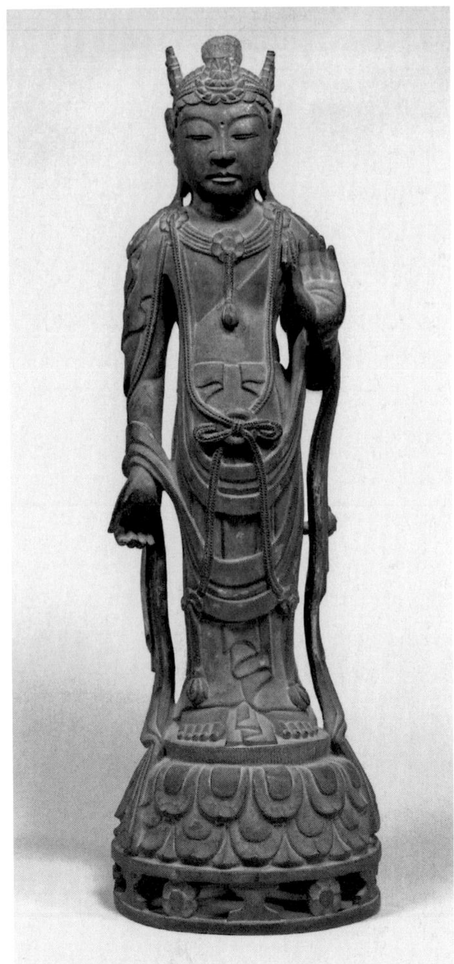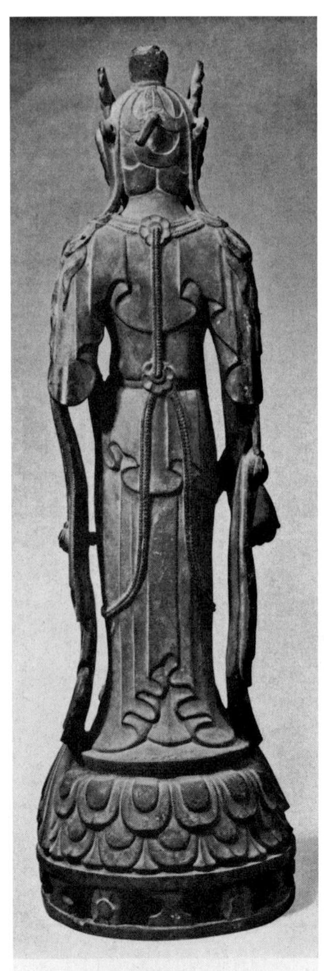

15   Standing Kannon No. 2, H: 54.1 cm. Hōryūji Museum   a. front   b. back
Photo courtesy of TNM

sides of the body, rather than crossing over in front of the legs. Kannon no. 179 shows the "quivering line" incised at the lower right area of the skirt, which I take to be a characteristic trait of this studio's production.[40] Their jewelry arrangements are similar, but with different details, indicating that the sculptor(s) were free to create variants. Consequently, there can be little doubt that the two are based on a common prototype or, perhaps, one on the other. Their very minor differences in no way diminishes their overall close resemblance, which affords evidence about the nature of Hakuhō studio practice.

Two relatively large Kannon images (no. 1, figs. 14a,b; no. 2, figs. 15a,b) in the Hōryūji Museum are, like the preceding pair, characterized by plump, round faces and child-like expressions and proportions.[41] Their

EARLY HAKUHŌ SCULPTURE

clothing and jewelry are nearly the same. They are, of course, essentially identical in overall configuration and evidently were both made in a single studio close in time to each other. It seems to me fairly certain that they are versions of the same icon.

Turning to subtle differences between the two, one notes that the *kebutsu* of no. 1 is standing, that of no. 2 seated.[42] The eyes of no. 1 have a double upper eyelid, no. 2 the more common single eyelid. Other minor differences can be observed in the arrangement of hair, configuration of crown, and facial expression. Elaborate detailing in both fabric and jewelry areas greatly enhances the surface of no. 1 only. Since the "quivering line," which was incised onto the surface after the image was cast, is present on no. 1 and absent on no. 2, it appears that the artist was free to use it or not. The differences in the lotus petals on the pedestals were created in the mold rather than by cold chisel work after casting, but also show individual design decisions.

The significance of these two figures is essentially the same as that of no. 179 and no. 188, since they all clearly demonstrate that the sculptors might design and execute several slightly varied images on the basis of a single prototype. In studying them, one observes very subtle differences of motif and execution, and from this observation, one can begin to discern more complicated relationships between images less directly related to each other.[43]

A small group of meditating bodhisattvas, including no. 159, no. 160, and one in a private collection, are all associated with the "boyish" group, since each has facial expression, bodily form, and a kind of decorative detailing of the drapery typical of that group.[44] They constitute a rare case of a group of three closely related images, although no. 160 and the private collection image share the most characteristics.

Meditating bodhisattva no. 159 (figs. 16a,b) is likely the earliest of the three and belongs to the "boyish" group of early Hakuhō considered above. Like the Hōryūji Kannon no. 1, meditating bodhisattva no. 159 has a double eyelid, a trait frequently seen in the group, as is the elaborate patterning of the drapery. Consequently, I believe that no. 159 was made in the same studio as the other members of the "boyish" group. Assuming that no. 159 is the first in a sequence of meditating bodhisattvas, likely no. 160 (figs. 17a,b) and the private collection image (fig. 18) were made a little later, perhaps in the same studio as no. 159, although this is not certain.

Differences within the faces, crowns,[45] and bodily proportions can be detected in the group, but it is in the drapery decoration that the most telling variations are found. The skirts of the three are very similar, but the sense of tension and dynamism that informs the drapery folds of no. 159 is lacking in the other two. One of the most striking features of these images is the presence of landscape elements on the drums of the pedestals.[46] The landscape of no. 159 is most fully articulated, consisting of craggy peaks, sometimes with trees along their ridges, extending around the entire circumference of the drum. On the

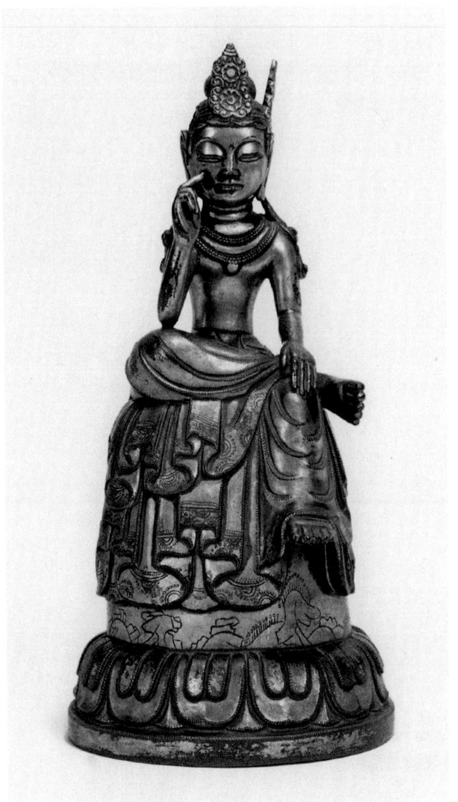 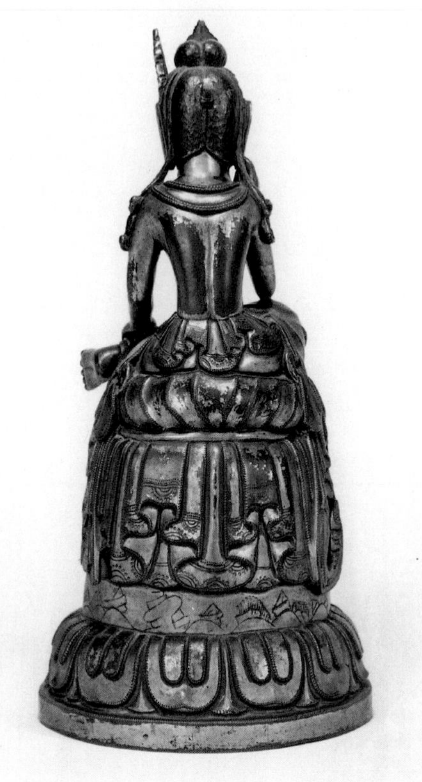

16   TNM Meditating Bosatsu no.159, H: 16.8 cm.   a. front   b. back
Photo courtesy of TNM

private collection image the landscape is less precisely detailed, but it does encircle the drum; that of no. 160, which is similarly undetailed, only appears at the front and sides of the drum. Perhaps the imprecise, rather inelegant landscapes of the latter two images were copied from either no. 159 or its model.[47]

By way of summary, I propose, at least tentatively, a chronological relationship among the three meditating bodhisattvas. Undoubtedly, no. 159 is the earliest and was probably made in what I refer to as the "boyish" group studio; perhaps no. 160 was made somewhat later; and the private collection image a little later still.

It is not my contention that the descriptive analyses of the preceding images have yielded unfamiliar data, since the relationship between the members of each pair, as well as within the larger group, has long been known. The presence of the "quivering line" on Buddha no. 153, Kannon no. 179, and Kannon no. 1 of the Hōryūji Museum should perhaps be emphasized, however, since this detail, together with common features in the decorative detailing of

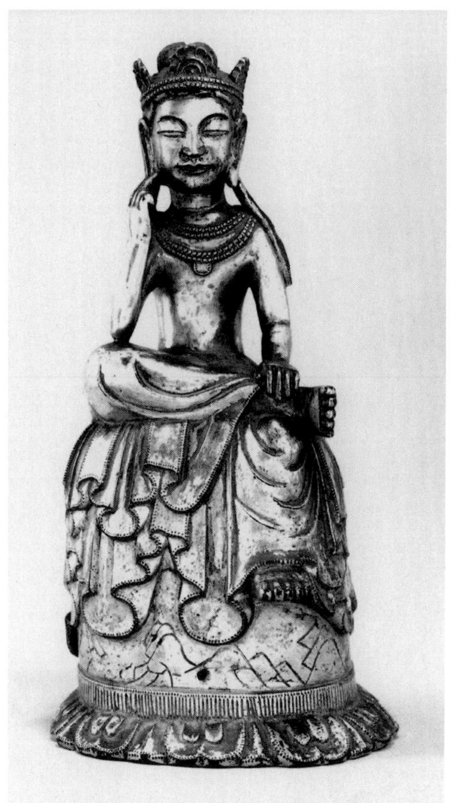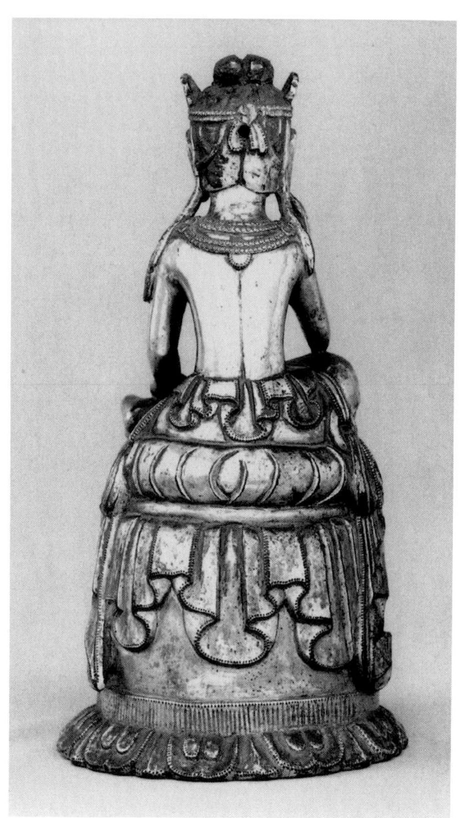

17 TNM Meditating Bosatsu no.160, H: 15.7 cm. a. front b. back
Photo courtesy of TNM

the fabric areas, suggests that all of these images may have emerged from the same studio. Although it is perhaps still premature to put forth a firm hypothesis, one can tentatively argue that all of the images listed at the beginning of this section came from the same general time and place, and doubtless some came from the same studio, perhaps made by the same artist.

CONCLUDING REMARKS

More general statements as to the evolution of Hakuhō sculpture will be reserved for the last chapter. Here, however, it might be useful to make a few broad remarks about the early phase. The beginning of the period is marked by a certain tentativeness, characteristic of a transitional phase and not unexpected, as the artists began to master a new stylistic vocabulary while also to some extent still rooted in older modes. Very soon we begin to see the first buds of definable Hakuhō style appearing in images such as the Kanshinji Kannon (fig. 6), the Yamadaden Amida triad (fig. 7), and the Ichijōji Kannon (fig. 8). Most observers would

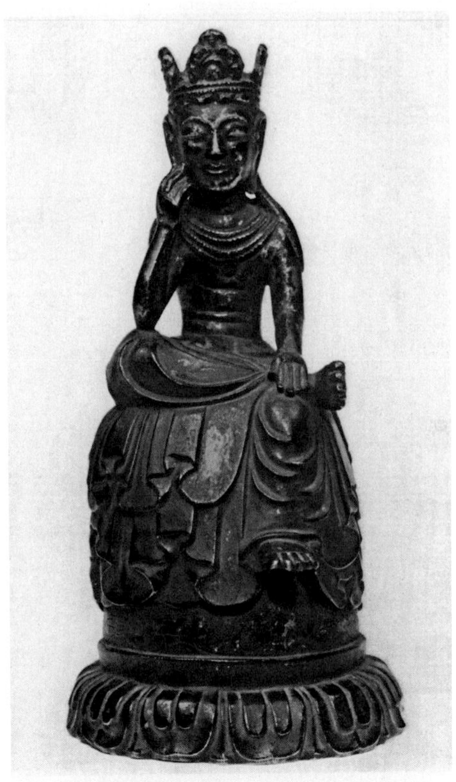

18   Meditating Bosatsu, H: 15.2 cm. Private Collection
Photo after TNM, *Kondō butsu* (1988), pl. 42

probably agree that the "boyish" group is perhaps the high point of early Hakuhō sculpture. Mōri and other scholars have searched for related images in China and Korea, finding some significant parallels, but this youthful mode never seems to have been as popular in those countries as in Japan. Japanese critics characterize these youthful images as *"adokenai,"* a term roughly translatable as "innocent," "artless," or "naïve." The term is highly positive, exemplifying qualities particularly valued in Japanese society. Certainly, most of the early Hakuhō images are significantly different in this respect from the few images from the Asuka period studied above.

Middle Hakuhō Sculpture

TRINITARIANISM IS PERVASIVE THROUGHOUT THE WORLD, AND I am fully cognizant of the risks in adopting a tripartite chronological scheme, given the strong ideological baggage that this concept carries.[1] Why not two or four subdivisions? (Presumably nobody would suggest five, or even a decade-by-decade consideration!) I am reasonably confident that all, or most, of the images dealt within the previous chapter should be

placed in the first couple of decades of the Hakuhō period (i.e., circa 650–670). In the final years of the period (circa 690–710), there are several extraordinary sculptures that appear, at least to me, to represent the full maturity of the tradition. Since there is a gap between the early and late periods of Hakuhō sculpture, one can reasonably suggest a search for intermediate works.

That being said, we must acknowledge difficulties in establishing a firm chronology for Hakuhō sculpture, and we might further wonder if a group of images can be plausibly attributed to the years circa 670–690, even allowing some leeway at either end. During the years in question, significant developments occurred in the political and religious spheres; new models may have come from the Korean peninsula and China; and continuing activity in the studios inevitably would have led to change. Despite such developments, perhaps it is impossible, even unnecessary, to develop a precise chronology for these years because sculptures proceeding from quite different stylistic currents could have been made at roughly the same time. In my best judgement, the images to be analyzed in this chapter appear to fall in the "Middle Hakuhō period," but I am certainly willing to be convinced of

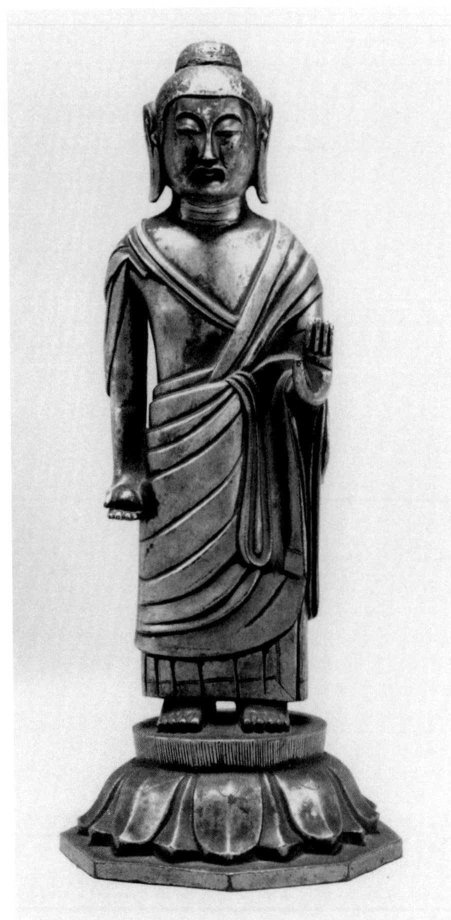 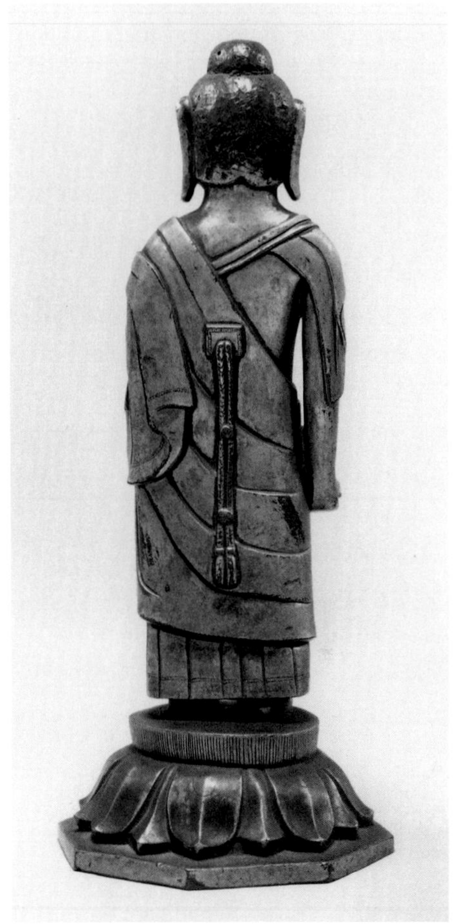

19   TNM Standing Buddha no.152, H: 30.1 cm.   a. front   b. back
Photo courtesy of TNM

other conceivable attributions. In any event, most of the images studied in this chapter are intrinsically interesting in various respects, so regardless of their absolute positions in time, all are extremely significant and, I expect, likely to appeal to the viewer.

TWO BUDDHA FIGURES

I would like first to consider a fascinating piece, standing Buddha no. 152 (figs. 19a,b). Certainly, this is one of the strangest representations of a Buddha in Hakuhō sculpture, and some of its iconographical and stylistic elements are especially difficult to interpret. As for iconography, the right arm is pendent, the hand palm upward and grasping what appears to be a jewel, although it might be a medicine jar; both are among the defining appurtenances of Yakushi Buddha. The face is full and fleshy, with small eyes, a down-turned mouth, and

enormous ears; limited modeling can be
seen in the chest area.

Particularly noteworthy is the arrangement of the drapery, including the peculiar
piece of fabric covering the right shoulder,
attached front and back by a strap, and a
tassel on the great robe at the back. Possibly the shoulder covering is the *henzan*,
as suggested by Kuno and rejected by
Yoshimura.[2] Without a doubt, the most
idiosyncratic detail of the drapery is a pair
of jewel strings with tassels, affixed to what
looks like a rectangle attached to the great
robe at back. Jewel strings are common on
bodhisattva figures,[3] but there seems to be
no iconographical justification for their
appearance on a Buddha figure. One hesi-
tates to call it a mistake, but I am at a loss to
offer any other explanation.

What exactly was the sculptor thinking when he designed the image? This,
of course, is the type of question asked
repeatedly in this book, and I am the first
to acknowledge that there may never be
a satisfactory answer; nevertheless, some
suggestions can be made. A general prototype can easily be located on the Korean
peninsula for the position of the right arm
and hand, but such prototypes invariably have the right shoulder bare in one of
the canonical formats.[4] Could there have
been a direct model for no. 152's drapery
element on the right shoulder and mysteri-
ous jewel strings at back? I suspect we have
here an odd image for which the sculptor
apparently adopted elements from various
traditions, perhaps with not a great deal of
understanding.

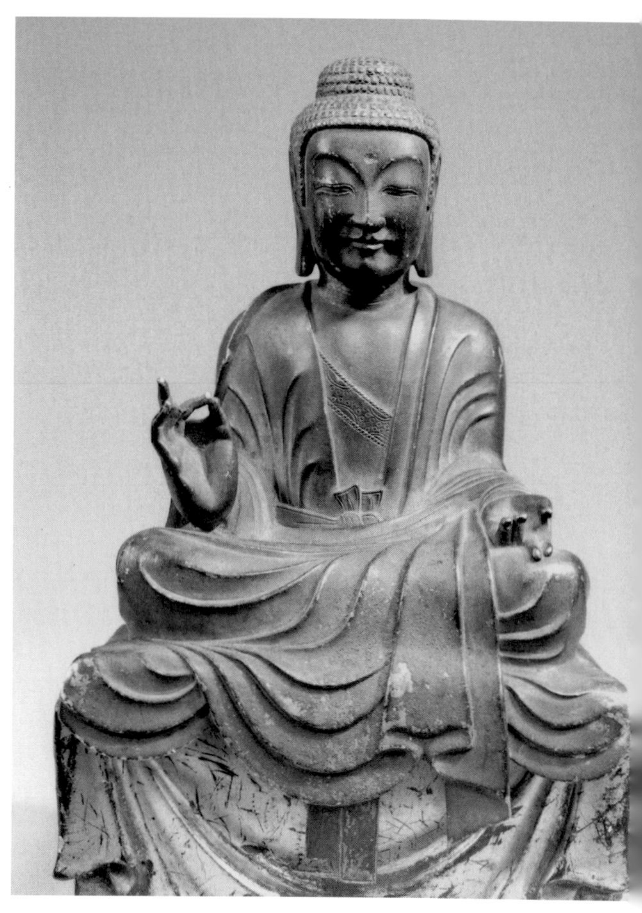

20   TNM Seated Buddha no.147, H: 17.2 cm.
a. front   b. left side
Photo courtesy of TNM

Turning now to seated Buddha no. 147
(figs. 20a,b), we encounter an equally puzzling image. As with no. 152, this sculpture
has a full, fleshy face although here the
individual features are more carefully
delineated, especially the elaborately rendered eyes. Most of the body is concealed
by the robes, in which two surprising
details are to be observed: first, here also is
a representation of a *henzan* or something
like it; and second, in the area of the bare

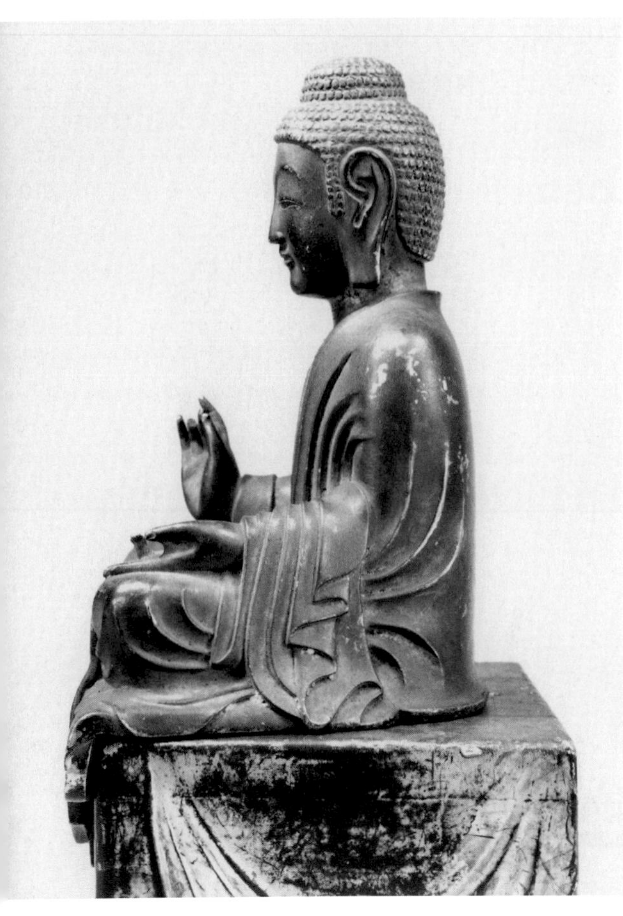

ing rather lengthy analysis will justify the expression of personal taste. This image is difficult to place, so that one cannot help wondering which aspects replicate an older image and which emerged from the sculptor's imagination. The head of Kannon no. 170 is very large, its body is quite slender, and, although its contours are clearly visible, the overall sense of modeling is minimal. Recalling Asuka sculpture (e.g., fig. 2), and some early Hakuhō images perpetuating Asuka traits (e.g., fig. 5), one is immediately struck by the X crossing of the scarf in front of the legs–and yet how different this motif is here![6] Obviously, the sculptor was drawing on an older motif, but here treating it in an extraordinary manner, with broadly sweeping folds, a feature echoed in the lower part of the belt-ends, the hem of the skirt, and the two ends of the scarf descending from the arms to the pedestal.

What can one make of this image? Having been unable to locate any closely related sculptures, I assume Kannon no. 170 was not widely copied and certainly did not inaugurate a new lineage. On the other hand, discounting a couple of awkward details, the image is superbly designed and cast, most certainly the work of a first-rate artist. The consistency of design, especially in the sweeping curves of the scarf, hems, and belt-ends, suggests a sculptor striving to achieve harmonious rhythms. Additionally, particular motifs, such as the hem overlying the scarf-ends just above the pedestal and the dip of the scarf at back to reveal the carefully crafted necklace, indi-

chest one sees the hem of an undergarment, but strangely, it moves from the right shoulder to the left side of the waist, opposite to the usual arrangement, and its hem has a type of decoration more typical for bodhisattvas. Its belt is tied in a prominent bow at the front of the waist, with the two ends emerging from under the lower hem of the great robe.[5]

THREE BODHISATTVAS

The extraordinary Kannon no. 170 (figs. 21a,b) is a sculpture that has intrigued me for a long time; I hope that the follow-

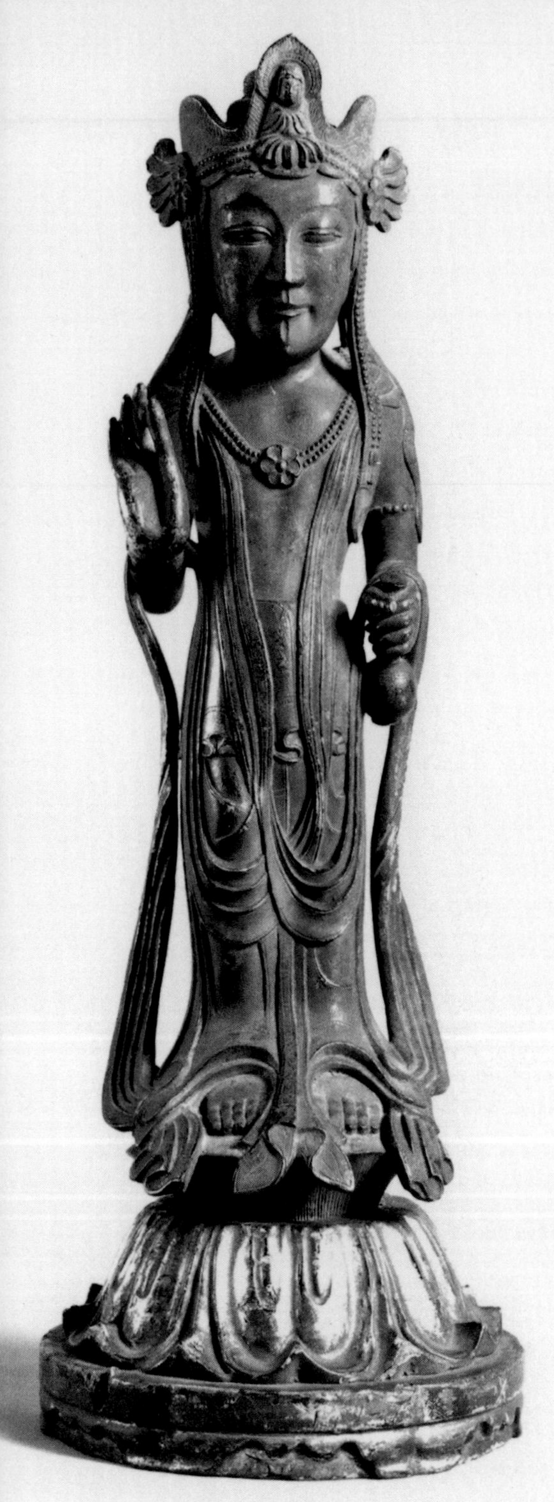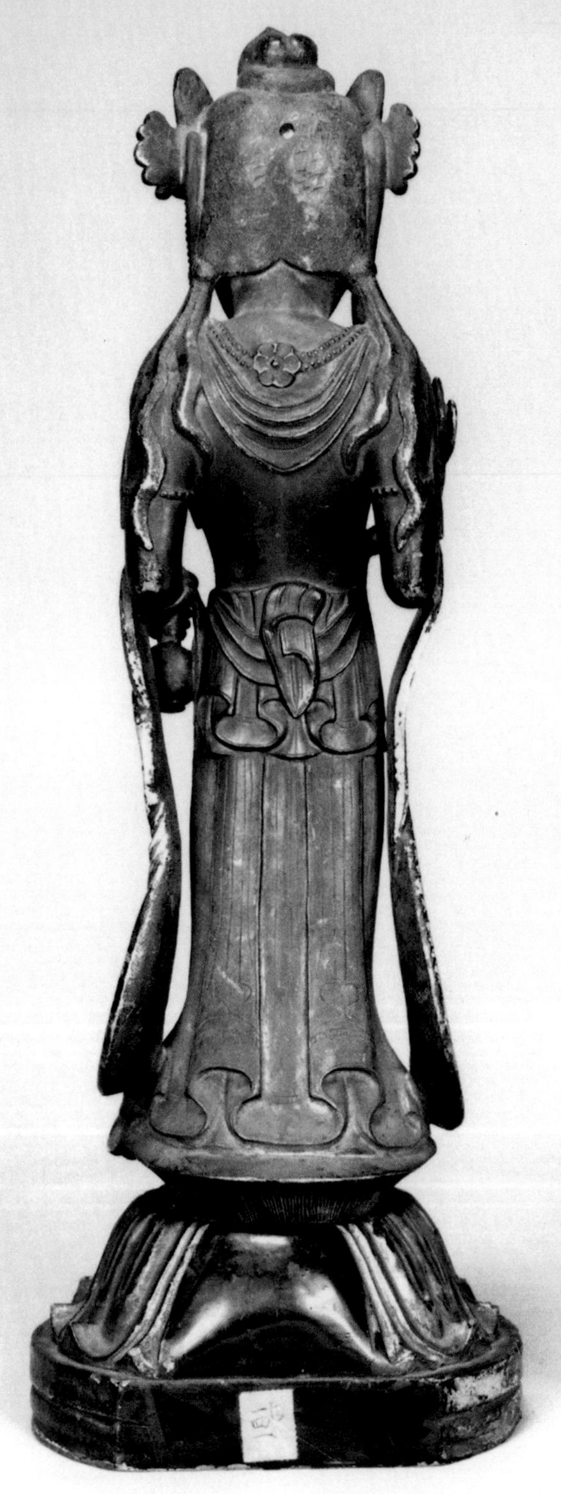

21 TNM Standing Kannon no.170, H: 28.8 cm. a. front b. back
Photo courtesy of TNM

CHAPTER 3

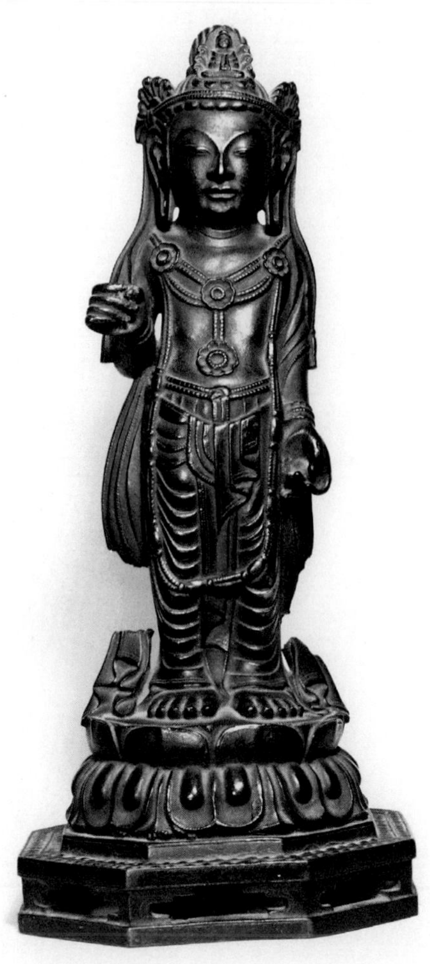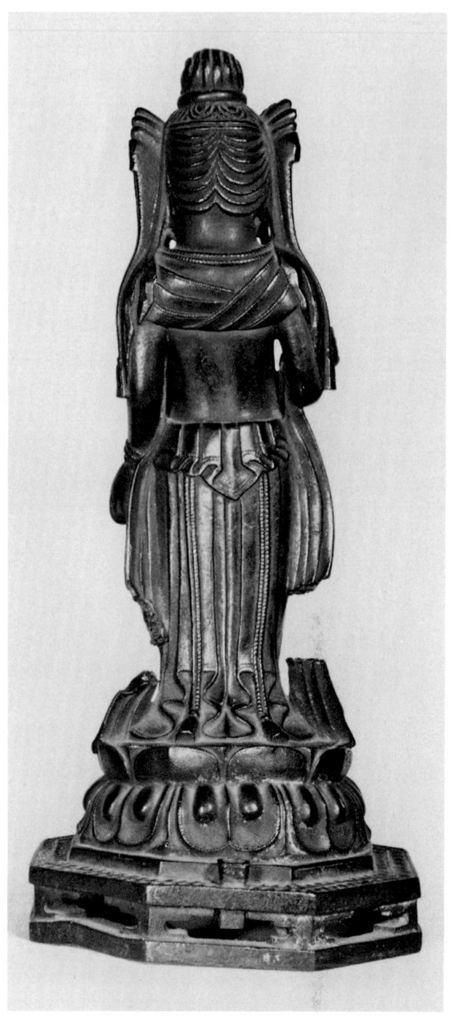

22   Standing Kannon, H: 37.7 cm. Sanzenji, Nagano   a. front   b. back
Photo courtesy of the Shinano Museum of Art

cate an artist conscious of contemporary trends in sculpture.[7]

The Japanese publication in which I have carefully analyzed the Sanzenji Kannon (figs. 22a,b) may not be generally accessible, so the following offers a summary of that earlier article.[8] Although this image has been associated with the "boyish" group, I believe it was made later than those sculptures considered in chapter 2, though presumably with full knowledge of the "boyish" characteristics. In my article, I commented on a number of features: the coiffure, having a beautiful topknot and a complicated arrangement of the hair at back, the latter being a feature rare in Hakuhō sculpture; the unusual treatment of the drapery at the abdominal area, with fabric showing between two belts; and the particularly complicated pedestal.

Comparing the Sanzenji Kannon with a standard example of the "boyish" group, such as Kannon no. 179 (fig. 12), reveals numerous differences. The proportions of the two are similar, but the Sanzenji Kannon has a heavier body and a mature and serious expression instead of a youthful and sweet one. Differences also occur in their jewelry and drapery, which are considerably more elaborate on the Sanzenji Kannon. I take such differences to indicate evolution within Hakuhō studios, as sculptors continually sought to vary their personifications of divinity.

Although I try to avoid enthusiastic superlatives in this study, I find the intriguing qualities of Kannon no. 176 (figs. 23a,b) impossible to exaggerate.[9] It is often included in the "boyish" category, which may be true of the face but seems less true generally, and especially of the sensuous profile created by the curving hips. Also, its legs are much longer than its upper torso, and in that respect, too, it differs from more typically "boyish" bodhisattvas, such as Kannon no. 179 (fig. 12) or bodhisattva no. 188 (fig. 13).

Careful examination of the drapery and jewelry arrangements reveal just how uncharacteristic this figure is. For example, at first glance the arrangement of the scarf appears standard. In fact, it is most peculiar. Rather than passing across the shoulders and either falling directly to the pedestal or passing in front of the body before looping over the arms, in this image the scarf does not cover the shoulders and

back at all, but makes a deep U in front of the legs and is draped over the two arms.[10] The skirt is relatively simple in arrangement, although the artist has taken pains to decorate all of the hems in the *hansetsu kuyo* pattern.[11]

Many unusual features are present in the jewelry, so many, in fact, that it might be best to list them:

1. The crown is complex, with two parallel diadem bands.[12]
2. The main jewelry arrangement at the front descends from the two side plaques of the crown, rather than coming from the sides of the necklace, as is ordinarily the case.
3. Three jewel strings descend in front, one from the necklace, and join at a central rosette at thigh level. From that rosette two other strings descend, diverging to encircle the back of the figure. Two small ring pendents, symmetrically placed, are looped over the lower strings.
4. At center back a jewel string descends from a central rosette on the necklace; here, at thigh level, is a ring through which the various strings are interwoven.

How should the jewelry and drapery arrangements of Kannon no. 176 be interpreted? I propose that the artist was striving to produce an image different from the norm. To that end, he utilized a variety of elements not frequently seen, certainly not combined as they are in this figure and in the Hōonji Kannon.[13]

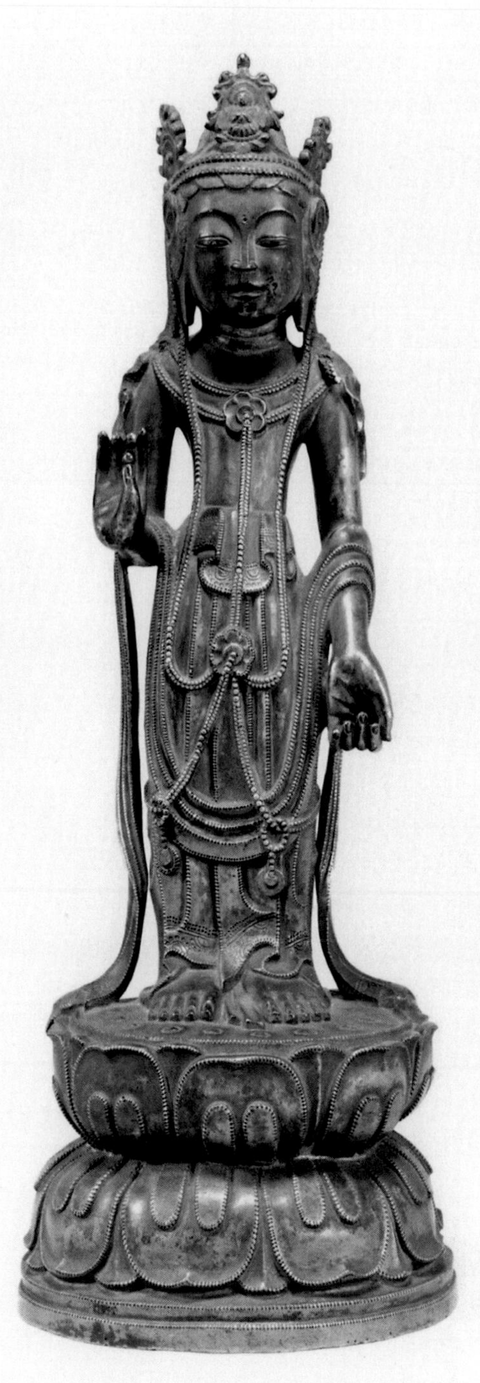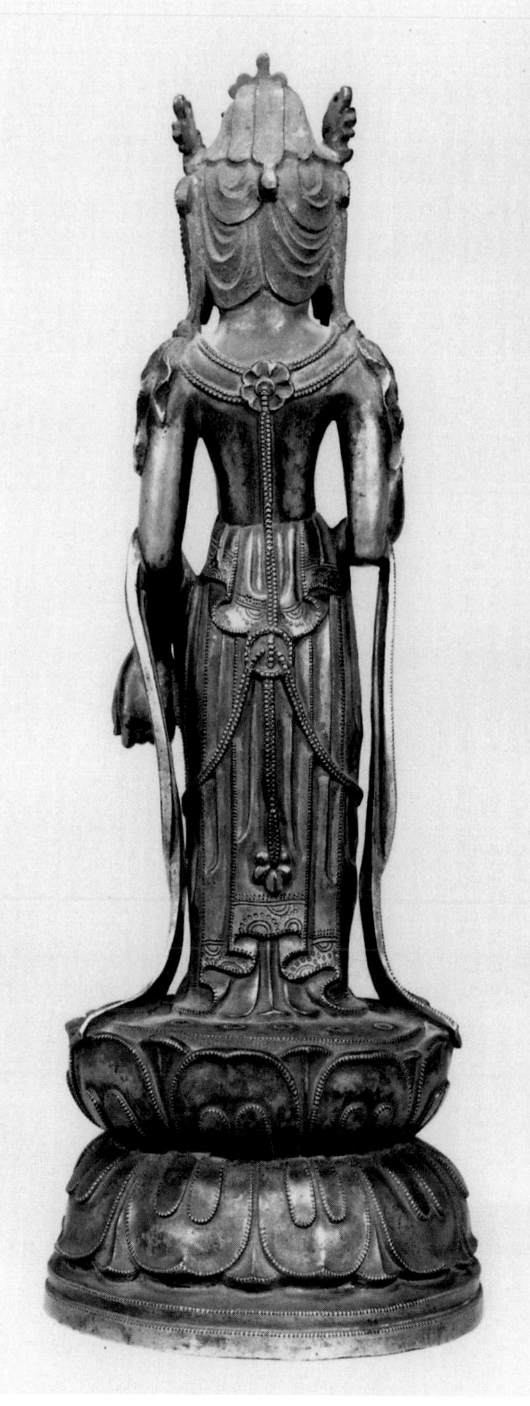

23 TNM Standing Kannnon no.176, H: 29.3 cm.   a. front   b. back
Photo courtesy of TNM

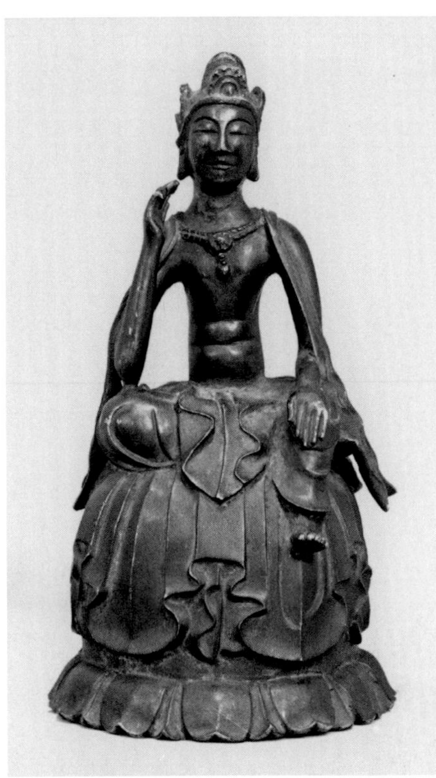

24 TNM Meditating Bosatsu no.161, H: 15.4 cm.
Photo courtesy of TNM

A GROUP OF MEDITATING BODHISATTVAS

Of the numerous meditating bodhisatt-vas in Hakuhō sculpture, several can be tentatively assigned to the middle period. Interestingly, they range from awkward, unattractive figures to others that are superb. Generally speaking, in this study I focus on images that manifest–at least to me–superior artistic quality. My justification for this is that by directing the reader's attention to what I perceive as excellent, I illuminate both the inferior and the super-lative.

Most observers will probably agree that meditating bodhisattva no. 161 (fig. 24) sits at the undistinguished end of the spectrum. A truly weird feature is its upper torso, unnaturally narrow in relation to the enormous, bulbous pedestal on which the figure sits. Arms and the right leg are in more or less proper proportions, but the pendent left leg is impossibly short. Most curiously, the right leg actually passes under the left, rather than resting on the knee as is correct. Apparently the sculptor who made no. 161 was not up to design-ing a proper icon, inevitably producing a surprisingly awkward piece. Much of the drapery covering the pedestal is reason-ably competent, if schematic, but even here there are odd touches. The image might be considered funny or cute, but it is unlikely that any critic would place it among the masterpieces of Hakuhō sculpture.

All of this being said, however, an inter-pretation or explanation is still required. Production of gilt-bronze sculptures was an expensive process, one not likely to be given to an incompetent craftsman, particularly in an important studio. Of course, all craftsmen had to learn their trade, but one assumes that this learning process was car-ried out in a lengthy apprenticeship during which the students assisted in routine mat-ters and then observed and helped the mas-ter before being allowed to do anything on their own. Perhaps meditating bodhisattva no. 161 is the product of a "provincial" studio, one lacking experienced and skillful artisans; or it might be spurious, although that seems unlikely given its provenance.[14]

CHAPTER 3

A remaining possibility is worrisome in the context of the present study. Could its clumsiness actually reflect the taste of patrons of the time? In response I can only say that an object deemed satisfactory or better in appearance would likely have been replicated, and the more it was admired the greater the likelihood of replications.[15] Presently, I hope to illustrate this correlation. At this point I can only propose that meditating bodhisattva no. 161 is merely the product of an incompetent artisan.[16]

Two images of a substantially higher level of achievement are the Kanshinji and Fukuoka Art Museum meditating bodhisattvas (respectively, figs. 25a,b, and figs. 26a,b). The former is one of the most charming of Hakuhō images; the latter, like many other examples here considered, is unusual in various respects. Looking first at the Kanshinji image, one is conscious of a very large head and a gentle face, broad shoulders and well-modeled torso, an elaborate necklace, and neatly arranged drapery folds in the skirt. Its pedestal is octagonal, and the pendent left foot rests on what appears to be a lotus blossom, none too clearly rendered. The Fukuoka meditating bodhisattva also has a very large head, but its expression is somewhat grim, and its hands and feet are also disproportionately large. Its left arm is held farther to the right than is customary, making the figure seem oddly unbalanced. Particularly striking is the enormous octagonal pedestal, each facet of which has a large opening.

Of all the meditating bodhisattvas considered, none has been more inten-

sively studied than the image at Yachūji in Osaka Prefecture (figs. 27a,b).[17] Its great beauty has not been the main motive for concentrated investigation: the Yachūji meditating bodhisattva has the characters for "emperor" (*tennō*) inscribed on the pedestal, a matter of compelling interest to historians of early Japan.[18] Furthermore, the inscription also contains the characters for Miroku, possibly the earliest instance of this term.[19]

Before moving to the question of date, let us look at the sculpture itself. Like practically all the meditating bodhisattvas studied thus far, the Yachūji Miroku has a very large head; moreover, it has an enormous topknot made up of two smaller topknots. The face, nicely presented, wears a meditative expression, and the body is well modeled. Great care has been taken with the articulation of the drapery folds falling in neat symmetrical rows and with incised patterns decorating the borders. Additionally, the designer has placed on either leg a panel containing the *hansetsu kuyo* pattern previously noted in meditating bodhisattva no. 159 (fig. 16).

In chapter 2, meditating bodhisattva no. 156 (fig. 3) was analyzed, including a brief discussion of its date. The cyclical characters inscribed on no. 156, most plausibly equivalent to either 606 or 666, also appear on the Yachūji Miroku. In the discussion of no. 156, I argued against the earlier date of 606 assigned by previous historians on account of its "archaic" qualities. Conclusions relating to the dating of meditating bodhisattva no. 156 need not

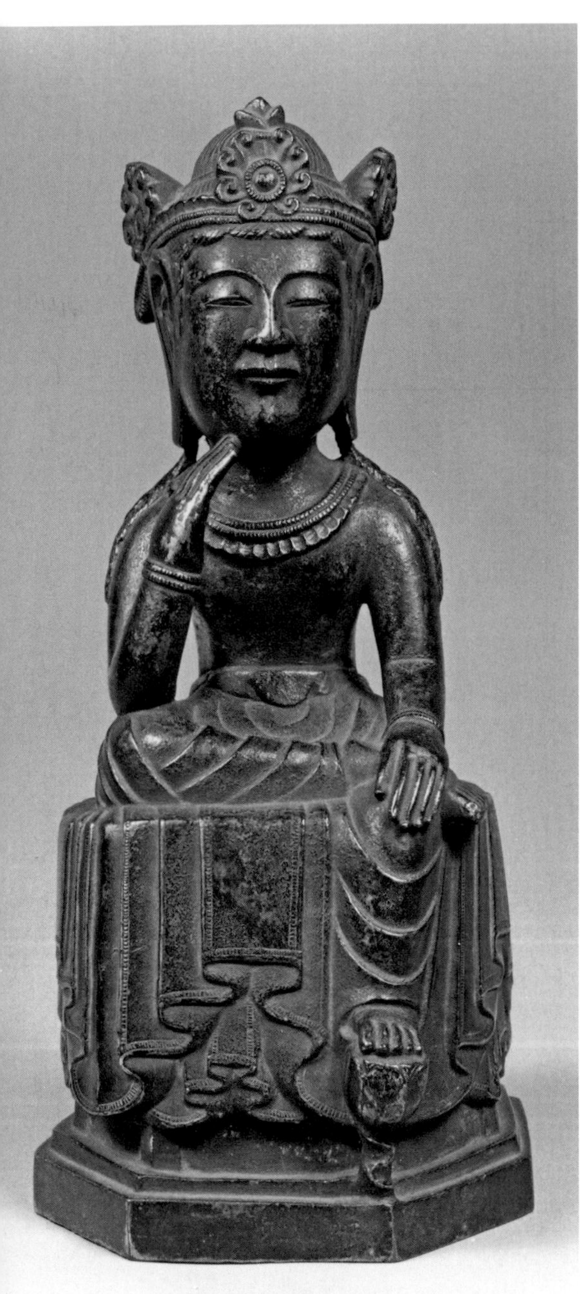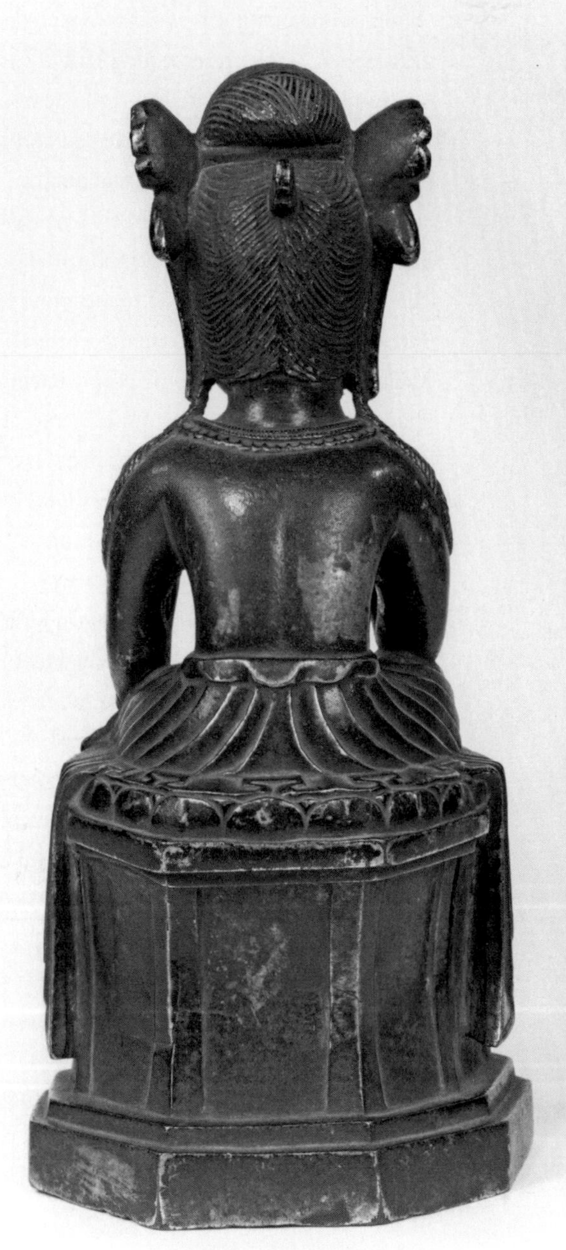

25   Meditating Bosatsu, H: 19.2 cm. Kanshinji, Osaka   a. front   b. back

Photo courtesy of NNM

                                                                CHAPTER 3

be repeated here, but the Yachūji inscription calls for careful consideration. One must always keep foremost in mind that the characters were incised rather than cast, which, logically, could have been done at any time after the image was made. On stylistic grounds the Yachūji Miroku probably dates from a decade or so later than 666, possibly about 680; furthermore the word *tennō*, in my view, more likely came into use in the reign of Tenmu (672–686).[20] At the very least, one should be cautious about too ready acceptance of the 666 date for the Yachūji Miroku.

A number of Hakuhō-period meditating bodhisattvas exist in addition to the ones just considered, but the latter, I believe, are enough to allow some tentative generalizations to be made. It goes without saying that such a large number reflects the great popularity of this icon type, one usually identified as Miroku. Evidently, there was significant demand for these, although apparently no single canonical prototype for the artists to follow, resulting in widely varying images.[21] As mentioned previously, more or less exact prototypes for each example *might* have been made in China or Korea. In my view this is an unlikely scenario, yet one that must be considered.

The basic form of the meditating bodhisattva was known in Japan from the onset of Buddhist practice, first through imported images and later in domestic productions.[22] As we have seen, the arrangement of arms and legs is constant; usually the head is large and the crown complex; the upper body is ordinarily fully modeled and adorned with nothing more than a necklace; and the drape of the skirt over the pedestal is often quite complex. Beyond these traits, however, significant variation appears, particularly in facial expression, which ranges widely from child-like to severe. Typically, the upper body is well designed and modeled, except in such images as no. 161 (fig. 24), where it is unnaturally slender, or in the Nittenji bodhisattva, where it is awkwardly handled.[23] Most of the figures we have studied lack an upper garment, but meditating bodhisattvas no. 161 and no. 162 both wear a vestigial scarf. Similarly, some meditating bodhisattvas wear side-belts (e.g., Yachūji Miroku, fig. 27), but most of the present group do not.[24]

Frequently, an analysis of a seemingly "unimportant" element is revealing. In the present group three variants of the pedestal base appear: the first is essentially absent, the second is round, and the third octagonal. Types one and two are usually relatively consistent.[25] More variety occurs in type three, for which at least two variants are apparent: in the Fukuoka City Museum figure the octagonal base has openwork in each facet (fig. 26), while the Kanshinji image has none (fig. 25). Clearly, the studios had models for these base forms, and the sculptors seem to have been free to use whichever they wished.

To sum up the discussion of the meditating bodhisattva category, I would argue that here, as with many other categories of Hakuhō sculpture, we are dealing with "complex variables." Each artist had access

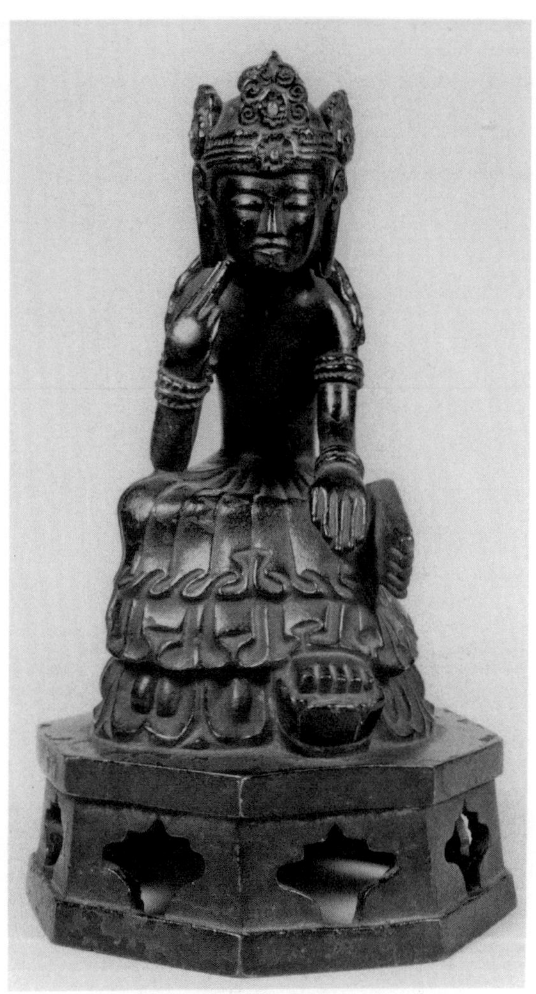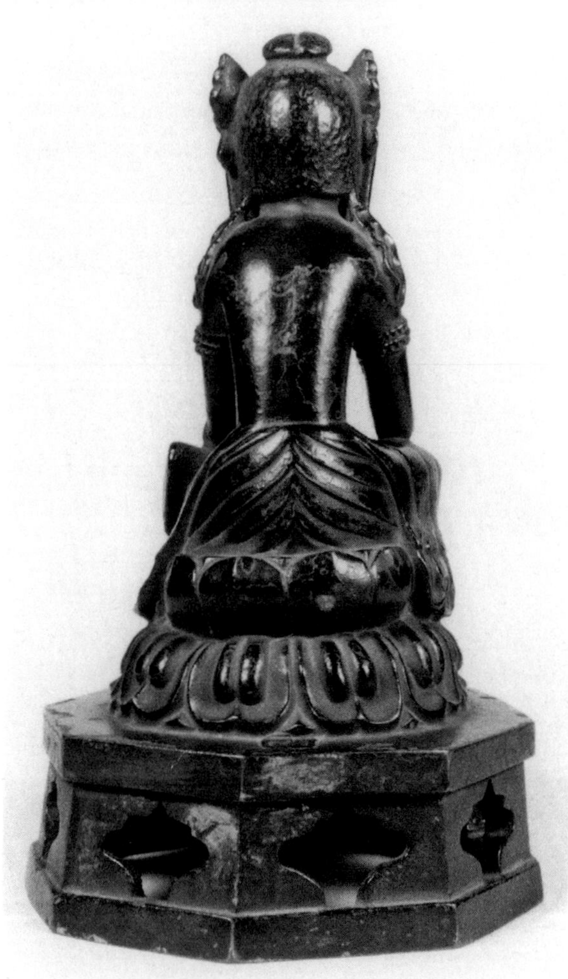

26   Meditating Bosatsu, H: 17.0 cm. Fukuoka City Museum   a. front   b. back

Photo after TNM, *Kondō butsu* (1988), pl. 53

to a variety of motifs and stylistic features that could be combined, within certain parameters, in various ways. Beyond this, the artist could experiment and introduce his own interpretation of the sculptural type in question, particularly in jewelry, drapery, and the like, but also in regard to facial expression, modeling, and overall interpretation.

TWO MORE STANDING BODHISATTVAS

Let us apply this idea of "complex variables" to some standing bodhisattva figures. Kannon no. 174 (figs. 28a,b) and Kannon no. 175 (figs. 29a,b) were probably made at about the same time, perhaps even in the same studio, although that is uncertain. In

CHAPTER 3

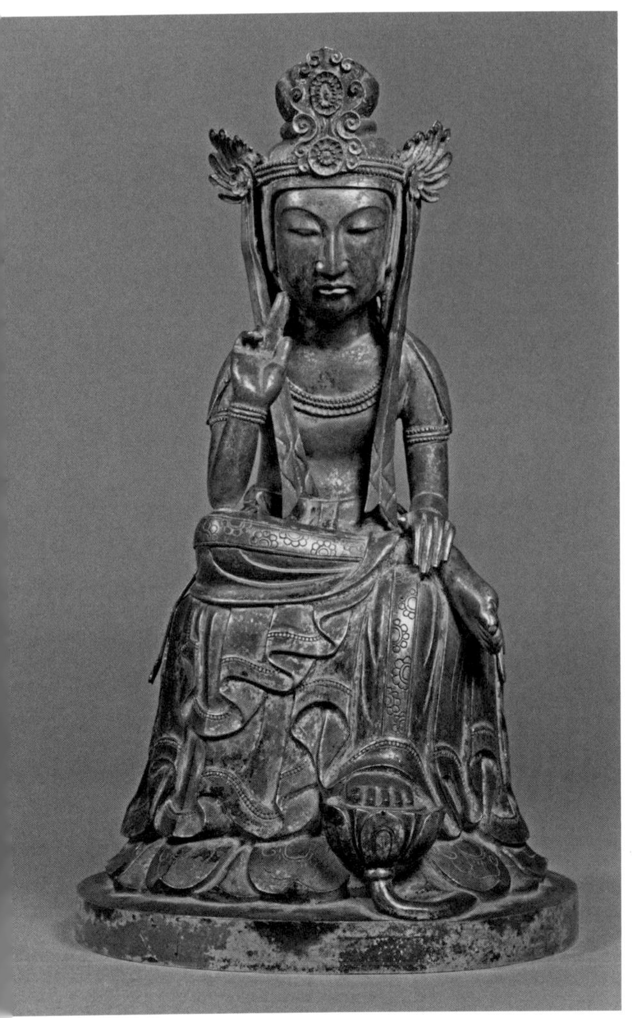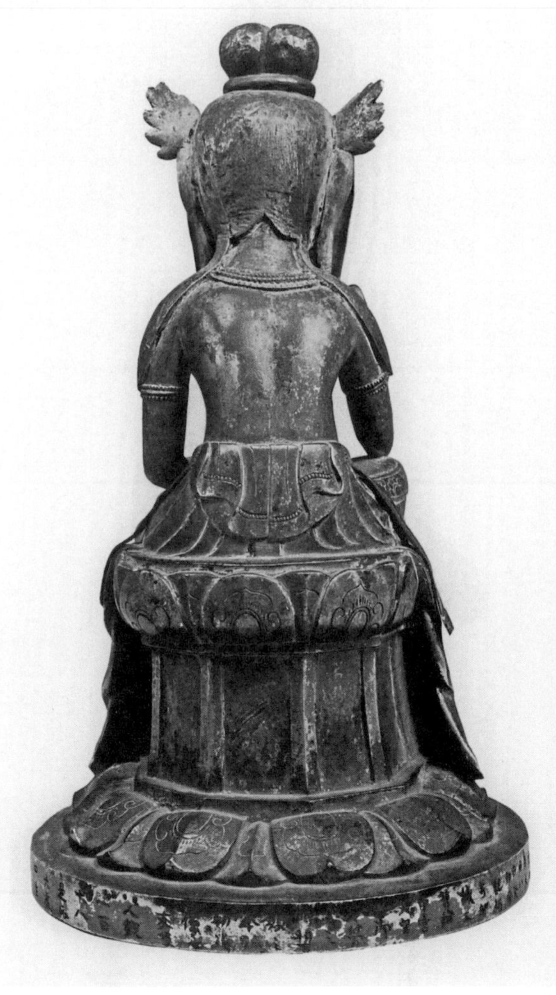

27   Meditating Bosatsu, H: 18.5 cm. Yachūji, Osaka   a. front   b. back
Photo courtesy of NNM

the treatment of the crown and face; the proportions and modeling of the body; the general articulation of the drapery folds; and the arrangement of the jewelry; they share several common features, but differences are more relevant to this analysis.

KANNON NO. 174
Standing *kebutsu*
Jewel in raised left hand
Scarf crosses in X format
Scarf with U loop at back
Round pedestal

KANNON NO. 175
Seated *kebutsu*
Jewel in pendent right hand
Scarf in "two-registers" format
Scarf straight across shoulders
Octagonal pedestal

MIDDLE HAKUHŌ SCULPTURE

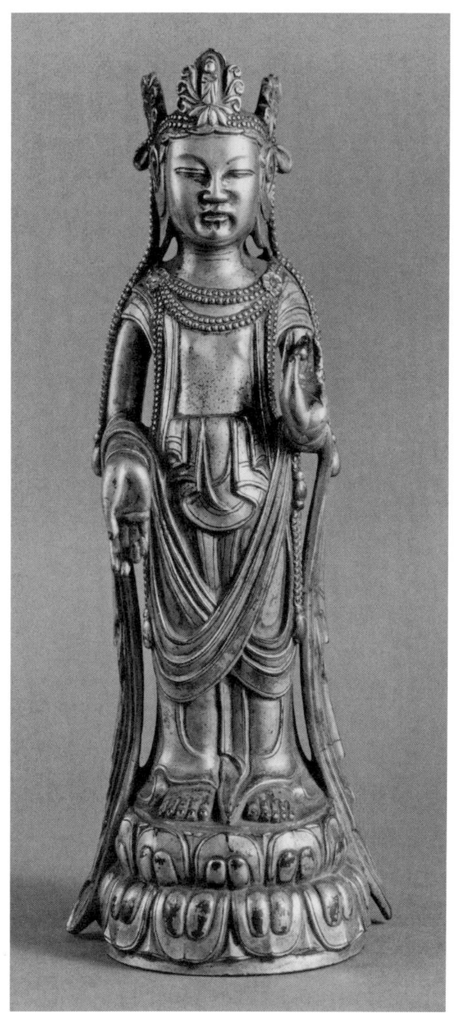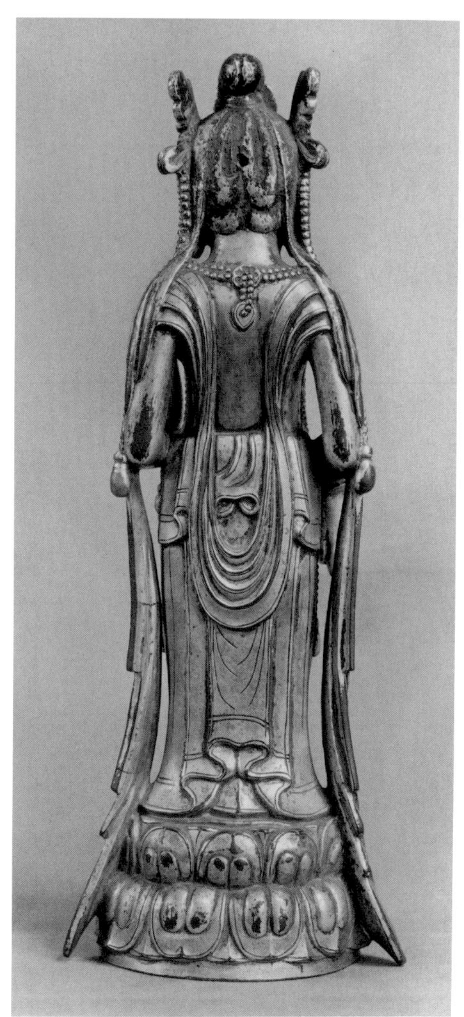

28 TNM Standing Kannon no.174, H: 26.4 cm.   a. front   b. back
Photo courtesy of TNM

How should these differences be interpreted? Taking them in turn, we might note that the standing versus seated *kebutsu* pose appears arbitrary; the jewel is iconographically significant, but its placement seems random; the scarf crossing in an X is an "archaic" trait, while the two-registers format is up-to-date, but the X is also occasionally found in Hakuhō sculpture; the U loop at back is frequently concomitant with the jewel, but the scarf straight across the shoulders is more typical of Hakuhō; and neither round nor octagonal pedestals appear to carry any specific meaning.

It is my belief that in Kannon nos. 174 and 175 it was the individual sculptor's prerogative to select among variant forms of the prescribed motifs. The jewel and

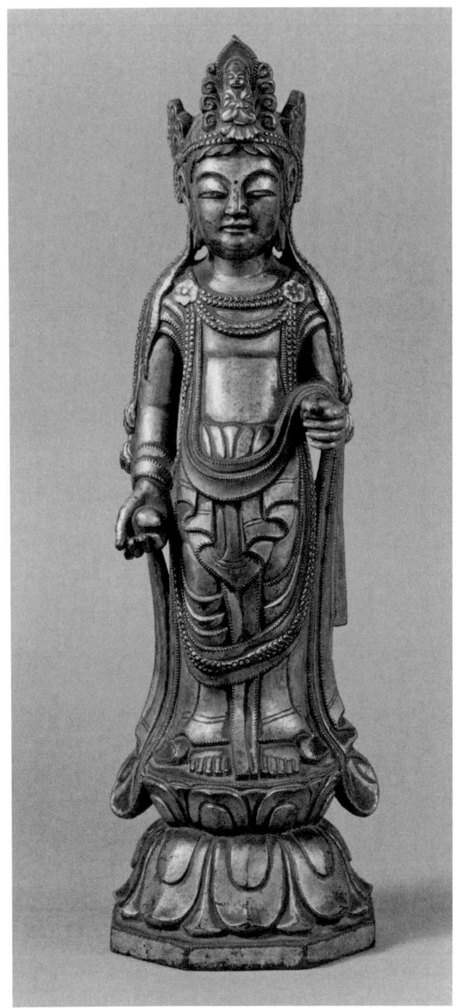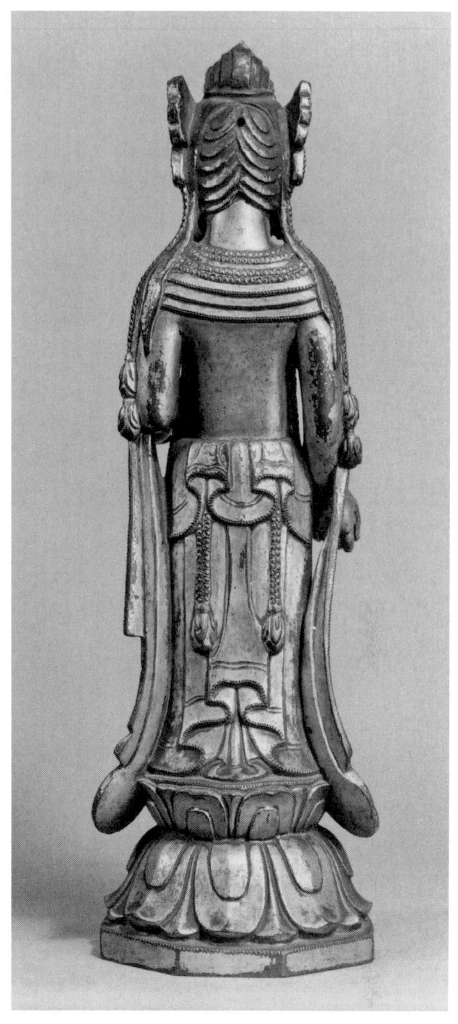

29   TNM Standing Kannon no.175, H: 31.0 cm.   a. front   b. back
Photo courtesy of TNM

scarf in U loop are frequently seen together, but by this phase of Hakuhō sculpture their combination does not seem to have been mandatory. Fundamentally, one cannot plausibly assume that, for example, a standing *kebutsu* mandated a jewel in the raised left hand, or that a seated *kebutsu* required a jewel in the pendent right hand. To this statement I append my constant caveat:

since the whole of Hakuhō icon production, firmly dated, is not available to us, the best one can do is to survey the surviving corpus and assert what seems reasonable. Could these two images have been made in the same studio and perhaps even designed by the same sculptor? Again, I can only say that a single studio is likely and the same artist possible, although the latter is hard to

MIDDLE HAKUHŌ SCULPTURE

demonstrate.[26] These are speculations, and I certainly would not want them thought of as foundational or essential to the broader argument.

CLOSELY RELATED IMAGES

Fortunately, it is possible to move to firmer ground, since a quite large number of "closely related images" demonstrate one of the key contentions of this book: that there are many interesting and significant sculptures which do seem to allow us to directly observe their creators making specific design decisions. Here I am referring to images whose relationships are unequivocal and have long been recognized, beginning with those pairs within the "Forty-eight Buddhist Deities" that lend themselves to being studied in juxtaposition. Expanded fieldwork in the postwar period identified additional relevant pieces throughout Japan, and with their publication further relationships became evident.[27]

Restrictions of space necessitate that I concentrate on just two pairs of standing bodhisattvas. One member of each pair comes from the "Forty-eight Buddhist Deities" group, the other from quite far away.[28] The first pair consists of the Daisenji bodhisattva (fig. 30), found in Tottori Prefecture, and bodhisattva no. 190 (fig. 31). So close to one another in form, their relationship cannot be doubted; apparently made in the same studio, perhaps even by the same artist. Of course their relative dates are uncertain: one could be a copy of the other, or both could be copies from a lost proto-type. Yet besides extraordinary similarities, they show numerous subtle differences, indicating that rote copying was not how either was made.

In posture and proportions the two images are close, each with the rhythmic contours created by their hip-shot pose; but the Daisenji figure has a substantially larger head and narrower shoulders. Presumably, such variation in figural style was permitted for the artist.[29] The two wear the standard costume of the Hakuhō bodhisattva, skirt and scarf, the latter arranged in the typical two-register format. At the right arm the scarf shows an extremely rare configuration. Instead of draping once over the arm and then hanging directly down to the base, in these two images the scarf passes over the wrist and then circles back, finally descending to the lower tier of the base. In addition, the lower register of the scarf is centered not at the lateral midpoint of the figure but over the right leg, and it is paralleled by a heavy jewel string centered on a large roundel, the whole creating a very effective rhythm. Though similarly configured, the motifs of scarf, jewelry strings, and roundel are far from identical in details on the two images. While adhering to a single form of the motifs, the sculptor felt free to introduce minor changes in these motifs.

Geographical separation also holds for the second pair, the Kaizōji Kannon (fig. 32) and Kannon no. 182 (fig. 33).[30] The former is from an island far south of present-day Tokyo and very distant from the Yamato region. These figures are not identical in

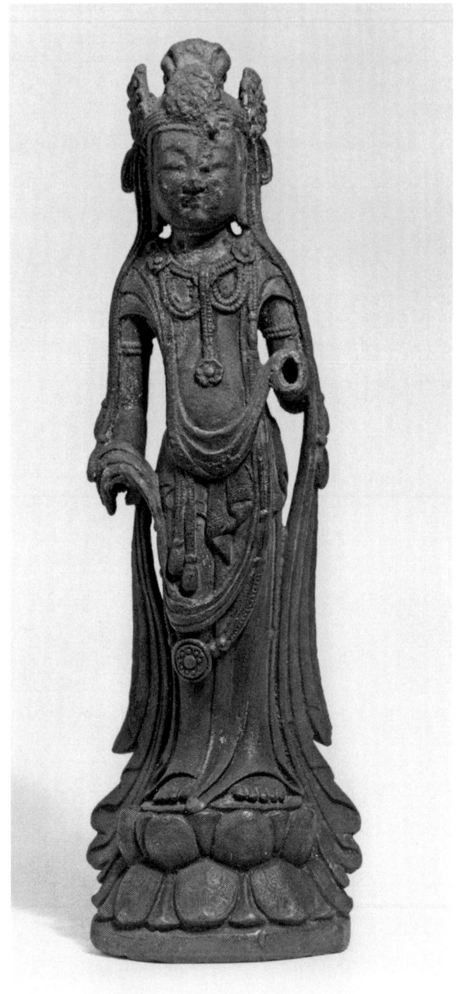

30   Standing Bosatsu, H: 32.0 cm. Daisenji, Tottori
     Photo courtesy of NNM

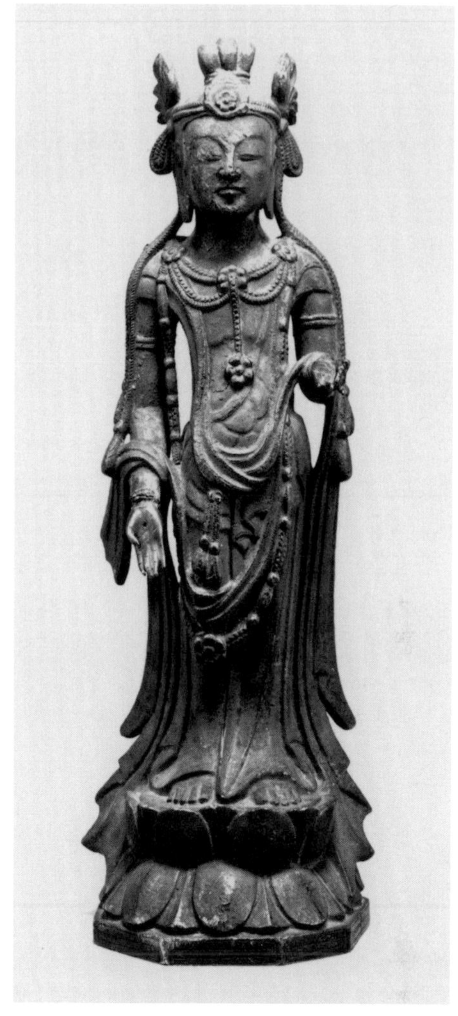

31   TNM Standing Bosatsu no.190, H: 30.8 cm.
     Photo courtesy of TNM

configuration, but mirror images of each other. Mirroring is frequently seen in pairs of bodhisattvas flanking a central Buddha (e.g., Yamadaden triad, fig. 7), but the present images, both being representations of Kannon, would never have figured in a single triad. Excepting arm positions, the two figures are extremely close in pose and proportions, yet, despite their overall strong resemblances, they differ in numerous subtle details. For example, the *kebutsu* is seated in the crown of the Kaizōji Kannon and standing in no. 182, a variation also noted above. Both images grasp a jewelry string at about waist level, but on the Kaizōji Kannon the string hangs plumb, while on Kannon no. 182, the artist has shown the string as being pulled slightly to

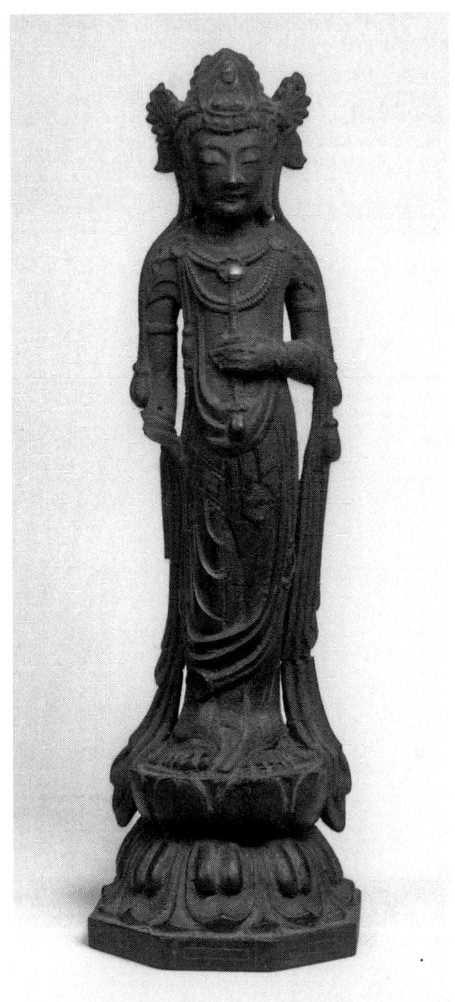

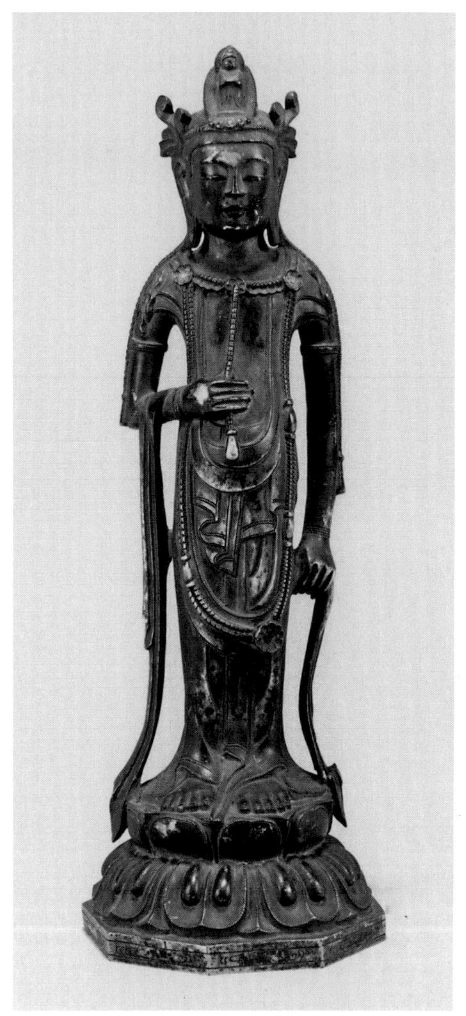

32 Standing Kannon, H: 29.8 cm. Kaizōji, Tokyo
Photo courtesy of TNM

33 TNM Standing Kannon no.182, H: 30.9 cm.
Photo courtesy of TNM

the right by the hand holding it.[31] Small differences also exist in the robes and jewelry systems of the two images.

Pedestals have been very much neglected in the study of early sculpture, but a focus on them here demonstrates that the four images were almost certainly made in the same studio. Each of the pedestals in this group of four sculptures has an octagonal base supporting two circular registers of lotus petals that point up in the top register and down in the bottom, all generally consistent in detail and basically related to standard Hakuhō treatments.[32] One intriguing trait, however, appears on the base of all four pedestals. Each bears an incised pattern. The two patterns closest in form appear on one pedestal in each of the two pairs. The Kaizōji Kannon and Bodhisattva no. 190 both have a long, narrow, horizontal rectangle incised into each facet of their base. The base of the Daisenji bodhisattva may have had a related design, but severe damage in this area makes it impossible to tell for sure. Finally, on the base of bodhisattva no. 182, a horizontal band runs continuously around all eight facets, enclosing ovoid shapes within each surface.[33] A survey of all the images in the "Forty-eight Buddhist Deities" group as well as other examples of Asuka and Hahuhō sculpture produced no other instances of this design on the pedestal base, reinforcing the conclusion that, despite minor differences in their pedestals, the four images constitute a clearly defined group. Even for icons as different as our two pairs, the artists apparently utilized a familiar pedestal type.[34]

KŌFUKUJI BUDDHA HEAD

Few monuments of Japanese Buddhist sculpture have more complex histories than the famous bronze Buddha head (fig. 34), now housed in the Kōfukuji Treasure House.[35] As noted earlier, in this study I do not concern myself particularly with historical background as it relates to specific images, but it would be impossible to present a reasonable account of this head without dealing with its circumstances. After this bronze was discovered in October 1937, during a routine repair of the pedestal of the main icon of the East Golden Hall of Kōfukuji, controversy arose over its identity; however, virtually all scholars now recognize that this large head is what remains of a monumental triad made for Yamadadera during the Hakuhō period.[36]

How the monument got to Kōfukuji is itself a fascinating story. The East Golden Hall was burned down in 1180 by the soldiers of Taira no Shigehira during the Taira-Minamoto war, which ended in the establishment of the Kamakura *bakufu*. When the hall was rebuilt in 1185, temple authorities were hard-pressed to finance the making of a new main icon.[37] An entry of 1187 (Bunji 3.3.9) in *Gyokuyō*, the diary of the courtier Kujō Kanezane (1149–1207), tells us how the monks of Kōfukuji went about solving this problem. According to Kanezane, armed monks attached to the East Golden Hall traveled to the southern part of Yamato Province, to Yamadadera, where they stole the sixteen-foot (*jōroku*) Yakushi triad. Yamadadera, prominent during the seventh and eighth centuries, was quite weak by the late twelfth century and certainly unable to resist the military power of the great Nara temple. Consequently, the monumental triad was transferred to the East Golden Hall of Kōfukuji, where Kanezane worshiped it in 1189.[38]

In 1356, the rebuilt East Golden Hall burned down once more, the result of a lightning strike. This time the main icon was saved and temporarily installed in another hall, but an additional fire in 1411 entirely destroyed the pagodas, East Golden Hall, and their icons. Scholars were conscious of the transfer of the Yamadadera sixteen-foot icon to Kōfukuji, and they

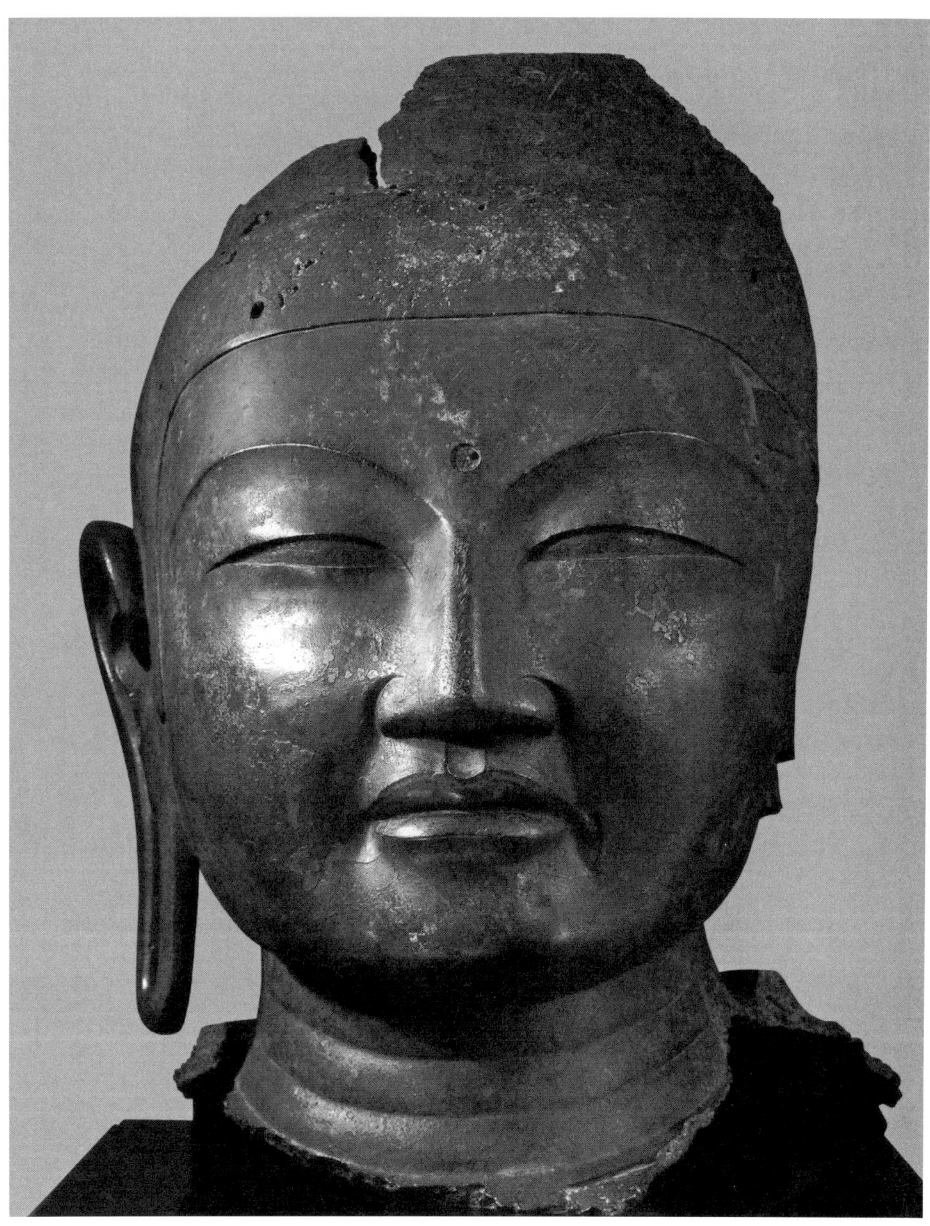

34   Buddha Head, H: 98.3 cm. Kōfukuji, Nara   Photo courtesy of Kōfukuji

                                                            CHAPTER 3

quite naturally assumed that the fire of 1411 had totally consumed it. This mistaken surmise accounts for the considerable surprise when the magnificent Buddha head came to light in 1937.

Yamadadera's early history was briefly discussed in the previous chapter. Following the long hiatus caused by Yamada Ishikawa Maro's enforced suicide, work began once more in the 660s, at a time when his daughters had become royal consorts and were thus in a position to finance a grand project. Sources inform us that the casting of a monumental sixteen-foot triad began on 678.12.4 and the dedicatory service was held on 685.3.25.[39] The head is by far the largest extant Buddhist sculpture from the Hakuhō period, and in that respect has considerable significance for this book, which of necessity concentrates on small, gilt-bronze images with only limited discussion of larger examples.

Despite serious fire damage, the Kōfukuji Buddha head remains a work of remarkable beauty. Modeling is perhaps as developed as in any sculpture dealt with here, and the features are beautifully articulated, particularly the eyes and the mouth. The head of the Yakushi of the Yakushiji triad in Nara naturally demands comparison, yet that reveals, at least from my perspective, a gap of some decades between the two icons. Scholars who place the Yakushiji triad in the late seventh century are hard-pressed to explain its evident stylistic advances. I firmly believe that the differences can only be accounted for by the assumption that the Yakushiji triad was made in the 720s or 730s, decades after the completion of the Yamadadera triad.[40]

Later Hakuhō Sculpture

IN CHAPTERS 2 AND 3, I WAS CAREFUL TO INDICATE A CERTAIN fluidity in my chronological scheme, and the same caution applies here. Bodhisattvas no. 186 and no. 187, as well as meditating bodhisattvas no. 163 and no. 164, come under the rubric "closely related images," and as such could have been considered at the end of chapter 3. On account of their general maturity of style, it seemed best to place them in the present chapter.

FOUR "INDIAN"-STYLE SCULPTURES

No pair of images within the "Forty-eight" is more intriguing than the two that apparently manifest an "Indian" style: bodhisattvas no. 186 (figs. 35a,b) and no. 187 (figs. 36a,b).[1] Buddhist icons made in East Asia generally derived from an Indian source, but the transformational power of China was so strong that the sculptural styles reaching Korea and Japan normally bear only remote traces of an Indian aesthetic. In that regard bodhisattvas no. 186 and no. 187 are definitely atypical, since they do look more like Indian images than any other extant works of the period. Salient characteristics include facial expression, conception of the body forms and pose, and, most importantly, the lower garment, which closely resembles a *dhoti*.

Strictly speaking, the two should not be referred to as closely related, since they show a variety of differences; but they are so similar to each other in overall expression that they seem undeniably to be products of the same studio and perhaps of the same artist. They differ especially in their jewelry forms; the side belt tie-ends

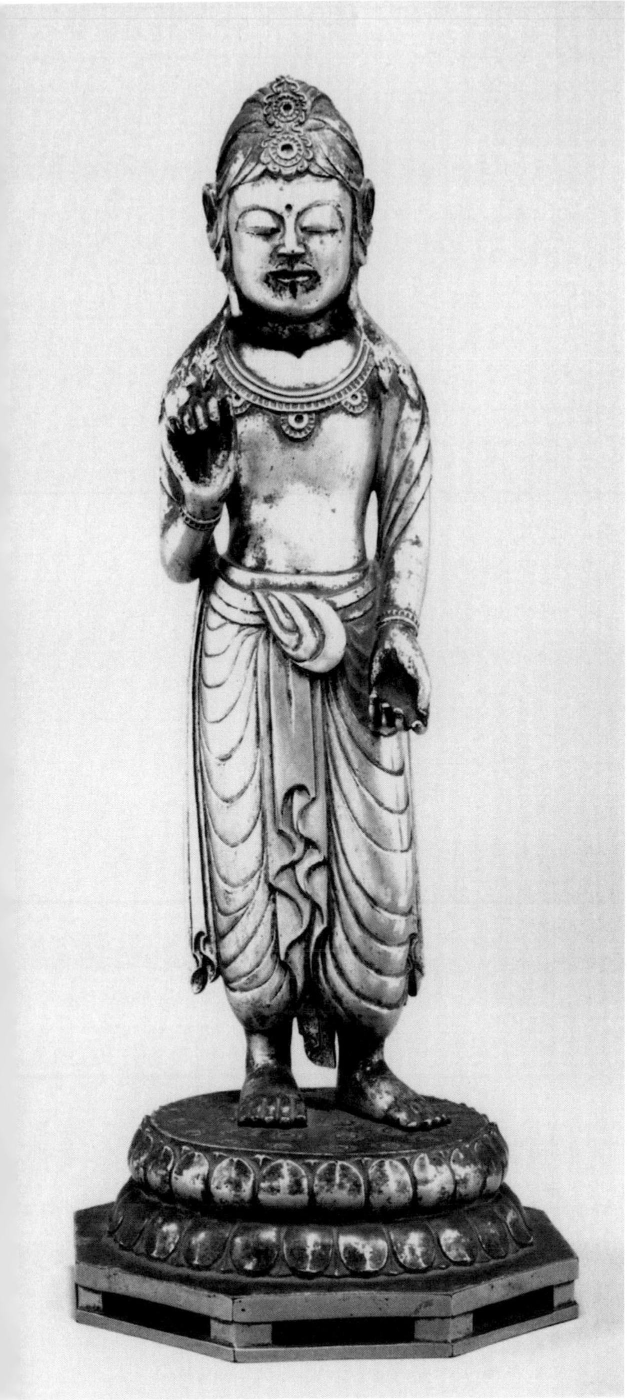

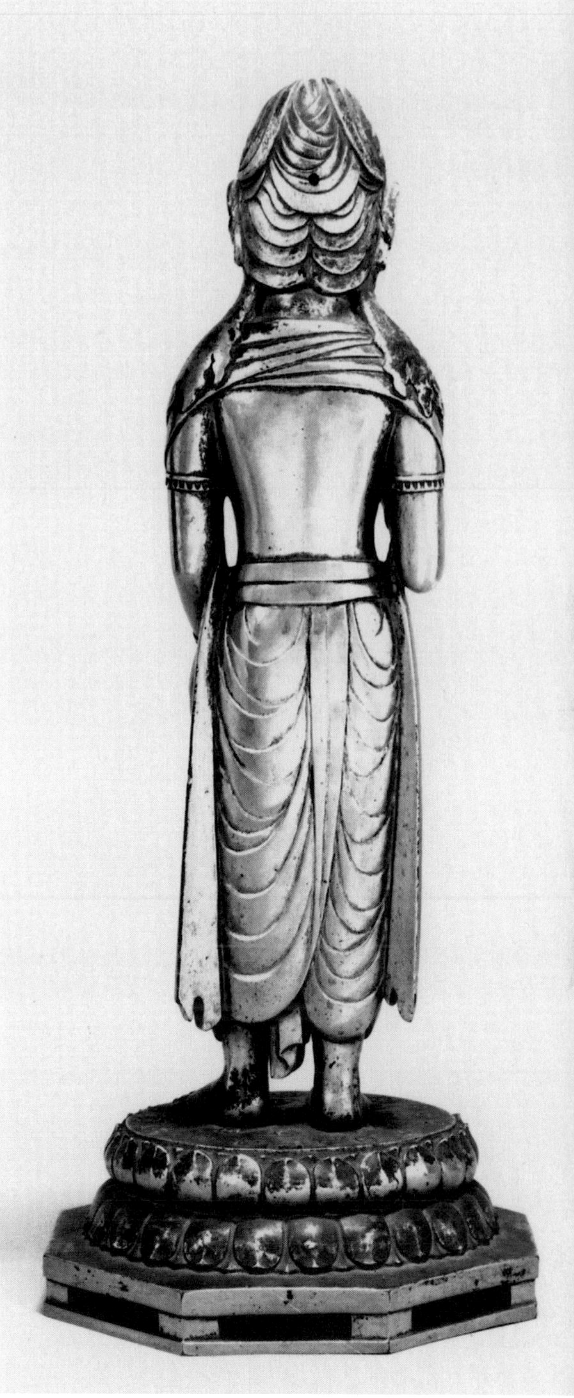

35   TNM Standing Bosatsu no.186, H: 38.0 cm.   a. front   b. back
     Photo courtesy of TNM

LATER HAKUHŌ SCULPTURE

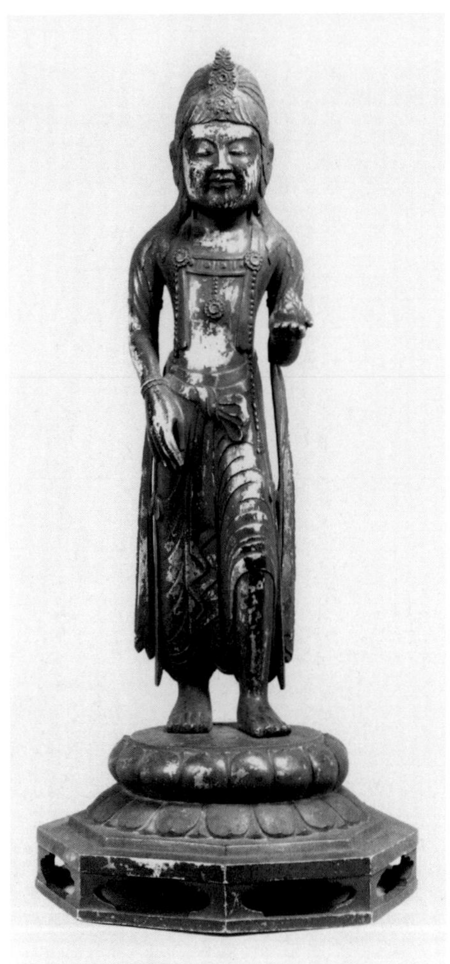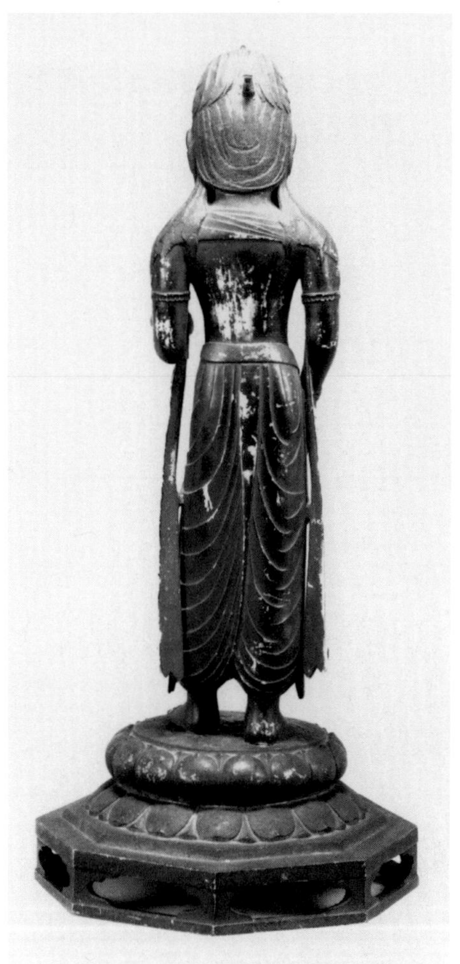

36   TNM Standing Bosatsu no.187, H: 42.3 cm.   a. front   b. back
Photo courtesy of TNM

of no. 187, lacking in no. 186; the lotus bud held in the left hand of no. 187, absent in no. 186; and the drapery raised to reveal part of the left leg of no. 187, not present in no. 186. I find the first difference inconsequential and might explain the second as a motif borrowed from another icon type by a sculptor wishing to add a touch of variety in his piece. It is more difficult to explain the combined presence of the lotus bud and the raised drapery in no. 187, since these two elements seem to have been imported from two separate lineages.

Meditating bodhisattvas no. 163 (fig. 37) and no. 164 (fig. 38) are also so closely related that unquestionably they were made in the same studio, most likely by the same artist. Needless to say, there are also numerous subtle differences between the two, including details of pose and articula-

CHAPTER 4

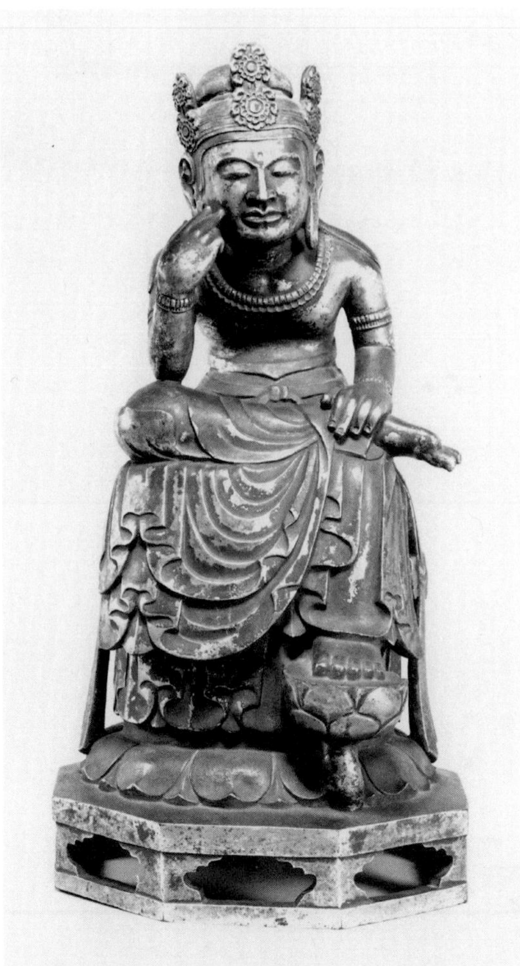 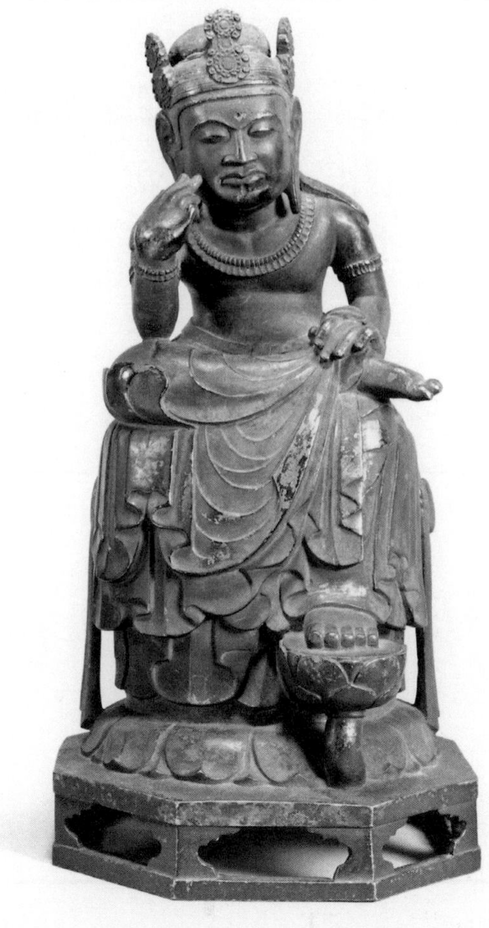

37 TNM Meditating Bosatsu no.163, H: 23.6 cm.
Photo courtesy of TNM

38 TNM Meditating Bosatsu no.164, H: 21.9 cm.
Photo courtesy of TNM

tion of drapery elements. A more prominent difference is the belt that appears above the skirt on no. 163, a form lacking in no. 164. Surely this has no iconographical significance and must indicate an individual artist's design decision. More tentatively, I call attention to resemblances in facial expression among meditating bodhisattvas no. 163 and no. 164 and bodhisattvas no. 186 and no. 187. It would be rash to assert an "Indian" complex here, but I think the two pairs are in some way related.

THREE KANNON FIGURES

Particularly impressive among these three figures is the Kongōji Kannon (figs. 39a,b).[2] This image has the large head usual among later Hakuhō images, shoulders of moderate breadth, a chest area that tapers in

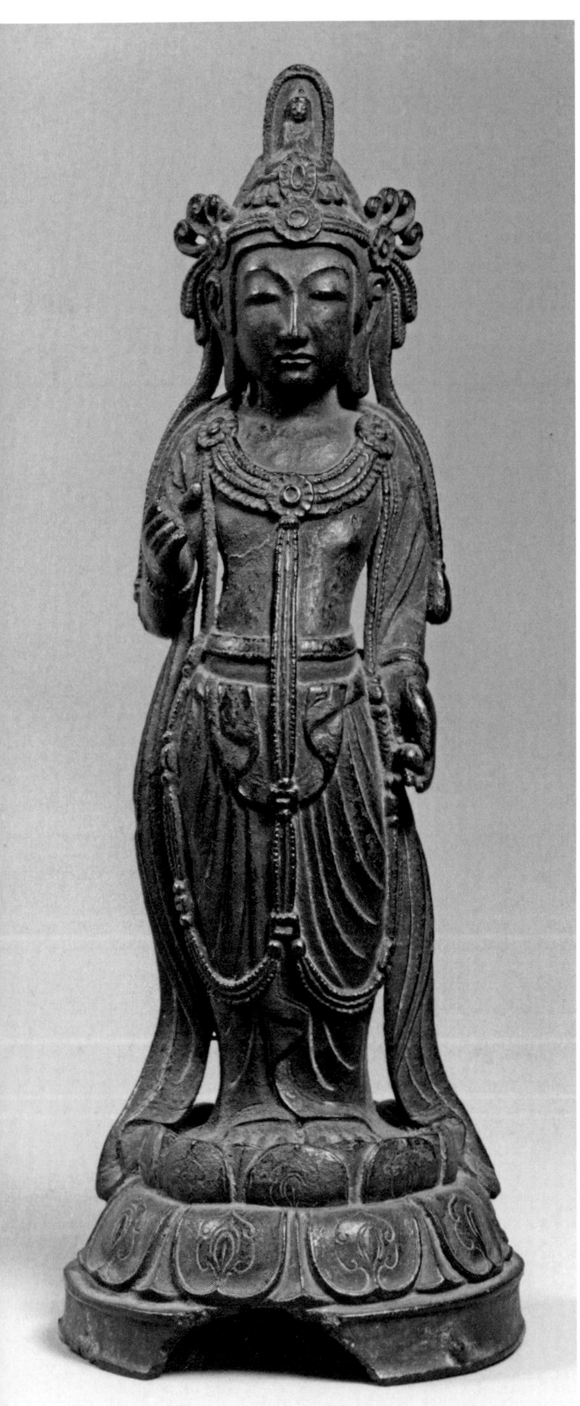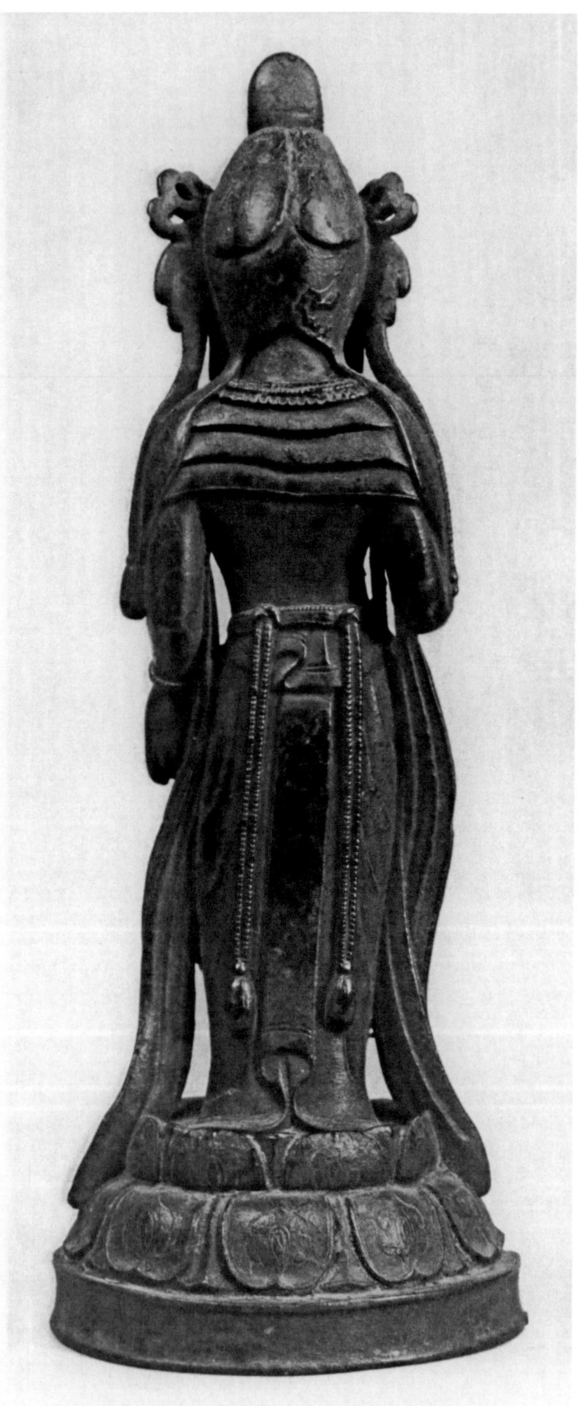

39   Standing Kannon, H: 29.1 cm. Kongōji, Osaka   a. front   b. back
     Photo courtesy of NNM

                                                          CHAPTER 4

strongly to the waist, hips that flare out
from the waist, and a pose that is determined by the outward thrust of the right
hip. Seen from the side, the modeling of the
chest and marked protrusion of the abdomen are evident. The design of the three-
plaque crown is a little unusual, as the
central plaque has two rosettes, one above
the other, with a rather large seated *kebutsu*
placed above the rosettes. As is typical of
this period, the face is full and fleshy, the
expression somewhat brooding. In the
pendant left hand is a jewel. Details of dress
and adornment are meticulously articulated, as seen in the quite complex jewelry
system and in the drapery, which includes
a belt visible at front above the upper hem
of the skirt.[3] The two ends of the scarf fall
along the sides of the image without first
passing in front of the body, as is more
typical. Elaborate designs are incised on
the upward-and-downward-pointing lotus
petals supported by a ring base, all of which
make up the pedestal.[4]

Kannon no. 181 (figs. 40a,b) is a charming icon, rather simply—or even naively—
composed. A quite large head with a
prominent topknot looms over the body,
and the facial features are sharply yet deli-
cately carved to produce a calm, meditative
expression. Great simplicity characterizes
the body in modeling, drapery arrangement, and jewelry, which is limited to a
single necklace. There is a limited sense
of volume in the chest area. The scarf is
arranged in the standard two-register format, the skirt is schematic in design.

As I have recently devoted a long article

to Kannon no. 178 (figs. 41a,b) a truncated
discussion will suffice here.[5] The earlier
publication was motivated by a sense that
this image is one of the finest examples of
its type and critical to an understanding of
Hakuhō sculpture. In particular, the artist
has achieved a superb sense of compositional balance in all aspects: proportions
and modeling, facial expression, drapery
arrangement, and jewelry details. Additionally, Kannon no. 178 is an outstanding
example of the bronze-caster's art.

Kannon no. 178 has a *kebutsu* placed
on its large topknot rather than in the central plaque of a "three-plaque crown," as
is more typical. The face is full and fleshy
with gently rounded cheeks, eyes downcast
for a meditative expression, and a very
small mouth. To my eye, this face resembles the "Indian" group just discussed.
Perhaps the most surprising element in
this image is its distinctive earrings: fifteen
small stacked rings topped by two larger
ones that are attached to the earlobe.
This type of earring, rare in East Asian
sculpture, is also suggestive of Indian
influence.[6] Since in the article I provide a
full analysis of all drapery elements, here
I shall limit the discussion to the possibility that a "sash" (*jōhaku*) is represented.
Sashes, frequently seen in Tang, Unified
Silla, and Nara images, are rare in Hakuhō
sculpture. On Kannon no. 178, the band
of drapery crossing the chest diagonally
from left shoulder to waist might be a sash,
although at back it is not represented, On
balance, I do not think the artist was especially interested in this motif.

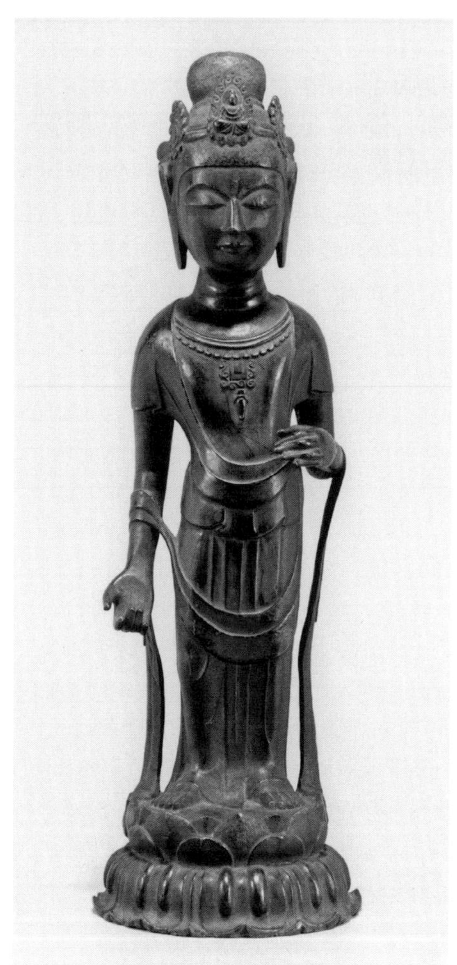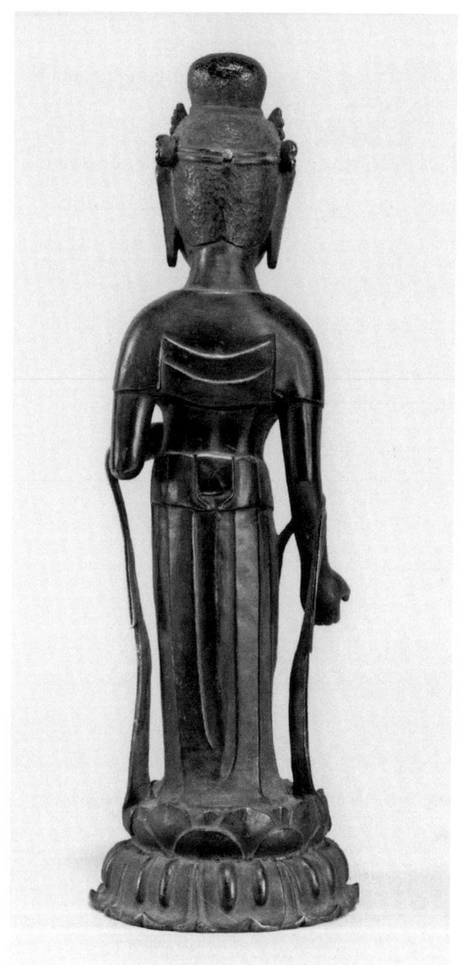

40   TNM Standing Kannon no.181, H: 32.5 cm.   a. front   b. back
Photo courtesy of TNM

THE TACHIBANA SHRINE AMIDA TRIAD

Perhaps no monument in Hakuhō sculpture, or even in all of Japanese sculpture, is of greater interest than the Amida triad of the Tachibana Shrine (figs. 42–43), a monument of substantial complexity in both design and iconography. Why is the name "Tachibana" associated with the shrine and its Amida triad? Lady Tachibana (d. 733), a member of an extremely prominent aristocratic family, is herself important as the mother of Empress Kōmyō (701–760) of the Nara period. Romantic as it would be, no documentary evidence associates the shrine directly with Lady Tachibana. Furthermore, it is evident that the shrine itself is later than the Amida triad called by its name.[7]

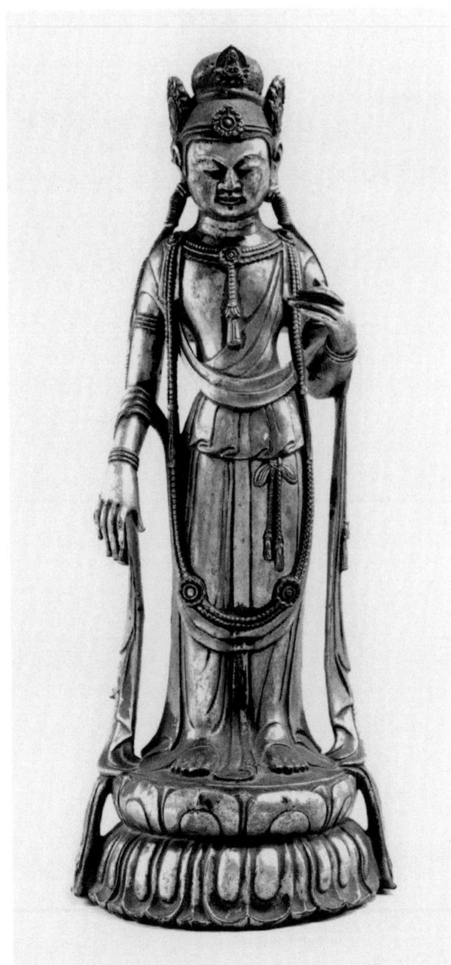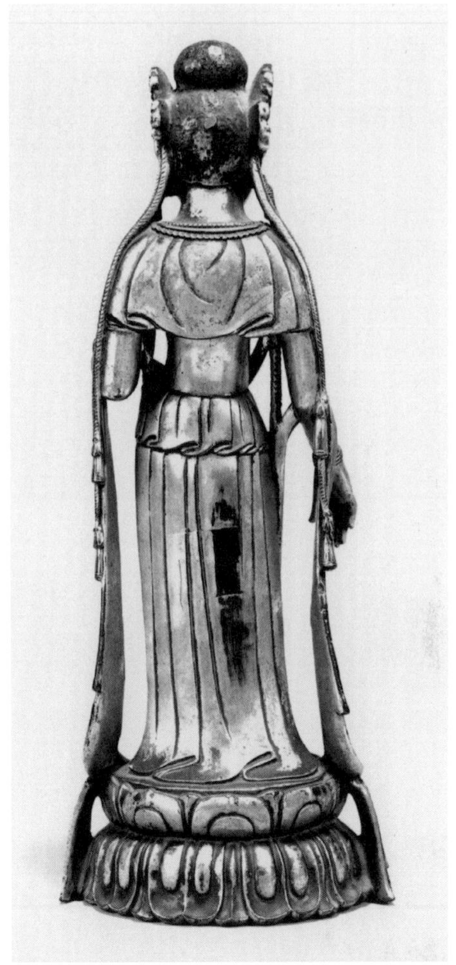

41   TNM Standing Kannon no.178, H: 30.8 cm.   a. front   b. back
Photo courtesy of TNM

As mentioned at the beginning, this book does not in general deal with iconography, because practically all of the images discussed belong to a limited number of types; but the Tachibana Shrine Amida triad transcends those types, as it includes a screen that is a marvelously evocative representation of the Western Paradise of Amida Buddha. That representation begins on the base of the triad, which is cast as a lotus pond out of which the lotuses that form the pedestals of the three deities grow. On the screen behind the triad are representations in relief of newborn souls in the Western Paradise as well as other iconographical details, such as the Buddhas of the Past. Wherever the triad was originally enshrined, and whoever owned it, it must have been perceived as a supremely moving representation of the wished-for rebirth in paradise.[8]

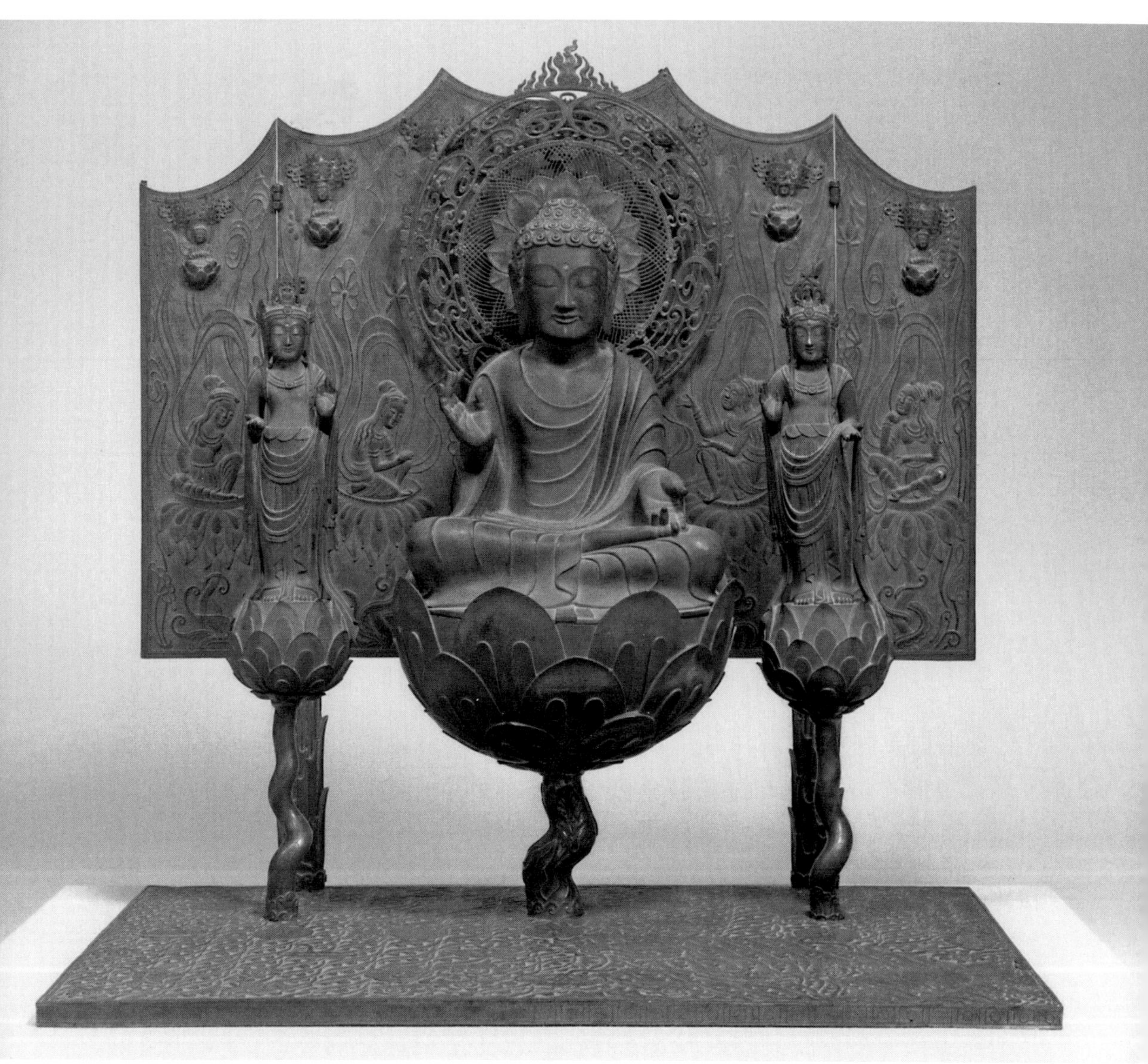

The Tachibana Amida triad can usefully be compared with the Yamadaden Amida triad (fig. 7). If, as presumed, the latter triad dates some decades earlier than the Tachibana image, some sense of stylistic development between early and late Hakuhō may be ascertained. Their poses are notably different: the Yamadaden Amida is seated with legs pendent, the Tachibana Amida in yoga posture. Of course, the Tachibana Amida exhibits much more naturalism in its modeling and drapery treatment. The Amida's head is relatively large in proportion to the body, its face is full and fleshy, and the individual features are precisely and sharply delineated. The drapery folds curve more gently, and the *henzan* is also present. Kannon and Seishi reflect the same sort

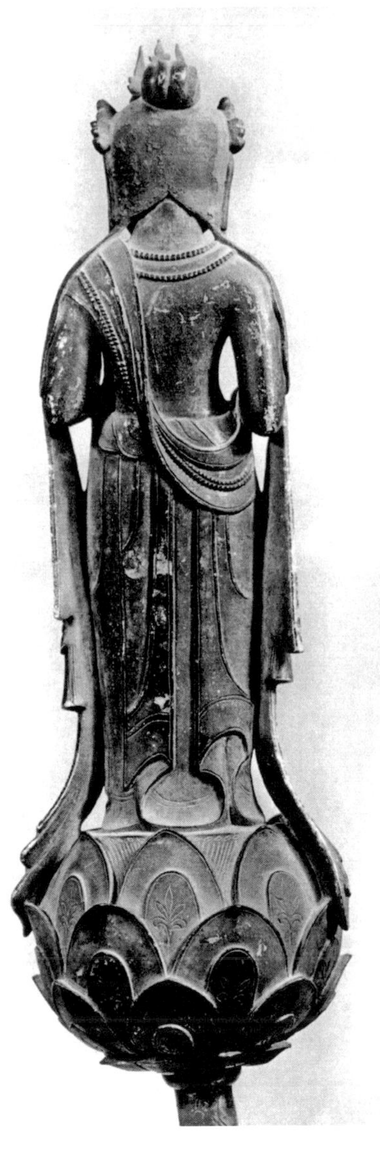

42   (*opposite*) Amida Triad, H: Buddha, 34.0 cm.
Tachibana Shrine, Hōryūji Museum
Photo courtesy of TNM

43   Amida Triad, Tachibana Shrine,
Flanking Bodhisattva H: 28.8 cm.
Hōryūji Museum
Photo courtesy of TNM

of development and thus seem to belong far more to our world than do the earlier, somewhat remote bodhisattvas of the Yamadaden triad. In the later triad drapery and jewelry systems are some peculiar features: for example, the two-register scarf is in generally standard format in front, but at the back it is shown passing over the left shoulder, crossing the back diagonally, and then lying along the right hip (fig. 43).

The pedestals of the three figures in the Tachibana Shrine are elaborate. That of Amida has four layers of overlapping, upward-pointing lotus petals, each petal having two long, narrow new leaves. The pedestals of the flanking bodhisattvas are similar, but they are further enhanced with decorative patterning on the new leaves.

Several of the greatest of all Japanese sculptures will be discussed in this chapter. Most appear to me to belong to the last couple of decades of the Hakuhō period (circa 685–710), but as with the middle-period images discussed in chapter 3, neither the period nor most of its assigned icons can be precisely dated.

FOUR GREAT KANNON IMAGES

Four relatively large Kannon images are here attributed to the later Hakuhō period: the Hōryūji Museum Kannon no. 4, the Kakurinji Kannon, the Gakuenji Kannon, and the Hōryūji Museum "Yumechigai" Kannon. Although each deserves monographic treatment, it is impractical to discuss them in appropriate detail here. This study has emphasized variation among generally similar images, and we have indeed seen many such variations in the last two chapters; one can, however, reasonably maintain that it appears most fully among these four images.

Presumably, by this stage readers have realized that I am fascinated by details of drapery and jewelry. Hōryūji Museum Kannon no. 4 (figs. 44a,b)[9] is certainly one of approximately ten images of the period most notable for complexity of detail and stylistic sophistication. A complete descriptive analysis would require far more space than is available here, although further study would certainly be desirable.[10]

Hōryūji Museum Kannon no. 4, at 61.5 centimeters, is substantially taller than most Hakuhō images. It is sturdy-looking,

well modeled, and exceptional in the complicated articulation and elaboration of such elements of the head as the double-winged topknot. Obviously, the artist had the time and resources (not to mention ability) to lavish attention on seemingly minor details, such as the arrangement of curls at the back of the head. The three-plaque crown with seated *kebutsu* manifests complex detailing, and the face is sharply and precisely carved, including the very rare trait of continuous eyebrows. The body displays ample modeling in the chest and generally a very plastic, three-dimensional quality. A small jewel grasped in the left hand contrasts with the heavy water jar in the right.

Suspended from both sides of the heavy necklace are precisely rendered jewel strings, which cross in an X at the waist, then loop around at the level of the knees, and continue to the back. The drapery system is atypical in its forms, including a ribbon that forms a long U loop at knee level and is fastened at each side roundel of the diadem band. The configuration of the scarf follows a normal Hakuhō mode, but the long ribbon draped over either arm, just above the wrists, is exceedingly rare. The tie-ends of the belt emerge from under the standard apron. The pedestal is elaborate, including three layers of lotus petals in the top tier instead of the more usual two layers. Additionally, the ends of the belt and the strings of jewelry at either side hang down as far as the lower register of lotus petals, providing further visual interest in this zone.

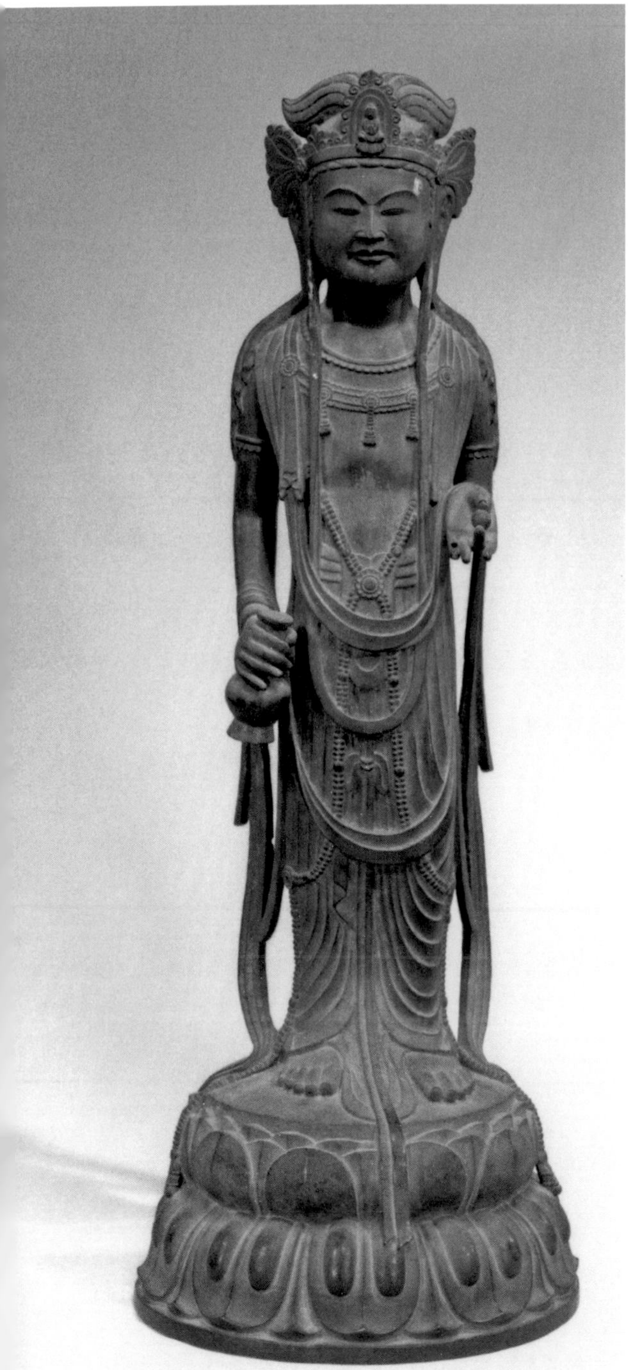

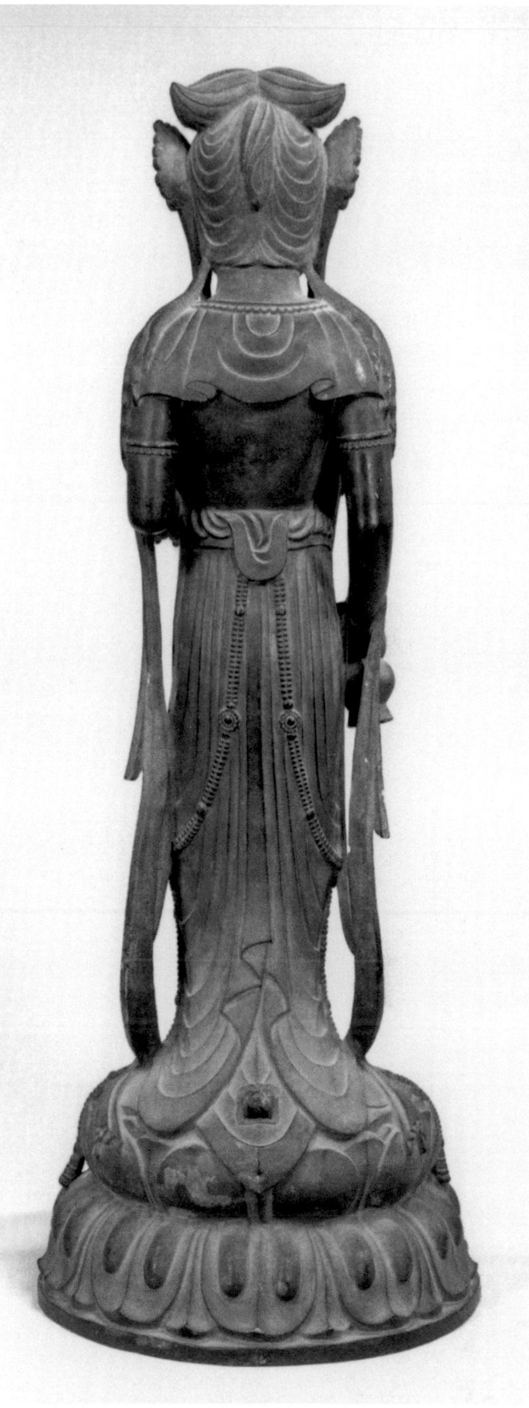

44   Standing Kannon No. 4, H: 61.5 cm. Hōryūji Museum   a. front   b. back
      Photo courtesy of TNM

LATER HAKUHŌ SCULPTURE

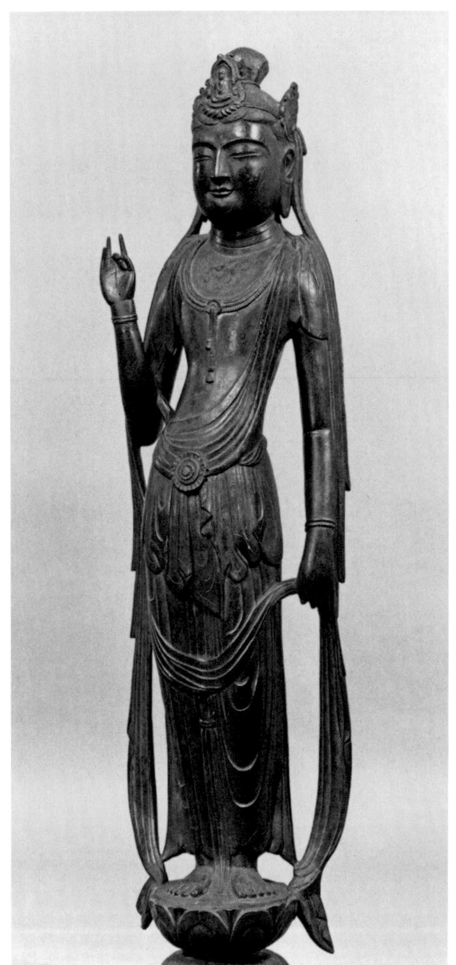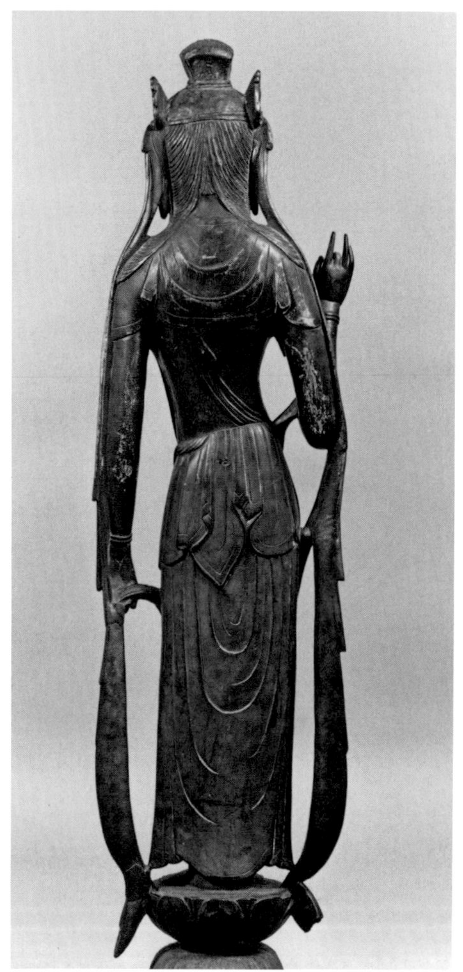

45   Standing Kannon, H: 82.4 cm. Kakurinji, Hyogo   a. front   b. back
Photo courtesy of NNM

Surely one of the most remarkable Hakuhō images is the Kakurinji Kannon (figs. 45a,b): 82.4 centimeters tall, sensuously modeled, and with a beautiful, curving contour and drapery fold lines. It displays traits that will be fully formulated in the Nara period, yet here are still rather tentative.[11] The head is large in relation to the body, which itself assumes the distinctive hip-shot pose, causing the upper torso to exhibit an oblique angle while the legs remain vertical. A certain awkwardness pervades this pose, as if the artist were still striving to master a new stylistic vocabulary.[12] In profile we again note a pronounced forward projection of the abdomen. Its head and face are worthy of detailed analysis: a distinctive topknot and carefully articulated curls, an exquisite three-plaque crown with seated *kebutsu*, and heavy locks of hair and fabric streamers hanging down to the shoulders and onto the arms. In the approximately square face, the eyebrows and eyes are placed horizontally, the mouth is small, and the cheeks are gently rounded.

Unusual details appear in the drapery and jewelry. Looking at the drapery first, the following seem distinctive: the configuration of the scarf, with the section coming over the right shoulder hanging straight down to the pedestal in a fairly standard arrangement, while that from the left shoulder crosses to the right arm, passes over the crook of the elbow, and then loops back across the body in a lower register before being grasped by the left hand and finally falling to the pedestal. Equally odd is a more than usually prominent apron with complex folds. The main folds over the legs and at back are arranged in broad arcs. Over the inner sides of the legs are vertical "panels" and between these a very visible tie-end of the belt. Finally, at the back, what appears to be a sash (*jōhaku*) emerges from under the shawl area of the scarf and then moves diagonally across to the right hip, where it then disappears under the upper hem of the skirt.

Careful inspection reveals the folds of the sash just above those of the scarf as the latter crosses from the left shoulder to the right hip. How should this sash-like component be interpreted? As mentioned earlier, the sash is standard among Nara-period bodhisattvas, but not at all typical of Hakuhō imagery. Possibly we are seeing here an initial, rather tentative, employ-

ment of the sash, which might explain why it is somewhat awkward at back and barely visible at front.[13]

With regard to jewelry, the necklace is precisely rendered with two tasseled jewel strings of unequal length hanging plumb from its center over the chest.[14] There are bracelets but apparently no armlets, and a prominent rosette is placed conspicuously by itself at waist level. This is an extremely limited jewelry ensemble for such an ambitiously designed icon, and only when we recognize traces of holes on the surface of the image does it become apparent that originally the jewelry ensemble was much more elaborate.

Suave elegance and sophisticated aesthetics are not qualities one would associate with the Gakuenji Kannon (figs. 46a,b). It stands bolt upright at 79.8 centimeters in height, the surface is rough, the face not especially appealing, and the drapery somewhat nondescript. Nonetheless, this is an image of extraordinary historical significance, because the inscription incised on the base tells us that the image was commissioned in a year equivalent to 692 by an individual named Wakayamatobe no omi Tokotari of Izumo for the sake of his parents.[15] Izumo (present-day Shimane Prefecture) was a politically powerful region during the seventh century, apparently quite independent of the central Yamato area.[16] That it faces Silla across the East Sea/Japan Sea is highly significant for our subject, as the Gakuenji Kannon clearly displays Sillan characteristics.[17]

Apart from the over-large head, the

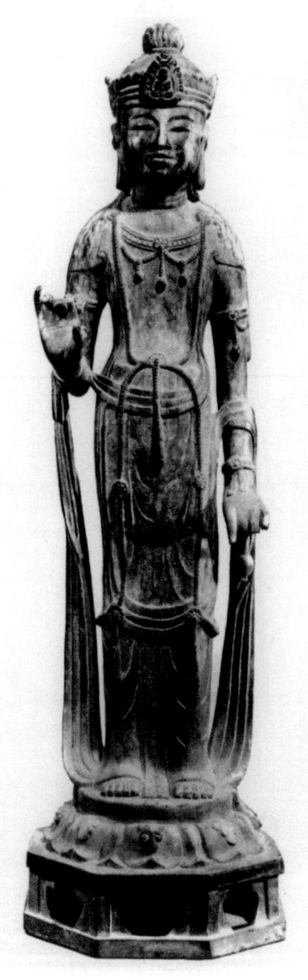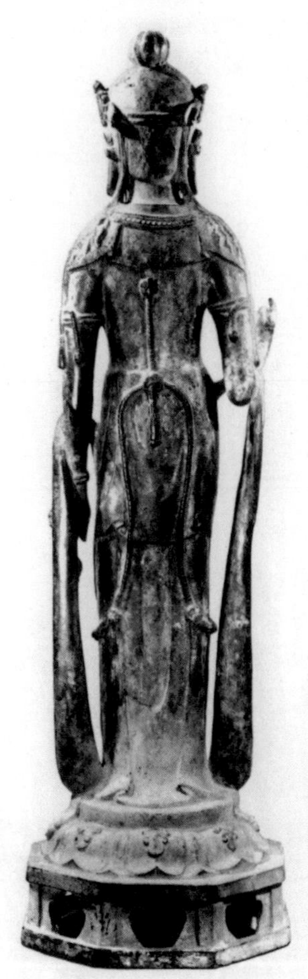

46   Standing Kannon, H: 79.8 cm. Gakuenji, Shimane   a. front   b. back
Photo after TNM, *Kondō butsu* (1988), pl. 145

bodily proportions are fairly natural, even with the exceptionally long legs. Modeling is generally schematic with little sculptural quality in the chest. The figure has a large topknot and a heavy three-plaque crown with a seated *kebutsu* in the central plaque. A profusion of heavy jewelry is symmetrically disposed over the body. Drapery is entirely standard in form, although the scarf ends are somewhat ungainly. Particu-

larly interesting is the eight-sided pedestal with openwork at each facet and incised floral ornament on the lotus petals, as these details relate closely to Sillan sculpture.

One of the most familiar and best-loved monuments of early Buddhist sculpture in Japan is the Yumechigai Kannon (figs. 47a,b). An image as famous as this is hard to assess spontaneously; nevertheless, we must attempt to isolate its various

CHAPTER 4

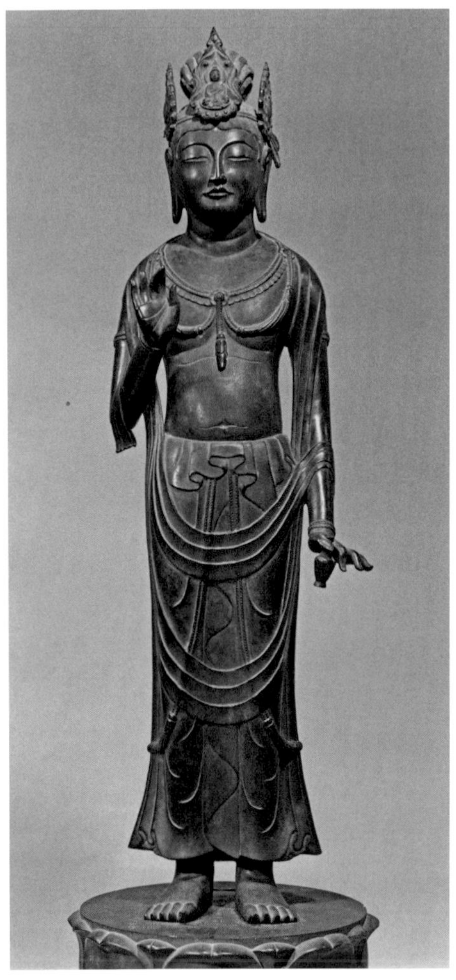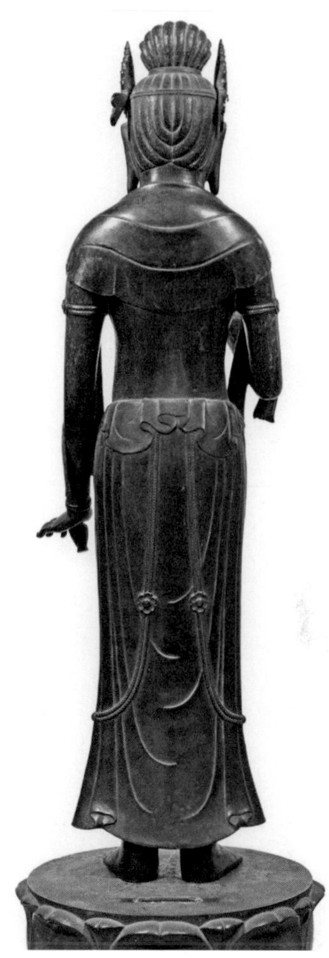

47   Yumechigai Kannon, H: 87.0 cm. Hōryūji Museum   a. front   b. back
Photo courtesy of NNM

characteristics in the context of Hakuhō sculpture.[18] At 86.9 centimeters tall, the Yumechigai Kannon is among the largest statues of the Hakuhō period. Like the Gakuenji Kannon just discussed, it is axially posed but even more bolt-upright than that image, since its right hip is not outthrust in the usual way. Clearly, it was made as an independent icon, and the sculptor seems to have concentrated on the central vertical axis, thereby increasing its hieratic quality. In its proportions it approximates the human with its head, upper body, and lower body having an approximately 1:2:4 ratio. Perhaps the only disproportion is in the arms, which seem a little short, especially as canonical requirements call for long arms.

In overall composition the most noticeable feature is the artist's intense concern

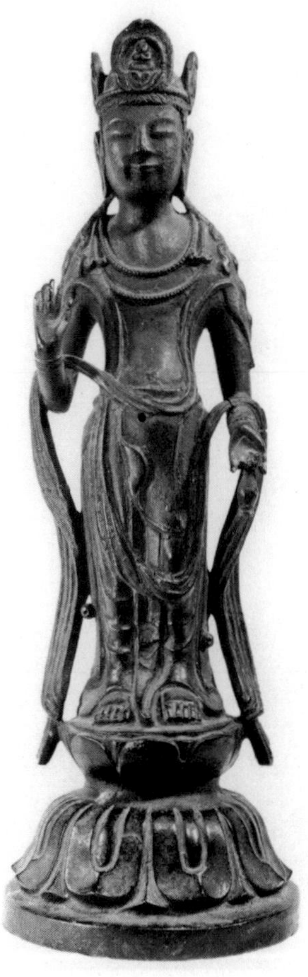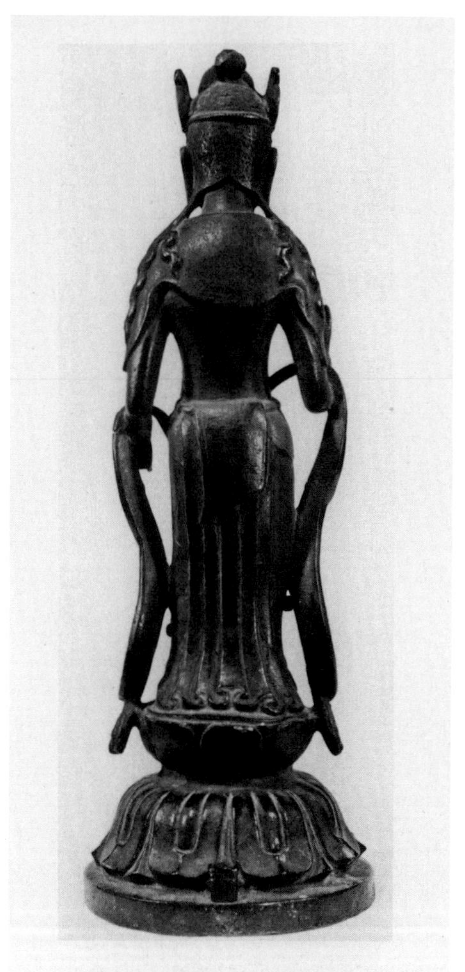

48 Standing Kannon, H: 39.4 cm. Hasedera, Oita   a. front   b. back
Photo courtesy of Hasedera

with curves in the face, the shoulders, the arrangement of the necklace, the modeling of the chest, the two registers of the scarf, and the jewel strings suspended from the belt. These linear curves are complemented and enhanced by the rather sensuous modeling of the body. Unfortunately, the two ends of the scarf are lost, but one imagines that they, too, contributed to the curvilinear effect. The head has a prominent topknot and a carefully designed three-plaque crown with a seated *kebutsu*. The full modeling of the face is most obvious in the cheeks, and the features are sharply carved, especially the beautiful bow-shaped mouth.

Jewelry is symmetrically arranged, and the various elements of the necklace show extremely detailed execution; two jewel strings, descending from about the level of the abdomen, cross the legs and con-

                                                           CHAPTER 4

tinue on to the back of the image. Drapery
is conventional, consisting of a standard
Hakuhō two-register scarf and a simply
designed skirt. In descending to cross the
legs, the two jewel strings pass under both
levels of the scarf in a surprisingly realistic
manner: the scarf fabric is represented as if
raised over the jewel strings. An additional
example of this realism is the forward curl
of the sideburns just below each temple. In
these respects the figure seems closer to our
world than does a remote figure such as the
Hōryūji Museum Standing bodhisattva (fig.
2) of the Asuka period.

I have seen the Yumechigai Kannon
many, many times over the years, and as
mentioned above, its very familiarity may
get in the way of reasoned aesthetic judgement. Recently, I have begun to think of
it in terms of a chilly perfection in every
aspect, and for that reason less appealing than an image such as the Kakurinji
Kannon, which manifests a sort of quirky
beauty; but taste is subjective, and I am sure
many people experience the Yumechigai
Kannon differently.

TWO "PROVINCIAL" SCULPTURES

Another image dated to the end of our
period is the Hasedera Kannon (figs. 48a,b)
of 702, just ten years after the Gakuenji
Kannon.[19] It would be useful if the
Hasedera figure could serve as a chronological benchmark in the evolution of
Hakuhō style, but I am not sure that it fills
that role very satisfactorily, being a pleas-
ant enough sculpture, but not outstand-

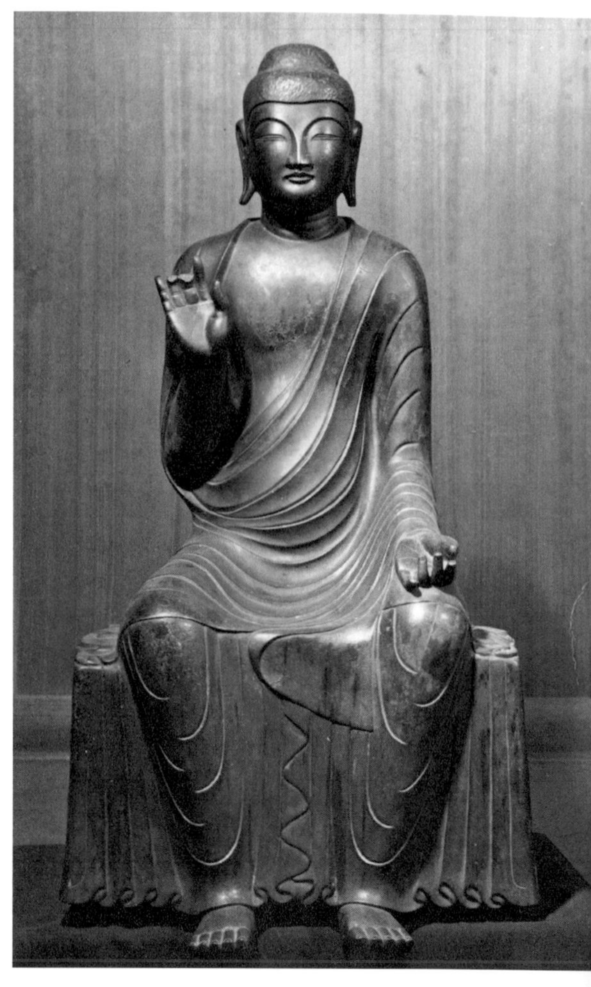

49   Seated Shaka, H: 60.6 cm. Jindaiji, Tokyo
Photo courtesy of Jindaiji

ing. The crown is rather awkward and the
face poorly articulated, although the body
displays a reasonable amount of modeling
and the scarf is arranged in nicely undulat-
ing curves. Small holes in various places
indicate jewelry strings that have regret-
tably been lost. Despite my general lack
of enthusiasm for this sculpture, I see no
problem with dating it to the first decade of
the eighth century.

Continuing our discussion of larger monuments, let us look at the Jindaiji Seated Shaka (fig. 49).[20] At the beginning of the twentieth century this image was excavated on the grounds of the Tokyo temple Jindaiji, a fact that has aroused some controversy over its place of manufacture. Could such a fine image have been made in the Kantō area during the Hakuhō period or was it, perhaps, brought from the Yamato region? Beyond that issue is a question of much greater significance: how many icons of this size existed in provincial temples? Study of ruined foundations, and particularly of roof tiles, makes clear that the distribution of Buddhist temples during the second half of the seventh century was extensive.[21] Presumably, each of these temples had at least one large-scale icon as its principal object of worship and probably more, as well as ritual equipment, sutras, and the like. It is highly likely that only a fraction of the provincial temple icons survive today. Of course, some may have been wood sculptures, but it also seems likely that some fraction were gilt-bronze. Acceptance of this hypothesis places a heavy burden on the Jindaiji Shaka as one of the very few surviving representatives of larger-scale icons outside of the capital region.[22]

As the only extant relatively large Hakuhō image seated in Western pose, the Jindaiji Shaka deserves close attention. It has been through at least one fire, as can be seen by its surface, where little gilt remains, and in the loss of three fingertips of the right hand; nevertheless, its state of preservation is quite good, allowing detailed examination. Although generally quite simple in conception, the figure displays full modeling of the body, and drapery folds cross the upper body in broad, sweeping arcs that create a strongly rhythmical movement, counterbalanced by the more staccato vertical folds of the drapery covering the seat. At back the drapery folds are very much simplified. The face, one of the most mature encountered in our study, is comparable in its fine articulation with the Kōfukuji Buddha head (fig. 34) and arguably more advanced than the latter.

Conclusion

MANY YEARS AGO, IN MY DOCTORAL DISSERTATION, I ATTEMPTED to define a sculptural style I called "Tenth Century Mannerism."[1] My thesis was that between the so-called Jōgan period (usually considered to be the ninth century) and the so-called Fujiwara period (eleventh and twelfth centuries), there lay a period of approximately one hundred years in which sculptures manifested a particular cluster of stylistic characteristics. Contrary to the conventional opinion of Japanese scholars, who typically have seen this as a "transitional" era, I postulated a continuing development and exaggeration of key elements of the major ninth-century styles. Rather than leading into the new currents of Late Heian sculpture, the very numerous images on which I focused appeared to push the ninth-century forms as far as they could go, primarily with expressive distortions in pose, proportions, facial features, modeling, drapery arrangements, and jewelry components. In actuality, most of those images led nowhere beyond the often rather bizarre experimentation that they themselves manifested. This is not to say there were *no* "transitional" works, since the assiduous efforts of historians of sculpture have succeeded in isolating a small group of images that could, possibly, be seen as bridging the enormous gap between the ninth and eleventh centuries. Nevertheless, my point was that the vast majority of tenth-century sculptures constituted a stylistic category having an independent existence, one basically unrelated to the imagery of the Late Heian period, which was just beginning to emerge in recognizable form during the first decades of the eleventh century.[2]

COMPARISON WITH "TENTH-CENTURY MANNERISM"

A constant theme in Japanese writings about their own art is the search for uniquely national characteristics, the earlier the better. I argued, perhaps too emphatically, for "Tenth-Century Mannerism" as the first truly native sculptural style. This theory was based on the idea that continental prototypes could be located for virtually all imagery of the seventh through the ninth centuries. With some significant modifications, I would still maintain this theory today as a general proposition. Should this be seen as contradicting a key premise of the present book? Perhaps not. While believing that prototypes in China and Korea can be found for practically all the stylistic traits of seventh-century sculpture, I also believe that careful investigation reveals unmistakable innovation on the part of Hakuhō artists. Their creations may be less striking or strange, but to my mind the Hakuhō period and the tenth century share certain characteristics resulting from the relative freedom of sculptors to try out various new ideas as they worked. Of course, what I am calling "freedom" is the absence of a precisely defined canonical style during the two periods in question. In contrast, the styles of the Asuka, Nara, Early Heian (ninth century), and Late Heian periods manifest dominant stylistic lineages to which most sculptors adhered quite closely.[3]

ARTISTS AND STUDIOS

The preceding paragraphs offer merely thumbnail theoretical accounts of sculptural styles during the Hakuhō period and the tenth century. Each Hakuhō image was made by one or more sculptors, in some cases supervised by a studio master. Who were these artists and what can we know about them? How were they trained? Where did they work and under what circumstances? What was their relationship with patrons? How free were they to make design decisions? Such questions may be essentially unanswerable; and yet simply broaching them might shed light on our topic. After all, Hakuhō statues were made by human beings, not by extraterrestials! Naturally, we must exercise the utmost caution in conjuring up the working lives of people far distant from us in time and culture. On the other hand, to claim that nothing, or very little that is meaningful, can be known about their activities smacks of the scholarly defeatism recently so fashionable. Is there any real value in merely saying, "They made Buddhist images," and then stopping with that?

This study exemplifies a more optimistic approach, one that assumes close inspection of individual sculptures and of some groups of sculptures will provide information and insights that potentially allow us to achieve a deeper and fuller understanding of our corpus. As I tried to make clear in my introduction, I am not claiming that this methodology is universally useful. I do maintain that when applied cautiously, it can yield information helpful in formulating a more precise picture of a body of material: in the present case, Hakuhō sculpture.

There can be little question concerning the status of seventh-century sculptors. They would not have lived like peasants, and yet they were ineligible for ranks even barely approaching those of the bureaucracy or the aristocracy.[4] Judging from what is known about traditional Japanese society, we can reasonably assume that an apprentice system was the training vehicle. Casting bronze images is a complicated task that requires extensive knowledge and experience only to be acquired during a long learning period. Perhaps there were also technical "secrets" passed from master to disciple, although we cannot be certain about this. Because of the various processes involved in the making of gilt-bronze images, there would have to have been carefully structured studios where the work was done. An extensive network would also be needed to gather the raw materials for bronze, the gold and mercury for gilding, and a less extensive one for the fuel to produce the necessary temperatures for casting.[5] Clearly, all of this would have been too complex and expensive to be accomplished by a single individual; rather, the quite substantial investment required to establish and supply a studio suggests that a group of some power must have acted as backers. The most likely candidate for this role would have been one of the guilds (*be*) so prominent in ancient Japanese society.[6]

Presumably, a studio would be structured hierarchically with a master at the top, then journeymen, followed by apprentices, and at the bottom, laborers. Based on what we can deduce from the organization of the Tori studio, the person of highest rank would not have been an artist, but rather a supervisor in charge of overall organization. Such an administrator would have possibly had a variety of duties in various realms and thus would not necessarily be constantly at the studio.

Needless to say, it is the artist responsible for the actual design of images who is of the greatest interest here. Division of tasks seems likely, but the designer must have been generally familiar with the relevant technical matters. I also assume that he was the person who dealt directly with the patrons, a topic that will be discussed shortly.

The preceding paragraphs are replete with qualifying words and phrases such as "assume," "perhaps," "presumably," "what we can deduce," and "seems likely," making for a decidedly weak argument; but such qualifications are essential, given the paucity of data from the seventh century. Some information is available about sculpture studios in the Nara period, and much more for the Heian and Kamakura periods, but whether these data are applicable to Hakuhō is questionable. As just noted, the *be* system was central to guild organization during the seventh century, but over time sculpture studios gradually became independent entities. An obvious question to be asked is just when did this happen?

At the very least, I am quite confident that independence had not yet occured during the Hakuhō period. The initial stages of autonomy may have been connected to the formulation of the *ritsuryō* system of governmental organization, but the chronology of that process is itself highly debatable.

THE COMMISSIONS

Who or what determined the appearance of an icon? Most of the images discussed in this book are small gilt-bronzes (*shō kondō butsu*), and as such would have been made for individuals, not for temples, where large-scale icons were normally enshrined. That being the case, we must think about the relationship between patron and artist. A reasonable assumption is that the patron would arrive at the studio having decided what deity he or she desired, perhaps having been advised by a priest. Several possibilities seem likely at the next stage. The studio may have had a stock of images or maybe a sketchbook showing different renditions of each deity; the patron himself might have brought an idea for the master to work on; or some combination of these three modes, even of other scenarios, may have occurred. Numerous examples of variant details have been adduced in our discussions, such as closely related pairs in which the shawl section of the scarf lies flat on one member and twisted on in the other,[7] or pairs of Kannon images with one seated and one standing *kebutsu* (e.g., figs. 34, 35). To what extent individual clients specifically requested particular details in their icons is unknowable, but it seems to me quite unlikely that most of these variations reflected the wishes of the patron. How then to account for such variety within a standard type?

In my opinion, the artists were responsible for most of this variety. Obviously they did not have total freedom to innovate, even if so inclined (itself unlikely), but they were allowed considerable license in minor details. Many back views have been studied in the previous chapters, and one wonders if patrons were really concerned with that aspect of the image. It is clear that they would have wanted a well-made icon with no flaws, one thought appropriate for the religious purposes for which it was intended, but they are highly unlikely to have concerned themselves with minor details or with the precise rendering of areas such as the back.

FAKES AND OTHERS

A matter of considerable interest is the existence of spurious sculptures purporting to be of the Hakuhō period. Forgery is a constant in world art, given the limited supply of genuine objects, the high demand for such objects, and the substantial profits accruing to successful forgers.[8] This is not a serious problem for Japanese sculpture, because practically all images have always been in temples, with a much smaller number in museums and private collections. It is within these latter that potentially spurious pieces may be found. Perhaps one of the most likely categories of Japanese sculpture to be forged is the small gilt-bronze image type we have been discussing, and I believe that a studio (or studios) for producing fakes existed, most likely during the later Meiji period.

Before considering a few probable candidates, some theoretical issues must be addressed. First, one must be very cautious about crying "fake" at an object that appears unique, since it may actually be an idiosyncratic piece made in antiquity. On the other hand, faked sculptures that are direct copies of images of unimpeachable authenticity are ordinarily easier to detect, as they usually include mistakes or misunderstandings of iconography or style, thus betraying their origins. (I am not referring here to "closely related" images, a totally different category.) As noted in chapter 4, some images of decidedly inferior quality (e.g., meditating bodhisattva no. 161, fig. 24) awaken a natural tendency to ascribe their inadequacies to an inept modern copyist. Needless to say, we must always consider the possibility that a doubtful piece was, in fact, the work of an ancient but untalented artist.

An especially inept fake is a copy of seated Buddha no. 147 (fig. 20), an unusual figure considered in chapter 3.[9] Buddha no. 147 has so many peculiar characteristics that it would be virtually impossible to imagine any process resulting in a spurious work other than direct copying. Let me state at the outset that the "copy" in question is extraordinarily ugly, making it unlikely that any reasonably well-informed person would mistake it for a seventh-

century sculpture. Still, it is interesting to observe what features the forger noticed and what he ignored. As an example of the latter, the bow of the belt at the waist is not clearly depicted and, more importantly, the two ends that emerge from under the drapery overhang are absent.[10] In many photographs this element is hard to see, and one imagines that our forger was not aware of its significance. More surprising is the treatment of the peculiar hem running obliquely from right shoulder to left hip, on which the elaborate decoration present in the original is missing on the forgery. As if to compensate for that lack, the forger added, below the hem, incised "frond" lines of no known significance.

This brings us to the British Museum's meditating bodhisattva of the "boyish" category mentioned in chapter 2, certainly a late piece, but just how late? A few years ago Professor William Watson published a study of the British Museum's meditating bodhisattva wherein he strove to prove its authenticity.[11] Apparently his article was completed prior to the British Museum exhibition of 1989, "Fake? The Art of Deception," since Watson states that there were no printed suggestions of its being spurious. In the catalogue, however, Victor Harris argues strenuously that the image was made in the early twentieth century.[12]

I saw the image in 1977 at an exhibition in Kyoto and was somewhat doubtful of its authenticity. When I asked a very qualified specialist in Japanese Buddhist sculpture about it, he answered, "It's a guest," implying that politeness forbade calling it a fake.[13] A few years later in a used bookstore I found a small volume containing a color illustration of the sculpture.[14] Many of the illustrations in this volume are of key monuments of Japanese art (e.g., a bodhisattva from the Yakushiji Yakushi triad; the Yumedono Kannon; Unkei's portrait of Muchaku at Kōfukuji; and numerous others). It turned out that our meditating bodhisattva was, at the time of writing, in the author's collection. One cannot help thinking that this piece and several others were planted in the book among this high company to enhance their aura. Needless to say, this provenance is not mentioned in Watson's article, although one assumes that he purchased it from Johnes for the museum.[15]

Space does not allow a careful analysis of the British Museum's meditating bodhisattva, but its dubious provenance and a variety of peculiar features seen in the statue do not inspire confidence.[16] Neither Watson's nor Harris's article is especially well informed, and I do not believe the last word has been said on this sculpture, although on balance its authenticity is rather doubtful.

Several doubtful pieces have long been in the collection of the Tokyo National School of Art and Music, including an odd standing bodhisattva.[17] Most of the elements of this figure also occur elsewhere, so our doubts do not proceed from a presumed "misunderstanding" on the part of the sculptor; rather, the overall awkwardness in the handling of details is problematic. It has an unusual crown and

the two ribbons hanging down to the chest at either side are devoid of articulation. The face is poorly executed and does not seem to be a Hakuhō type, and the treatment of the drapery is inept and schematic. There is also a markedly peculiar relationship between the feet, the end of the belt, and the top of the pedestal.[18]

A small group of standing bodhisattvas having quite consistent characteristics includes the following images: one each from the Nachi Sutra Deposit, at Rakanji, at Ichijōji, and in the Idemitsu Museum, Tokyo.[19] All have similar crowns and essentially the same arrangement of drapery, each holds a water jar in front of the abdomen, and all of the pedestals are related in form. When I first saw the Idemitsu figure, I doubted whether it was genuine, primarily because of the generally awkward handling of most elements. Subsequently, I learned of the other three images, and since they are in temple collections, ordinarily a guarantee of authenticity, I had to reconsider my initial impressions.[20]

The best published of the group, as far as I know, is the piece from Nachi. The excellent catalogue for this site has four illustrations, one for each side, allowing for careful analysis.[21] The fairly detailed entry describes most of the significant features of the image, but to my mind the telling feature is the author's own expressed uncertainty:

This image is not in the style of the Asuka period or of images of the Hakuhō period of Asuka lineage, but appears to be a work that copies an archaic mode. I do not believe it is a replication from the Kamakura period when many such images were made, nor do I believe it is a work of the Heian period. Although there is a theory that it might be a work of late Tenpyō, it does not manifest hints of the Tenpyō style, and so we are left with the problem of lacking real clues as to when it was made.[22]

It goes without saying that such uncertainty, which is not at all characteristic of Japanese scholars, increases one's doubts about all four images. Furthermore, the three temples holding these images are widely distributed, from Ōita Prefecture in Kyushu (Rakanji) to Hyōgo (Ichijōji) and Wakayama (Nachi Sutra Deposit) in Honshu. Given their geographical distribution, plus the consistency of characteristics among the four images and the doubts expressed immediately above, is it possible that they are products of a modern forger's studio?

Another image that should give one pause is a standing bodhisattva at Kōfukuji, Nara. This image, originally deposited in a large Thousand-armed Kannon, was apparently taken out in the late Meiji period.[23] Although somewhat finer than the preceding four images, it does share some traits with them. Since, among these four, I have adequate photographs only of the Nachi bodhisattva, I will limit the comparison to it. Both images have large crowns, small faces, and very thick necks; the bodies are not similar, but both hold a water vase, the Kōfukuji image in the pendent left hand.

Most striking is a detail at back, where we see the U loop of the scarf, an Asuka trait that also occurs in Hakuhō images, as discussed above. In the Kōfukuji bodhisattva a most peculiar, large lotiform element fills the lower area of the U loop, an anomaly in a genuine image. Serious misunderstanding of the configuration of lotus petals forming the pedestal precludes, in my view, the possibility of a Hakuhō date for this image, as does the awkward stance of the figure on the pedestal.

So, what can be said about the preceding group of four and the Kōfukuji image? Although they relate to the Hakuhō style, I do not think they were made during that period. Nevertheless, they do not seem to be spurious. Tentatively, I conclude that there must have been a studio during a later period making "Asuka-Hakuhō" sculptures to satisfy a demand for archaic icons.[24]

ŌHASHI ON HAKUHŌ SCULPTURE

At the beginning of chapter 2, I surveyed the major Japanese historiographical currents in the study of the Hakuhō period, concluding that a 650–710 chronology was most reasonable. During that discussion I did not focus on Ōhashi Katsuaki's research concerning Hakuhō sculpture, because I thought it might better be considered after I had laid out my own views on the subject.[25] A cursory glance through Ōhashi's long article will instantly highlight the stark differences between our approaches, for his twenty pages include not a single illustration! Perhaps for a "theoretical" study illustrative material is deemed superfluous,[26] but closer attention reveals the basis for this quite incredible lack. Ōhashi does not consider the sorts of images we have been studying to be particularly significant for an understanding of seventh-century sculpture.

In his article Ōhashi provides a detailed exegesis of Sekino Tadashi's observations concerning Hakuhō sculpture. One of Sekino's concerns was with periodization. Sekino altered a previous scheme that postulated three periods: Suiko, Tenji, and Tenpyō. He retained Suiko, but substituted Nara for Tenji and Tenpyō.[27] Realizing that the Nara period then became very long, he divided it in two, an "early phase" (*zenki*) and a "mature phase" (*honki*), the former called Hakuhō, the latter keeping the original name, Nara. Sekino was not committed to the term "Hakuhō," but apparently adopted it as a convenience. As noted in my preface, it quickly became the standard nomenclature. Of course, Sekino's study was not primarily focused on chronological designation, but rather was a discussion of the dating of the two Yakushi triads at Yakushiji, one in the Golden Hall, the other in the Lecture Hall. He decided the latter should be dated to the Hakuhō period, the former to Nara. Although most scholars today would disagree with the early date for the Lecture Hall triad, the majority would accept the later, Nara-period date, for the Golden Hall triad. (The latter will be discussed below.)

Ōhashi found Sekino's argument sympathetic because it proposed Tang influence on Japan at a quite early time. How early is not entirely clear because of ambiguities in Sekino's article, which is not surprising given the early year in which it was written. Ōhashi recognizes this weakness, especially the failure to identify representative examples. He nonetheless considers it to be a fundamental contribution on account of the basic conceptual scheme Hakuhō/Nara, with Hakuhō definitely manifesting Tang traits.

Ōhashi provides a long historiographical survey, similar to that given above in chapter 2. In Ōhashi's survey some crucial aspects must be noted. First, he completely rejects Mizuno Seiichi's explanation of the stylistic sources for Asuka, Hakuhō, and Nara sculpture and is particularly dismissive of Mizuno's suggestion that Hakuhō sculpture is characterized by variety.[28] Second, he depreciates the argument, made by both Matsubara Saburō and Mōri Hisashi, that Korean art, primarily that of Silla, had a significant impact on Hakuhō sculpture.[29] Although Ōhashi somewhat grudgingly acknowledges the possibility of influence from the Korean peninsula, his fundamental opinion resides in the following: "I think Early Tang culture was transmitted directly [from China], beginning in the fourth year of Jomei's reign."[30] That is to say, he postulates a strong impact of Tang culture as early as 632, the year when a number of students and priests returned from China. In this context, he finds Tang influence figuring importantly in Japanese sculpture from this date, referring to it as "Period I" of Tang influence. His "Period

II" encompasses the years 654 to 661, when "treasures" were being brought from Tang China, including what he suggests was the model for the great sixteen-foot, dry-lacquer triad enshrined at Kudara Ōdera, the first royal temple in Japan.[31]

By way of background, I remind the reader of my meticulous investigation of the "Four Great Temples," especially Kudara Ōdera, in a study frequently cited in the notes for this book.[32] Being fully cognizant of the extraordinary historical and religious significance of the four temples of Asukadera, Kudara Ōdera, Kawaradera, and Yakushiji, I agree with Ōhashi about the importance of these temples and their icons. With his assertion that much larger monuments, mostly associated with the great "official" temples, represented the mainstream while the numerous small, gilt-bronze images that remain are of only limited significance, I could not disagree with more strongly. I find his dismissal of the smaller images a thoroughly impoverishing viewpoint.

Ōhashi's project also contains a detailed analysis of the clay sculptures of Kawaradera, which he relates to direct Tang influence.[33] Finally, in his various studies of the *chokuganji* ("imperially vowed temples"), he endeavors to prove that these temples, because of their high statuses, had large-scale icons in the Tang style that constituted the most important monuments of Hakuhō sculpture, as we have seen.[34] Ōhashi readily acknowledges that only the Kōfukuji Buddha head (fig. 34) remains as an example of this style; nevertheless,

he seems determined to demonstrate the centrality of Tang influence flowering in the Hakuhō period. I cannot help wondering what has motivated this long-term, intense engagement with icons that cannot now be seen, while ignoring those that can. Tentatively, I suggest that the large corpus of extant Hakuhō images fails to fit his thesis because the great majority are not in the Tang style and many can be directly related to sculptural currents on the Korean peninsula, particularly that of Old Silla and especially during the succeeding Unified Silla period (668–935). Ōhashi seems bound and determined to demonstrate the centrality of Tang culture for developments in seventh-century Japan, beginning as early as 632, and fully flowering during the Hakuhō period.

WESTERN STUDIES OF HAKUHŌ SCULPTURE

In a previous discussion of the Gakuenji Kannon (fig. 46), I offered a detailed critique of Kuno's treatment of the image and also cited that of Mizuno.[35] These, although published in English, are translations of works that originally appeared in Japan, and consequently both are representative of Japanese approaches. What about the ideas presented by Western scholars in English? Langdon Warner's very large, elaborately illustrated book, *Japanese Sculpture of the Suiko Period*, got things off to a very bad start when he attributed the bulk of our Hakuhō images to his Suiko period.[36] In a later volume Warner has a chapter entitled

"Suiko and Hakuho [*sic*] Periods: A.D. 552–710," where the former is represented by six key monuments, while the latter must make do with two, the Tachibana Shrine Amida triad and the Yakushiji Yakushi triad's Gakkō. I attribute the triad (including Gakkō) to the Nara period and shall discuss it presently. Nevertheless, improvement must be acknowledged, since the Amida triad is here considered "Hakuhō, late 7th century," although I am at a loss to know on what evidence Warner based the sentence: "Though probably of Chinese or Korean workmanship, there is reason to believe this group begins to show some elements of the native Japanese style that developed during the next century."[37]

Not surprisingly, the Tachibana Amida triad has proved remarkably popular among Western scholars. The most important postwar volume on Japanese art, that of Paine and Soper, includes two full-page illustrations of the monument, the only sculpture so honored.[38] Unfortunately, the monument is called "Late Asuka" in the captions, even though the text discusses it under the heading "Hakuhō." (Even more unfortunately, this error goes uncorrected in later "revised" editions.) Paine's analysis of the triad is inadequate, although he does present a reasonably extended account of Hakuhō sculpture, including discussions of the Gakuenji Kannon (unillustrated) and the now lost Kō Yakushi, stolen from Shin Yakushiji during the Pacific War and never recovered (Paine's fig. 11 and p. 17).

A volume by William Watson devoted to Japanese sculpture also deals with the Tachibana Amida triad, here under the rubric "Early Nara, 671–710."[39] Watson dates it, in my view accurately ("early eighth century") and provides a not unreasonable assessment of its character, although he, like his predecessors, persists in seeing "Asuka" traits in its style. I believe this opinion results from the incorrect dating of the Yakushiji Yakushi triad and the same temple's Shō Kannon to the Hakuhō period, thereby distorting the analysis of works actually belonging to that period. It would be tedious to continue examining the earlier Western writings on the Hakuhō period, but I believe enough has been said to make it clear that these sources are generally inadequate in varying degrees. How is the Hakuhō period treated in more recent Western publications?

The principal successor to Paine and Soper is Penelope Mason's survey of Japanese art.[40] Although I reluctantly assigned this volume for a number of years, I was invariably annoyed by its totally inadequate account of Hakuhō sculpture. Entirely missing was any example of the small gilt-bronze images, not to mention key monuments such as the Yumechigai Kannon, the Tachibana Shrine Amida triad, or the Kōfukuji Buddha head, to cite only the most obvious candidates for inclusion. In fact, the sole Hakuhō piece illustrated and discussed is a wood image housed in the Hōryūji Museum (her fig. 69), inaccurately identified as "Kannon bosatsu."[41] The Yakushiji Yakushi triad is provided with an ambiguous "late 7th or early 8th century" date, although the text favors the earlier of

the two alternatives (p. 62). A recently published "revised" second edition is basically
no improvement.[42]

Far more modest in scale is Joan
Stanley-Baker's survey (163 plates in
comparison to Mason's 381), and yet the
author found room to illustrate three
examples of Hakuhō sculpture, including
the highly important Yumechigai Kannon
and the Tachibana Shrine Amida triad (her
pls. 29–30). The 688 date assigned to the
Yakushiji Yakushi triad is unfortunate.[43]
Stanley-Baker's characterization of Hakuhō
sculpture is somewhat misleading, naming
the Yakushi triad as the principal defining
monument for the period. Additionally,
associating the Tachibana Shrine Amida
triad and the Yumechigai Kannon with the
"Tori" school is not, in my view, acceptable.
Nevertheless, the reader of this volume is
at least alerted to the existence of Hakuhō
sculpture.

COMPARISON WITH ZENKŌJI
AMIDA TRIAD TRADITION

At the beginning of this chapter I juxta-
posed the sculpture of the Hakuhō period
with that of the tenth century, a strategy
that must have been seen by many readers
as comparing apples and oranges. There
was, however, method in my madness, for
in making this comparison I was focusing
on processes of stylistic evolution, not on
actual similarities between the two groups
of monuments. The time has arrived for a
comparison of more closely related images.
By far the largest group of bronze images

in Japan belongs to the Zenkōji Amida
triad lineage. Not only is their number
comparable to that of the Hakuhō corpus,
but many are clustered in a period similar
in length to that of the Hakuhō group,
between approximately 1249 and the early
fourteenth century.[44]

Zenkōji-lineage Amida triads belong
to a well-defined religious community,
and the cult icons, as objects of worship,
must conform more or less exactly to a
prescribed format; that is to say, they are
replications of a "secret image" (*hibutsu*)
enshrined at the Nagano Zenkōji. Of
course, the icons that have occupied us
in this study were also objects of worship
although not, I suspect, of such a precisely
formulated cult. Additionally, the icons
of the two groups are similar in size, as a
height of approximately 30 centimeters for
the bodhisattvas and 45 centimeters for
Amida is standard, although some variations appear.

What do we learn from comparing and
contrasting these two iconic traditions?
Most importantly, there are numerous
superlative Hakuhō images, whereas no
example of the Zenkōji tradition attains a
comparable aesthetic excellence. In fact,
the vast majority is of quite limited interest
from an artistic perspective. How should
this difference be explained? Obviously, the
sculptors who made Zenkōji Amida triads
were responding to specific commissions
in which a high premium was placed on
truth to prototype. If a specific example
did not resemble, or was thought not to
resemble, the prototypical "Living Buddha"

of Zenkōji, then it would not manifest the affective power of the prototype and thus the commission would be deemed a failure. Consequently, patrons were presumably willing to accept a modest level of quality as long as the canonical formula was respected. In my study of the Zenkōji-lineage icons I was able to isolate a few stylistic currents, but certainly the character of the group does not bring to mind variety or stylistic experimentation.[45]

In these respects Hakuhō sculpture differs markedly. The sculptors had to adhere to basic formats, but beyond that they were able to innovate and experiment, as we have seen repeatedly in the three preceding chapters. Usually, I have attributed these innovations and experiments to the personal predilections of individual artists, but in relation to our analysis of the Zenkōji images, we should also consider the role of the patrons of Hakuhō sculpture, whom, after all, the sculptors had to satisfy. If not, the patrons certainly would not have been willing to pay the presumably high prices for such icons, most of which required substantial effort to produce. In my Zenkōji study I sought to direct attention away from elite traditions toward broader religious and social complexes, but in this book I am dealing squarely with images made for an elite group of patrons, a situation that largely accounts for the differences in quality and expression between the two groups.[46]

THE YAKUSHIJI YAKUSHI TRIAD

Often lurking in the background of this

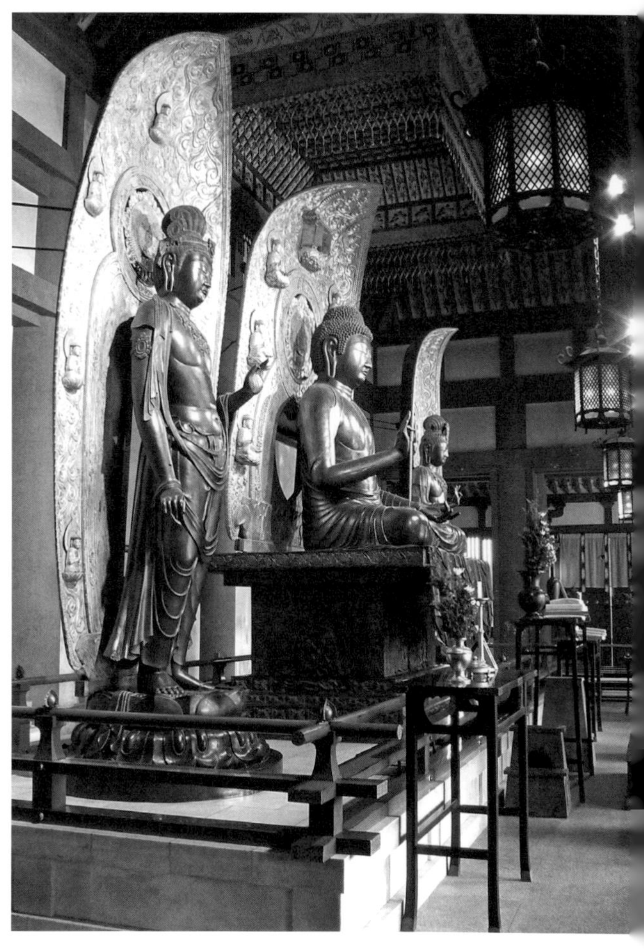

50   Yakushi Triad, H: Buddha, 254.7 cm. Yakushiji Kondō, Nara
Photo courtesy of Yakushiji

study is the dating of the Yakushi triad (fig. 50) of Yakushiji, Nara. Since this question of a relative date is of fundamental importance for an accurate conceptualization of Hakuhō sculpture, I propose to deal with it at some length. Necessarily, there will be some repetition of material I have presented in greater detail in *The Four Great Temples*, but in the interests of completeness, this is unavoidable.[47]

The central historiographical issues are the respective circumstances of the Fujiwarakyō and Heijōkyō Yakushiji and of their icons. Emperor Tenmu (r. 672–686) vowed the construction of Yakushiji in 680 for the sake of his seriously ill consort, Princess Uno (later Empress Jitō, r. 690–697), who had long outlived her husband at her death in 702. Although work on Fujiwarakyō Yakushiji probably began in 681, at the time of Tenmu's death (686.9.9) it was not yet ready for the performance of his memorial services. The first record of such a service is dated 688.1.8, by which time there must have been a finished main hall and a main icon, the minimum requirements for use. Stanley-Baker's 688 date for the present triad in Nara is based on this sequence of events.

Two entries in *Nihon shoki* of 697 (697.6.26 and 7.29) refer to the making of an icon at Yakushiji, and some scholars have dated the present triad to "late 7th century" (i.e., late Hakuhō) in light of this information. Frequently, "late 7th–early 8th century" is given, although I am unable to explain the sense of "early 8th century" unless "early" is meant to refer to the years after 710, when the capital was transferred from Fujiwarakyō to Heijōkyō.[48] This sort of ambiguous chronology should be eschewed by responsible scholars, for if one wishes to sit on the fence it is obligatory to indicate this position, using something like "late Hakuhō-early Nara period." As suggested above, I am convinced that the present Yakushiji Yakushi triad was made some time after 720, by which time the new temple in Heijōkyō would have been functional.

Recent archaeological investigations have proven conclusively that Fujiwarakyō Yakushiji continued to function long after the capital was transferred to Heijōkyō, and, in fact, new buildings were erected during the eighth century at the original site, including the very important West Pagoda. That being the case, it is inconceivable that the old temple would be disassembled, taken to the new site, and re-erected there. The concept of "transfer" as applied to Buddhist temples is too complicated to discuss here. Suffice it to say that each of the "Four Great Temples" continued to function in its original location.[49]

Many scholars, including myself, have long thought on stylistic grounds that the Yakushiji Yakushi triad could not date to the Hakuhō period.[50] A comparison of the faces of that Yakushi and of the Kōfukuji Buddha head (fig. 34) suggests a significant chronological gap between the two. If the Buddha head was made between 678 and 685, it seems unlikely that the Yakushi triad could have been completed by 688, or even at the end of the century. In any case, the full, fleshy modeling of the three figures appears to relate to Chinese styles that appeared after circa 700. Since there is no evidence for an early eighth-century date, the one remaining alternative is circa 720–730, at the time Heijōkyō Yakushiji was under construction. This time frame seems likely to me on the basis of style and technology; and now, because recent archaeological data proves that Fujiwarakyō

Yakushiji remained at its original site, no reasonable grounds exist for imagining an original icon (688 or end of the century) being moved to the new temple. It stayed where it had always been, while a new icon of the most advanced characteristics was made for Heijōkyō Yakushiji. Great as is my admiration for Hakuhō sculpture, the Yakushiji triad is not, and cannot be, an exemplar of that style.[51]

MEYER SCHAPIRO AND VISUAL ANALYSIS

In pondering matters of design while thinking about Hakuhō sculpture, I was enormously stimulated by a recent book of the great American art historian Meyer Schapiro (1904–1996).[52] As is well known, Schapiro's published corpus is relatively thin, considering the tremendous impact he has had on so many areas of art history. On a theoretical level, one probably thinks first of his seminal 1953 article "Style," a study I have read and reread continually throughout my professorial career.[53] Of course, the reader will have noted that *Language of Forms: Lectures on Insular Manuscript Art* is posthumous, appearing almost a decade after Schapiro's death. Although this may not be especially surprising given the trajectory of that author's career, it is very surprising indeed to realize that the lectures on which the book is based were delivered in 1968, almost forty years earlier. According to the director of the Morgan Library, Charles E. Pierce Jr., at a date as late as 1994 Schapiro was still very much interested in having his early projects published; and in 2002, his widow, Dr. Lillian Schapiro, continued to encourage publication of his lectures.[54] I wish to make clear that Schapiro did not regard this work as juvenilia (he was, after all, sixty-four years of age when the lectures were delivered), and certainly did not disavow its methodology.

What then is the methodology? I should like to focus on just one aspect of Schapiro's *Language of Forms*, a probing analysis of the illustrations of the *Book of Durrow* (probably circa 650–700). Rather than attempting my own summary of his position, perhaps it would be best to have Schapiro speak for himself:

> I must say from the outset that my concern is not essentially with the history of those Insular schools nor with solutions to the problems of authorship, localization, and dating that scholars have long debated. I wish rather to bring out certain aesthetic features of this art through close study of its forms and by means of comparisons with the work of other schools in order to make more evident the *individuality, original character, and inventive imagination* of Insular works. To this end, it may be fruitful to concentrate on a few pages from those manuscripts, suspending judgment as to where, when, and why they were done and in what tradition. *Let us scrutinize the works themselves, to acquaint ourselves more fully with their structure, their formal arrangements, and minute detail.* (p. 7, italics added)

The last sentence is especially pertinent for the present book, as it lays the foundation for my intense scrutiny of art here.

As might be anticipated, I strongly recommend that anybody interested in the matters considered in my analysis of Hakuhō sculpture immediately obtain a copy of Schapiro's book rather than depending on my inadequate exegesis. To choose one especially subtle example, Schapiro considers the formulation of the Lion symbol of St. John in detail. He asks why the lengthy lion is squeezed horizontally into the middle of a tall, vertical field, rather than being more symmetrically and spaciously arranged parallel to that long vertical axis. Instead of limiting himself to verbal descriptions of the visual potentially confusing to his audience, Schapiro illustrates his "new" version of the page with the animal aligned within the vertical field. By relating the form of the lion with the compositional elements of the border interlace, he demonstrates that this "new" arrangement would have destroyed essential aesthetic qualities of the original composition.

In analyzing the Man symbol of St. Matthew, Schapiro utilizes the same methodology, commenting first on the odd arrangement of the man's feet, which both point to the right, and then producing another "new" page where the feet point to the left *and* right, thereby showing how that arrangement is much less effective compositionally. (He also experiments with reversing the direction of the border interlace, with similar results.) Schapiro's

analyses are not limited to the *Book of Durrow*, but are also applied to pages from the *Echternach Gospels* and *The Book of Kells*.

I have no intention of equating my discussions of Hakuhō sculpture with Schapiro's brilliant analyses of Insular-style illuminated manuscript pages, but I do believe that they point to related artistic approaches. For example, in looking at Evangelist pages, the symbols are relatively canonical,[55] although their placement within the frame varies and internal differences are apparent. These questions of compositional arrangement and "minute detail" (to use Schapiro's term) are aspects directly attributable to the aesthetic concerns of the artists, since it is highly unlikely that they affect in any significant manner the iconographical meaning of the representations. As I have already acknowledged, artistic liberty within iconographic prescription is pervasive in world art, but in certain types it appears more clearly, as in Insular illumination and Hakuhō sculpture.[56] Neither Schapiro nor I would ever argue that additional issues are not of crucial importance for an understanding of artworks, but I would suggest that the approach outlined above unequivocally demonstrates Schapiro's intense commitment to precise, concentrated visual analysis.[57] Naturally, I can only speak for myself, and I do, of course, maintain such a commitment.

THE END OF HAKUHŌ SCULPTURE

What happened to the Hakuhō tradition in sculpture, especially images within the small gilt-bronze category? Earlier in this study I hinted at some of the factors for change, but it might be useful to review them again here. Most important is the formation of an increasingly centralized, bureaucratically administered state based on the *ritsuryō* codes. For our purposes, the significant aspect of this is the establishment of official government studios for the production of icons. Although very important images in bronze continued to be produced, other mediums such as clay and dry lacquer became increasingly popular, and wood statuary was also produced. Generally speaking, the government studios made icons for temples, and these would almost always be of large scale.[58]

Along with changes in government, one assumes that as more standardized statuary became the norm, artists enjoyed fewer opportunities to experiment or innovate. One can hardly imagine artistic liberty appearing in images such as the Tōdaiji Great Buddha! Stated differently, Nara culture and art had a degree of confidence and sense of self-satisfaction uncongenial to the type of variety seen during the Hakuhō period.

At the beginning of modern art history in Japan, an intensive search was carried out to locate styles comparable to those of fifth-century Greece or sixteenth-century Italy, with the almost inevitable result that the Nara period was anointed as the "Golden Age of Japanese Art" and Buddhist sculpture assumed a central position in this ideological construct. Naturally, this process was very much aided by the Nara establishment's wholesale adoption of Tang modes, which themselves emerged from a self-confident society. As stated in my preface, I see Hakuhō sculpture as arising primarily out of Sui styles via the Korean peninsula, especially Silla. I am willing to acknowledge a certain direct Tang contribution, but I believe that the style incorporating this contribution reached its full flowering only in the Nara period.

NOTES

PREFACE

1 Unfortunately, the most substantial study of Hakuhō sculpture in the West, Chie Ishibashi's 1990 Harvard dissertation, "Hakuhō Sculpture: Its Development as Viewed in the Context of the Chronology of Roof-Tile Motifs," remains unpublished.

2 Uehara Shōichi, *Asuka-Hakuhō chōkoku*, vol. 21 of *Nihon no bijutsu* (Tokyo: Shibundō, 1968); and Matsuura Masaaki, *Asuka Hakuhō no butsuzō: kodai bukkyō no katachi*, vol. 455 of *Nihon no bijutsu* (Tokyo: Shibundō, 2004).

3 *Shoku nihongi*, Jinki 1 (724).10.1. Although *Shoku nihongi* has the term "Suzaku," scholars assume that this is a mistake or a substitution for "Shūchō," a reign era assigned to Tenmu and his successor Jitō.

4 *Nihon shoki*, where Kōtoku 6 (650), is also designated Hakuchi 1; for the years from Kōtoku 1 to 645, the Taika era name is used.

5 Further discussion of the use of the term "Hakuhō" will be found in chap. 2, "Historiography," and in chap. 5, "Ōhashi on Hakuhō Sculpture."

6 Mizuno Seiichi, *Asuka Buddhist Art: Horyu-ji* (New York & Tokyo: Weatherhill/Heibonsha,1974), Chūgūji Miroku, plates 59, 77; Hōrinji Buddha, plates 60, 86, 87; Hōrinji bodhisattva, plates 85, 194; Hōryūji Museum "Six Kannon," plates 58, 88, 89; Taimadera Miroku, plate 128. For *senbutsu*, see *Kashihara Kōkogaku Kenkyūjo Fuzoku Hakubutsukan*, "Hakuhō no imeeji: Nara ken shutsudō senbutsuten" (The Image of Hakuhō: Exhibition of *senbutsu* Excavated in Nara Prefecture) (Kashihara: 2002). Yoko Shirai, "Senbutsu: Figured Clay Tiles, Buddhism, and Political Developments on the Japanese Islands, ca. 650 CE–794 CE," PhD diss., University of California, Los Angeles, 2006.

7 Gregory Levine, "Two (or More) Truths:
Reconsidering *Zen Art* in the West,"
in *Awakenings: Zen Figure Painting in
Medieval Japan*, ed. Gregory Levine and
Yukio Lippit (New York: Japan Society,
2007), 52–61. Levine italicizes "Zen
Art" in the title of his essay in order to
defamiliarize the term.

8 Ibid.

1. INTRODUCTION

1 The sculpture of Greece has frequently
been the subject of general mono-
graphs; see Rhys Carpenter, *Greek
Sculpture: A Critical Review* (Chicago:
University of Chicago Press, 1960), and
more recently, Andrew Stewart, *Greek
Sculpture: An Exploration* (New Haven:
Yale University Press, 1990). I have been
especially stimulated by Mary Stieber,
*The Poetics of Appearance in the Attic
Korai* (Austin: University of Texas
Press, 2004), and A. A. Donohue, *Greek
Sculpture and the Problem of Descrip-
tion* (Cambridge: Cambridge University
Press, 2005), both of which deal with a
corpus of sculptural images similar in
scale to Hakuhō sculpture.

2 For a good general discussion of casting
techniques, see Washizuka Hiromitsu,
"Techniques of Early Buddhist Sculpture in Japan," in Washizuka Hiromitsu
et al., *Transmitting the Forms of Divinity: Early Buddhist Art from Korea and
Japan* (New York: Japan Society, 2003),
128–35. More technical discussions are
found in Nishikawa Kyōtarō, "Hōryūji

Kondō Shaka-Yakushi ni zō to kennō
kondō butsu no izō gihō: Tori ha no
sakurei o chūshin to shite" (The Casting
Techniques of the Shaka and Yakushi
Images in the Hōryūji Golden Hall
and the Donated Gilt-bronze Images:
Centering on Works of the Tori School),
in *Hōryūji kennō hōmotsu: kondō
butsu* (Gilt-bronze Images Donated
by Hōryūji), ed. Tokyo Kokuritsu
Hakubutsukan, vol. 1 (Tokyo, 1996),
340–46; and Matsuyama Tetsuō, *Nihon
kodai kondō butsu no kenkyū: Yakushiji
hen* (Research on Ancient Japanese
Gilt-bronze Images: Yakushiji) (Tokyo:
Chūō Kōron Bijutsu Shuppan, 1990),
especially 37–65.

3 Donald F. McCallum, "A Standing Kannon in the Tokyo National Museum,"
Archives of Asian Art 53 (2002–2003):
7–25.

4 For penetrating comments on the
roles of craftsmen and supervisors, see
Martin J. Powers, *Pattern and Person:
Ornament, Society, and Self in Classi-
cal China* (Cambridge, MA: Harvard
University Press, 2006), especially chap.
4, "Craft," 83–98.

5 A general source for Chinese Buddhist
sculpture with many good illustrations
is *Chinese Sculpture*, ed. Angela F. How-
ard et al. (New Haven: Yale University
Press, 2006); see also Robert L. Thorp
and Richard Ellis Vinograd, *Chinese
Art and Culture* (New York: Prentice
Hall, 2001).

6 A typical example of this viewpoint
is Nishikawa Shinji, "Hakuhō jidai no

chōkoku" (Sculpture of the Hakuhō Period), in Bunkachō, ed., *Nihon no bijutsu* 5, *chōkoku, Asuka-Nara* (Art of Japan 5, Sculpture, Asuka-Nara) (Tokyo: Daiichi Hōki Shuppan, 1978), 88.

7 An early formulation of these ideas is my "Kankoku - Nihon no chōkoku ni ataeta Zui yoshiki no eikyō ni tsuite" (The Influence of Sui Styles on Korean and Japanese Buddhist Sculptures), in Nara Kokuritsu Hakubutsukan, ed., *Kenkyū kadai: Nihon ni okeru bukkyō bijutsu no juyō to tenkai* (Research Themes: The Reception and Development of Buddhist Art in Japan) (Nara, 1978), 1–10.

8 Lena Kim, "Tradition and Transformation in Korean Buddhist Sculpture," in Judith G. Smith, ed., *Arts of Korea* (New York: Metropolitan Museum of Art, 1998), 250–93, is a comprehensive survey of the subject; by the same author, see *Buddhist Sculpture of Korea* (Seoul: Hollym, 2007). Kang Woobang, *Korean Buddhist Sculpture: Art and Truth* (Chicago: Art Media Resources, 2005), has three chapters relevant to the present study. Kang believes that Koguryo was very important for the development of Three Kingdoms Buddhist art, but because of the eccentric nature of some of his arguments his work must be used with caution.

9 I have presented a detailed account of this matter in Donald F. McCallum, "The Earliest Buddhist Statues in Japan," *Artibus Asiae* 61, no. 2 (2001): 149–88.

10 *Nihon shoki*, Kinmei 13 (552).10 (hereafter, *Nihon shoki* will be abbreviated to *NS*); as is well-known, *Gangōji engi* tells a different story and gives a date equivalent to 538. Since this difference is not crucial to the present study, readers interested in it should consult the bibliography in McCallum,"Earliest Buddhist Statues," especially 151–53.

11 The question of "immigrants" is discussed at greater length in McCallum, "Earliest Buddhist Statues," 180.

12 Since I have analyzed in great detail the role of the Soga clan and the building of Asukadera in Donald F. McCallum, *The Four Great Temples: Buddhist Art, Archaeology, and Icons of Seventh-Century Japan* (Honolulu: University of Hawai'i Press, 2009), I refer readers to it for a discussion and bibliography.

13 Full bibliographical references for these images can be found in Donald F. McCallum, "Tori-busshi and the Production of Buddhist Icons in Asuka-period Japan," in *The Artist as Professional in Japan*, ed. Melinda Takeuchi (Stanford: Stanford University Press, 2004), 19.

14 Ibid., 25–36.

15 Donald F. McCallum, "The Buddhist Triad in Three Kingdoms Sculpture," *Korean Culture* 16, no. 4 (1995): 18–35.

16 For these two sculptures, see Washizuka et al., *Transmitting the Forms of Divinity*, Shaka triad, cat. 24, 238–39; standing bodhisattva, cat. 23, 236–37. Several of the sculptures that I will consider are illustrated and discussed

in this catalogue; since it has good color plates and is readily available, I shall cite these images in the text.

17 Tanaka Yoshiyasu, "*Boshi* nenmei Shaka sanzon zō no fukugen" (Reconstruction of the Shaka Triad with a *boshi* date), in *Arugama: Sawayanagi sensei koki kinen bijutsushi ronbunshū* (Arugama: Art Historical Essays Celebrating the Seventieth Birthday of Professor Sawayanagi) (Tokyo: Dōhōsha, 1982), 289–302.

18 The interpretation of the *sōgishi* has elicited a great deal of controversy; see Yoshimura Rei, "Butsuzō no chakui: 'sōgishi' to 'henzan' ni tsuite" (The Costume of the Buddha: Concerning the *sōgishi* and *henzan*), *Nantō bukkyō* 81 (2002): 93–120, and "Kodai no bikuzō no chakui to meishō: sōgishi, kansan, henzan, jikitotsu ni tsuite" (The Dressing Code and Terms as Evidenced by Ancient Monk Statues: on *sāṃkaksikâ, kansan, henzan, and jikitotsu*), *Museum* 587 (2003): 5–24.

19 Mizuno, *Asuka Buddhist Art: Horyu-ji*, Kudara Kannon, plates 55–56, 81–84; Shitennō, plates 53–54, 71–76.

20 Ibid., plate 78.

21 Ibid., plate 192.

22 Discussed in detail in McCallum, *The Four Great Temples*, chap. 2.

23 Joan R. Piggott, *The Emergence of Japanese Kingship* (Stanford: Stanford University Press, 1997), 102–5. I have reservations concerning "Prince Shōtoku" aka, "Prince Stable Door," but as this is a study concentrating on the

Hakuhō period, I will avoid that issue here.

24 Ibid., 105–13. For more detail, see Yokota Ken'ichi, "Soga honshū no metsubō to Taika kaishin" (The Downfall of the Main Line of the Soga and the Taika Reform), in *Kodai o kangaeru: Soga shi to kodai kokka* (Reflecting on Ancient Times: The Soga Clan and the Ancient State), ed. Mayuzumi Hiromichi (Tokyo: Yoshikawa Kōbunkan, 1991), 169–201.

25 *NS*, Kōtoku 1 (645).8.8. For a discussion of this entry, see Tamura Enchō, *Asuka-Hakuhō bukkyō shi* (History of Asuka and Hakuhō Buddhism), vol. 1 (Tokyo: Yoshikawa Kōbunkan, 1994), 221–29.

26 Asuka Shiryōkan, ed., *Saimei ki* (Nara, 1996), provides a detailed account of some of Saimei's building activities.

27 Piggott, *Emergence*, 116.

28 Ibid., 117–26, for the Tenji reign, and 127–66 for the reigns of Tenmu and Jitō. The first occurrence of the Japanese term for "emperor" (*tennō*) appears to be on a *mokkan* (small wooden tablet used for writing) excavated at Asuka Pond in a context dated circa 676; this issue is treated in more detail in my chap. 3 in the discussion of the Yachūji Miroku.

29 McCallum, *The Four Great Temples*, chap. 4, gives a full account of Yakushiji.

30 Convenient sources for this capital are: Terasaki Yasuhiro, *Fujiwarakyō no keisei* (The Formation of Fujiwarakyō) (Tokyo: Yamakawa Shuppansha, 2002);

and Kinoshita Masashi, *Fujiwarakyō* (Tokyo: Chūō Koron Shinsha, 2003). I am preparing a monograph devoted to Fujiwarakyō.

31 *NS*, Tenmu 2 (673).3. For Kawaradera, see McCallum, *The Four Great Temples,* chap. 3; here it might be noted that quite recently a structure was uncovered at Kawaradera that was either a Bell Tower or a Scripture Hall. Whichever it was, the very existence of one implies the other. Nabunken, ed., *Kawaradera jiiki hokugen no chōsa* (Nara, 2004).

32 See McCallum, *The Four Great Temples,* chap. 2, 93.

33 For this, see *NS*, Tenmu 2 (673).12.27.

34 *NS*, Tenmu 8 (679).4.5.

35 *NS*, Tenmu 9 (680).4. I give a detailed analysis of this edict in McCallum, *The Four Great Temples,* chap. 5, 237–38.

36 *NS*, Tenmu 14 (685).3.27.

37 For the early historiography, see Ishimura Kie, "Tenmu ki no *iegoto tsukuru bussha* shikō" (Thoughts on the *iegoto tsukuru bussha* edict in the Tenmu annals), in his *Nihon kodai bukkyō bunka shi ronkō* (Study of the History of Buddhist Culture in Ancient Japan) (Tokyo: Sankibō Busshorin, 1978), 11–24, especially 11–12, and notes 1–5 (p. 23).

38 Piggott, *Emergence*, 154; Piggott's notes refer to *Nihon shoki*, but she does not indicate the reasons for her interpretation. A comprehensive account of Japanese suggestions is Yoshida Kazuhiko, "Hakuhō bukkyō to chihō gōzoku" (Hakuhō Buddhism and the

Provincial Great Families), in his *Nihon kodai shakai to bukkyō* (Ancient Japanese Society and Buddhism) (Tokyo: Yoshikawa Kōbunkan, 1995), 20–24, and notes 28–36.

39 Yoshida, "Hakuhō bukkyō," 20.

40 Tamura Enchō, "Kokka bukkyō no seiritsu katei" (The Process of the Formation of State Buddhism), in his *Nihon bukkyō shi,* vol. 1: *Asuka jidai*) (History of Japanese Buddhism I: The Asuka Period) (Kyoto: Hōzōkan, 1982), 208–26, especially 220–23.

41 Ibid., 223; *NS*, Suiko 2 (594).2.1.

42 Yoshida, "Hakuhō bukkyō," 20–21.

43 Ibid., 22–23.

44 Kuno Takeshi, "Asuka-Hakuhō shō kondō butsu no hatsugansha, seisakusha" (Donors and Artists of Small Gilt-bronze Buddhist Images in the Asuka and Hakuhō Periods), Part 1, *Bijutsu kenkyū* 309 (1979), 172–86, especially 183.

45 Ibid., 184. We should note that many of the images of the "Forty-eight Buddhist Deities" group were originally at Tachibanadera in the heart of Asuka, and they were not transferred to Hōryūji until much later.

46 Ibid., 183.

47 The term *butsuden* (or *butsudono*), translated here as "Buddhist Halls," may require some further thought. As is well known, *Hōryūji engi*, 749, speaks of two *butsuden*, presumably the Tamamushi shrine and the Tachibana shrine; of course, neither are buildings, a standard meaning for "*den*" or "*dono*,"

suggesting considerable flexibility in definition. Could it be that *"sha"* and *"bussha,"* discussed above, had a similar range of meanings, including both "shrine" and "hall"?

48 *NS*, Jitō 5 (691).2.1. This entry is discussed by Katata Osamu, "Shoki ritsuryō bukkyō kōryū no ichi sokumen" ("One Aspect in the Rise of Ritsuryō Buddhism") in his *Nihon kodai shinkō to bukkyō* (Ancient Japanese Religion and Buddhism) (Kyoto: Hōzōkan, 1991), 186–93. He disagrees with the idea that the 691 edict is related to the 685 edict, arguing that two terms in the former imply the capital, not the provinces: "Ministers" (*maetsukimi*) has a different referent from "all the houses in the various provinces" (*kuniguni ie goto*), and the *ōtoneri* who were despatched must have been capital officials.

49 For the burial of Tenmu and Jitō, see *Asuka-Fujiwarayō ten*, ed. Nabunken (Nara, 2002), 119–20.

2. EARLY HAKUHŌ SCUPTURE

1 Reign or era designations such as "Suiko," "Tenpyō," "Jōgan," "Fujiwara," etc. have been discarded by practically all art historians, and only Hakuhō remains.

2 Sekino Tadashi, "Yakushiji kondō oyobi kōdō no Yakushi sanzon no seisaku nendai o ronzu" (Considering the dates of Manufacture of the Yakushi Triads in the Golden Hall and Lecture Hall of Yakushiji), *Shigaku zasshi* 12.4 (1901): 425–45. Sekino's article is discussed in detail in Ōhashi Katsuaki, "Hakuhō chōkoku ron" (Theory of Hakuhō Sculpture), *Bukkyō geijutsu* 223 (1996): 37–56, especially 37–40. A fundamental source for the analysis of historiographical theories is Mōri Hisashi, "Hakuhō chōkoku no Shiragi-teki yōso" (Silla Elements in Hakuhō Sculpture), in *Shiragi to Asuka-Hakuhō bukkyō* (Buddhism of the Asuka and Hakuhō Periods), ed. Tamura Enchō and Hong Soon-chang (Tokyo: Yoshikawa Kōbunkan, 1975), 113–45.

3 Mizuno Seiichi, "Asuka-Hakuhō butsu no keifu" (Lineages of Asuka and Hakuhō Sculpture), *Bukkyō geijutsu* 4 (1949): 23–51, especially 47–51.

4 Minamoto Toyomune, "Asuka jidai no chōkoku" (Sculpture of the Asuka Period), originally published in *Bukkyō bijutsu* 13 (1929), more conveniently found in his collected works, *Minamoto Toyomune chosaku shū: Nihon bijutsu shi ronkyū 2, Sosetsu - kodai* (Kyoto: Shibunkaku, 1995), 88–109. See also Machida Kōichi, "Jōdai chōkoku shi jō ni okeru yōshiki jiki no mondai" (Problems in the Stylistic Periodization of Ancient Sculpture), in his *Jōdai chōkoku shi no kenkyū* (Research in the History of Ancient Sculpture) (Tokyo: Yoshikawa Kōbunkan, 1977), 1–75; originally published in *Bukkyō geijutsu* 38–39 (1959). (Hereafter abbreviated as Machida, *Jōdai chōkoku shi*). Nishikawa Shinji, in *Nihon no bijutsu 5, chōkoku,*

Asuka-Nara, 14–15, presents a variant of the modified Hakuhō, seeing a break between Asuka and Hakuhō about the year 663.

5 Kobayashi Takeshi, "Hakuhō chōkoku shi ron" (Historical Analysis of Hakuhō Sculpture) in *Nihon chōkoku shi kenkyū* (Research in the History of Japanese Sculpture) (Nara: Yōtokudō, 1947), 57–78; originally published in *Kōkogaku zasshi* 30.8 (1940).

6 Kanamori Jun, "Hakuhō chōkoku shi ron" (My Views on Hakuhō Sculpture), *Bijutsu kenkyū* 125 (1942): 181–91. Also published in *Nihon chōkoku shi no kenkyū* (Research in the History of Japanese Buddhist Sculpture) (Kyoto: Kawahara Shoten, 1949), 36–53. Kanamori saw the first half as a continuation of Asuka, the second as the start of Nara. Andō Kōsei, "Hakuhō jidai wa sonzaishinai" (The Hakuhō Period Did Not Exist), in *Nara bijutsu kenkyū* (Research in Nara Art) (Tokyo: Kokura Shōbō, 1962), 9–31; originally published in *Geijutsu shinchō*, 1958. Andō generally follows Kanamori, but sets the dividing point at 678, the year work began on the Yamadadera Lecture Hall triad (i.e., the Kōfukuji Buddha Head). Kuno Takeshi, "Hakuhō jidai wa sonzaisuru ka" (Did the Hakuhō Period Exist?), in *Hakuhō no bijutsu* (Hakuhō Art) (Tokyo: Rokko Shuppan, 1978), 7–34, argues against Andō and advocates the standard Hakuhō dates of 645–710.

7 The "Forty-eight Buddhist Deities" group of sculptures was transferred from Hōryūji to the new Imperial Household Museum in the late nineteenth century. As noted above, prior to being at Hōryūji, many were housed at Tachibanadera in Asuka, closer to their original locations. The sculptures are numbered 143–96, and this system of designation will be used here.

8 Two cyclical characters together indicate a specific year in a sixty-year cycle. Since it is known when the cycles began, hypothetically a pair could be associated with an infinite number of cycles; but stylistic and historical evidence make it highly unlikely that, for example, no. 165 could be dated to 531 or 711 (or to any other earlier or later date).

9 Asuka Shiryōkan, ed., *Asuka/Hakuhō no zaimei kondō butsu* (Dated Gilt-bronze Images of the Asuka and Hakuhō Periods), 2d ed. (Nara, 1979), no. 2, plates 57–60, 149–51, 174–75 (hereafter abbreviated to *Asuka/Hakuhō zaimei*); Yabuta Kaichirō, "Heiin nen Takaya no taifu zōzō ki kōshaku" (Interpretation of Record of Manufacture of the Image of the Heiin Cycle bearing the Inscription Takaya no taifu [name and title]), *Bijutsu kenkyū* 148 (1948): 89–101. Koizumi Yoshihide, "Hōryūji kenno hōbutsu 156-go to Yachūji Miroku zō: heiin nenmei motsu nitai no hanka shii zō" (Two Meditating Bodhisattvas Having a Heiin Date: The Hōryūji Treasure House no. 156 and the Yachūji Miroku), in *Ronso Nara bijutsu* (Controversies in Nara Art), ed. Ōhashi

Katsuaki (Tokyo: Heibonsha, 1994), 97–124, especially 107–13.

10 These traits will be examined later in the discussion of the formulated Hakuhō style; here it is adequate to state that their presence, especially the three-plaque crown, precludes a 606 date for the image.

11 *Asuka-Hakuhō zaimei*, no. 4, 152–54, 178–79, plates 67–69; Machida Kōichi, "Hōryūji denrai no shōkondō butsu to *shingai* mei Kannon bosatsu ritsuzō ni tsuite" (Concerning the Small, Gilt-bronze Images transmitted at Hōryūji and the Standing Kannon with a *shingai* inscription), in his *Jōdai chōkoku shi*, 77–103.

12 The Amida figure in the crown is referred to in Japanese as a *kebutsu* ("transformation Buddha"), and this term will be used here.

13 Kim Lina [Lena Kim], "Hōju hōji bosatsu no keifu" (The Lineage of Jewel-clasping Bodhisattvas), in *Hōryūji kara Yakushiji e: Asuka-Hakuhō kenchiku-chōkoku* (From Hōryūji to Yakushiji: Architecture and Sculpture of the Asuka and Hakuhō Periods), ed. Mizuno Keizaburō et al., vol. 2 of *Nihon bijutsu zenshū*, (Tokyo: Kōdansha,1990), 195–200. An earlier Korean version is "Samguk sidae ui pongi pojuhyong posal ipsang yon'gu: Paekche wa Ilbon ul sang ul chungsim uro," *Misul charyo* 37 (1985): 1–39.

14 As we shall see, the scarf is one of the elements most frequently showing variation; a particularly striking instance

can be seen at the backs of the flanking bodhisattvas of the Tachibana Shrine Amida, where sections of the scarf that cross in the back do so on the diagonal.

15 It should be noted that the inscriptions on the two images include terms of great historical interest, although there is no space here to consider these matters.

16 The identification of the "tassel" is controversial; on some images it may represent a *stupa*. This motif is seen in the Kanshōin Meditating Bodhisattva, an image I dealt with in my "Earliest Buddhist Statues," 175–76, as a pre-Asuka import from the Korean peninsula.

17 Much more could be said about the drapery, as some elements are very difficult to understand. In this regard, there are common features with the Yumedono Kannon, especially in the relationship between the lower sections of the scarf and the wider parts over the shoulders.

18 A similar arrangement of jewelry strings can be seen in the Sekiyama-jinja bodhisattva, a pre-Asuka import discussed in my "Earliest Buddhist Statues," 177. This image also has the U loop at back and presumably clasped a jewel in the now missing hands. One might ask if elements seen in this image and in the Kanshōin meditating bodhisattva were perhaps ignored during the high point of the Soga-Tori style, only to reappear in early Hakuhō.

19 Ordinarily in this study I do not adduce Chinese or Korean prototypes for ele-

ments such as the three-plaque crown, but I cannot resist citing one interesting Sui Guanyin, a large stone figure in the Gansu Provincial Museum. See Annette L. Juliano and Judith A. Lerner, eds., *Monks and Merchants: Silk Road Treasures from Northwest China, Gansu, and Ningxia, 4th–7th centuries* (New York: Abrams, 2001), no. 71, 196–98.

20 For a detailed discussion of the halo, see *Asuka/Hakuhō zaimei*, no. 5, 70–76, and 154–55, 78–180. For the controversy, see Matsubara Saburō in Matsubara Saburō and Tanabe Saburōsuke, *Shō kondō butsu* (Small Gilt-Bronze Images) (Tokyo: Tokyo Bijutsu, 1979), 338; Yamamoto Tsutomu in Tokyo Kokuritsu Hakubutsukan, ed., *Tokubetsuten, Kondō butsu: Chūgoku, Chōsen, Nihon,* (Special Exhibition, Gilt-Bronze Icons: China, Korea, Japan; hereafter abbreviated to *TNM, Kondō butsu, 1988*) (Tokyo: Ōtsuka Kogeisha, 1988), 413–14; Iwasa Mitsuhara in Mizuno Keisaburō, ed., *Hōryūji kara Yakushiji e: Nihon bijutsu zenshū,* vol. 2: *Asuka-Nara no kenchiku/chōkoku* (From Hōryūji to Yakushiji: Collection of Japanese Art, vol. 2: Asuka-Nara Architecture and Sculpture) (Tokyo: Kōdansha, 1990), 209. Those scholars generally accept that this halo was attached, although each indicates some room for doubt. Kuno Takeshi, in "Hakuhō jidai wa sonzai suru ka," 13, and in *Kodai shō kondō butsu* (Ancient Small Gilt-bronze Images) (Tokyo: Shōgakkan, 1982), 161,

has greater reservations than do other authorities about the likelihood that the above image and halo were attached.

21 See *NS*, Kōtoku 5 (649).3.24 for Himuka's report to Prince Naka no Ōe of Ishikawa Maro's purported treason, and 3.25 for his death. By an implausible coincidence, Abe no Ōomi, Minister of the Left, had already died a few days earlier, and although we are told that there was great mourning for him, I suspect that he was poisoned or otherwise done in by Naka no Ōe and Nakatomi no Kamatari, who apparently wished to clear the decks; see *NS*, Kōtoku 5 (649).3.17 for Abe's death.

22 *NS*, Kōtoku 5 (649).3; the day is not specified, but it obviously was after 3.25. Given political realities of this period, it is difficult to decide if Ishikawa Maro was innocent or guilty. For a detailed consideration of these sordid events, see Shinokawa Ken, "Itsushi no hen to Soga Kura Yamada Ishikawa Maro" (The "Itsushi" [=645] Disturbance and Soga Kura Yamada Ishikawa Maro), in Saeki Arikiyo, ed., *Nihon kodai seiji shi ronkō* (Studies of Ancient Japanese Political History) (Tokyo: Yoshikawa Kōbunkan, 1983), 59–84. ("Itsushi no hen" is a more neutral term than Taika Reform.) For an English account, see Mary Neighbour Parent, "Yamadadera: Tragedy and Triumph," *Monumenta Nipponica* 39.3 (1984): 307–31.

23 For discussions of the Western, or European, pose, see Alexander C. Soper, *Literary Evidence for Early Bud-*

dhist Art in China (Ascona: Artibus Asiae, 1959), 2, 15; and Soper, "Some Late Chinese Bronze Images (Eighth to Fourteenth Centuries) in the Avery Brundage Collection, M. H. De Young Museum, San Francisco," *Artibus Asiae* 31, no.1 (1969): 36–37.

24 Sheila L. Weiner, *Ajanta: Its Place in Buddhist Art* (Berkeley and Los Angeles: University of California Press, 1977), 62–63. For China, see the discussions by Soper cited in the preceding note. Also, Mizuno Seiichi, "Iza bosatsu ni tsuite" (Concerning the Bodhisattva Seated in the Western Pose), in *Chūgoku bukkyō bijutsu* (Buddhist Art of China) (Tokyo: Heibonsha, 1968), 251–55 (originally published in *Tōyōshi kenkyū* 6.1, 1940.)

25 Nara Kokuritsu Hakubutsukan, ed., *Amida butsu chōzō* (Sculptures of Amida) (Tokyo: Tokyo Bijutsu, 1975), 210, plate 15.

26 See Kuno Takeshi, "East Asian Buddhist Sculpture and the *Henzan*," in *Tokyo National Institute of Cultural Property—Inter-regional Influence in East Asian Art History* (Tokyo, 1981), 15–17. A Japanese version will be found in Kuno's *Kodai shō kondō butsu*, 241–49.

27 Various ratio schemes are seen in Buddhist sculpture. A classic expression is 1:2:4, referring to the relationship of the height of the head, upper part of the body, and lower part of the body, including legs.

28 In making this comparison, I shall refer to the Seishi of the Yamadaden triad.

29 Kannon no. 167 is a typical jewel-clasper/U-loop figure, but the flanking bodhisattvas of the Yamadaden triad display a variant, as they seem not to grasp jewels. Other variations will be seen later.

30 Tazawa Yutaka et. al., *Hōryūji shiryō chōkoku hen 1, Hōryūji Kondō Shaka sanzon zo* (The Hōryūji Golden Hall Shaka Triad) (Tokyo: Iwanami Shoten, 1949), 33–34, plates 64–76. Of course, the Yamadaden triad lacks the Sumeru form of the lower pedestal of the Shaka triad.

31 Most Hakuhō bodhisattvas have this two-register arrangement of the scarf, but there are also some on which the ends of the scarf hang down from the shoulders, parallel to the sides of the body. It is essential to realize that there is only one scarf in the bodhi-sattva costume; "scarves" is incorrect. See my "Buddhist Sculpture of the Seisuiji, Matsushiro," *Oriental Art* 25, no. 4 (1979–1980): 466 and note 19, for a discussion of later developments in the arrangement of the scarf. I have prepared an article, as yet unpublished, entitled "Scarves, Ribbons, and the Scarf, as well as some Sashes and Belt-ends: the Bodhisattva Costume in the Early Buddhist Sculpture of East Asia," containing a detailed analysis of the dress of these deities.

32 I believe the style of this triad is related to the sculpture of Silla and prob-ably reflects influence coming directly across the East Sea; therefore, I find the

"provincial style" hypothesis unconvincing. I presented my hypothesis in "East Sea/Japan Sea: A Neglected Area for Early Korean-Japanese Relations in Buddhist Sculpture," Annual Meeting, Association for Asian Studies, Washington D.C., March 25, 1984; a later version appears as "Silla and the East Sea: A Neglected Area for Early Korean-Japanese Relations in Buddhist Sculpture," in Silla Cultural Heritage Research Group, ed., *Silla in the World—The World in Silla: Gyeongju International Symposium on Silla Studies*, Gyeongju, 2007, 19–36, especially 23–25 (hereafter abbreviated to "Silla Symposium").

33 Asai Kazuharu, "Hyōgo, Ichijōji Kannon bosatsu ritsuzō ni tsuite" (Concerning the Standing Kannon at Ichijōji, Hyōgo), *Bukkyō geijutsu* 158 (1985): 117–20; *TNM, Kondō butsu, 1988,* no. 93: 194–95 (plates), 425 (text); Japan Society, *Transmitting Divinity*, no. 22: 234–35. I commented on this image in "Silla Symposium," 25.

34 The most important study of these images is Mōri Hisashi, "Asuka-Hakuhō no dōgyō butsu to sono genryū" (Boyish Images of the Asuka and Hakuhō Periods and Their Origin), in *Shiragri to Nihon no kodai bunka* (Silla and Ancient Japanese Culture), ed. Tamura Enchō (Tokyo: Yoshikawa Kōbunkan, 1985), 25–53. Mōri's conception of the category is broader than mine.

35 These two numbers are arbitrary, assigned only for convenience, and will be explained later. (They should not be confused with the museum numbers assigned to the Forty-eight Buddhist Deities at the TNM.)

36 This figure, in Kinryūji, Nara, is a representative member of the group. See Nara Kokuritsu Hakubutsukan, ed., *Nihon bukkyō bijutsu meihōten* (Exhibition of Masterpieces of Japanese Buddhist Art) (Nara, 1995), no. 43, 75, 304. Also related are the wooden "Six Kannon," mentioned in my preface.

37 Donald F. McCallum, "A Standing Gilt-Bronze Buddha of the 'Boyish' Category in the Tokyo National Museum," *Orientations* (January 1990): 64–70.

38 Yoshimura Rei, "Butsuzō no chakui: 'sōgishi' to 'henzan' ni tsuite" (The Costume of the Buddha: Concerning the *sōgishi* and *henzan*), *Nantō bukkyō* 81 (2002): 93–120, and "Kodai no bikuzō no chakui to meishō: sōgishi, kansan, henzan, jikitotsu ni tsuite," 5–24.

39 Mizuno, *Asuka Buddhist Art*, plate 82.

40 I discuss the "quivering line" in my "Boyish Buddha," 69–70. Japanese scholars refer to this motif as *dakō kyokusen* ("serpentine line").

41 Designating images at Hōryūji is a problem, because there are so many. I have arbitrarily numbered a group of larger images in the Museum according to their order of appearance in the standard work *Nara rokudaiji taikan 2, Hōryūji* 2, and so will refer to these two as no. 1 and no. 2. Kannon no. 1 is illustrated on plates 22, 102–7; Kannon no. 2 on plates 23, 108–13. Excellent pho-

tographs and detailed analyses of the two can be found in an earlier source, Tazawa Yutaka et al., eds., *Hōryūji shiryō chōkoku hen 2, Hōryūji hōzō shō kondō zō* (Hōryūji Research Materials: Sculpture Series, vol. 2, Bronze Buddhist Statuettes in Hōryūji) (Tokyo: Iwanami Shoten, 1949), 27–32, English summary, 17–19, and plates 20–34. At the Hōryūji Museum the two figures are identified as the flanking bodhisattvas for the Kondō Yakushi, but this is not possible.

42 Other pairs of closely related images, such as the Kaizōji Kannon and Kannon no. 182 (plates 30 and 31), to be considered below, are also differentiated by a standing *kebutsu* in one and a sitting in the other. I am unable to account for this variation other than to suggest that it too indicates a certain freedom of choice for the sculptor(s).

43 Many of these observations are taken from a very long unpublished essay entitled "Studio Practice in Hakuhō Sculpture," wherein I provide detailed analyses of practically every aspect of the sculptures in question. Unfortunately, the vicissitudes of publication do not allow for so many pages of text and a very large number of illustrations, so here all I can offer is a summary of the evidence of relationships within this group of images.

44 A fourth, related example now in the British Museum will be discussed later.

45 In no. 159 the diadem band of the crown does not extend around to the back, as it does in no. 160 and the private collection image; significantly, the latter two have a prominent bow where the diadem band is tied at back. This sort of detail suggests that the two were designed by the same sculptor, working on the basis of the model employed for no. 159, but introducing a new element.

46 For a study of the development of archaic landscapes in China, see Michael Sullivan, *The Birth of Landscape Painting in China* (Berkeley and Los Angeles: University of California Press, 1962).

47 A further indication of a direct relationship between no. 160 and the private-collection figure is the presence of a *renniku* zone below the landscape and above the lotus petals, a motif absent in no. 159. *Renniku* refers to the stems of the seeds, indicated by vertical striations.

3. MIDDLE HAKUHŌ SCULPTURE

1 I have considered the trinity/triad issue in "The Buddhist Triad in Three Kingdoms Sculpture."

2 Yoshimura, "Butsuzō no chakui: 'sōgishi' to 'henzan' ni tsuite," 114–15.

3 See, for example, the jewel strings with tassels on Kannon no. 167 (fig. 8).

4 For a representative Korean example, see Yamato Bunkakan, ed., *Higashi Ajia no kondō butsu* (Gilt-bronze Images of East Asia) (Nara, 1999), no. 24. In addition to Korean examples, seated Buddha no. 146 has the right shoulder bared.

5　This quite unusual treatment of the belt with ends emerging from under the lower hem is also seen in a tiny Buddha image (18.2 cm) housed at Iōji in Niigata, so to that extent no. 147 is not unique; see *TNM, Kondō butsu, 1988,* no. 111: 215, 432; Matsubara and Tanabe, *Shō kondō butsu,* no. 33.

6　The crown is a sort of combination of the Asuka "three mountain" form and the more typical Hakuhō "three plaque" configuration.

7　Kannon no. 169, which I date to about the same time, is diametrically opposite to Kannon no. 170 in most respects. While the latter is generally suave and elegant, no. 169 has a rather awkward, even ungainly appearance, resulting in part from the very heavy, clunky jewelry. It seems inconceivable that both could have come out of the same studio, and one wonders what fills the gap between the two. Perhaps so many Hakuhō images have been lost that evidence is lacking.

8　Donald F. McCallum, "Sanzenji Kannon bosatsu zō to Hakuhō dōgyō chōkoku no mondai" (The Kannon of Sanzenji and the Problem of the Hakuhō "Boyish" Sculptures), *Bijutsu Forum* 21 (2001): 20–23.

9　In "Studio Practice in Hakuhō Sculpture," I make a very detailed comparison between this image and a Kannon at Hōonji; see *TNM, 1988,* no. 107: 210 and 430. The two are essentially identical in jewelry and drapery arrangements, but their figure styles are quite different. That of the Hōonji Kannon is later, indicating that its sculptor used certain elements of Kannon no. 176, but chose to employ a more up-to-date treatment of the body.

10　This scarf arrangement can be found, although rarely, in China and Korea. One example is a Northern Zhou or Sui Guanyin excavated near Xi'an, now in the Xi'an Institute of Cultural Relics and Archaeology; see Li Jian, ed., *The Glory of the Silk Road: Art from Ancient China* (Dayton: The Dayton Art Institute, 2003), 149–50, plate 70. Another is the Three Kingdoms (Paekche?) standing bodhisattva now in the Kyongju National Museum; see *Transmitting Divinity,* 212–13, plate 11. I propose, perhaps unwisely, that this motif is rare because it is fundamentally impractical, even illogical, with a long strip of fabric (the scarf) in front of the body with no apparent function other than decoration. Presumably the heavy jewelry on the Chinese, Korean, and Japanese images reflects tendencies developed during the Northern Zhou period and then propagated during the Sui.

11　The *hansetsu kuyo* pattern consists of a large half circle with a border of several small circles.

12　Despite my desire to avoid excessive detail, I cannot resist pointing out a particular of the diadem bands of both Kannon no. 176 and the Hōonji Kannon. At the sides, two small jewels can be seen between the bands, just above the ears. This motif can have no icono-

graphical significance and was probably employed to produce an attractive
transition from side plaque to ear. The
crucial point here is that the two artists
employed exactly the same very rare
element, thereby displaying the preci-
sion in copying deemed necessary or
desirable, even though the figure styles
of the two images are so different.

13 Why the artist of the Hōonji image
chose to utilize this strange combination of odd drapery and jewelry
elements is a hard question to answer.
Evidently, the combination was thought
to be either aesthetically pleasing or in
some way religiously effective, while the
figural style was not of much relevance.

14 I highlight "provincial" as this term
is often used as a dumping ground for
sculptures that are otherwise hard to
interpret.

15 Of course, icons seen as particularly
powerful and efficacious, although
lacking in beauty, are copied, but even
this is not the norm.

16 The Nittenji meditating bodhisattva is
another example of the work of a sculptor below the highest level of achievement, and although less idiosyncratic,
meditating bodhisattva no. 161 also has
strange features. For the Nittenji image
see *TNM, 1988*, no. 50: 139 and 409.

17 See Iwasa Mitsuhara, "Yachūji Miroku
bosatsu hankazō ni tsuite" (Concerning the Miroku Bodhisattva Image in
hanka Posture at Yachūji), in *Tokyo
Kokuritsu Hakubutsukan kiyō* (1991):
151–224, with 53 illustrations following

the text. This is possibly the longest
study devoted to a single Hakuhō
image, and new studies continue to
appear on a regular basis, primarily
concerned with historical context.

18 The initial appearance of the term *tennō*
is not of much relevance to this study,
but at least a few words should be said
about its historiographical significance.
Japanese scholars, especially the more
nationalistic, attempt to date the use of
tennō in place of the earlier *ōkimi* (great
king) as early as possible. At present
the appearance of the term *tennō* on
this pedestal would be, if accepted, its
first inscribed instance. This relates
to the inscribed date equivalent to the
year 666 on the pedestal, a matter to be
considered next.

19 All of the meditating bodhisattvas
studied in this book may be representations of Miroku (Sks. Maitreya),
although there is also a possibility that
some represent the youthful Shaka,
prior to his enlightenment; consequently, most scholars have adopted
the more cautious term "meditating
bodhisattva." A tile was excavated at
Kawaradera with the Miroku characters; see my *Four Great Temples* for a
discussion and illustration of this object
(184 and fig. 3.18).

20 My position on this matter has been
strengthened by the discovery at Asuka
Pond of a *mokkan* (small wooden tablet
used for writing) dating to approximately 676 with the characters for
tennō. Historical developments make

the Tenmu reign seem most likely for the appearance of the title. For the *mokkan,* see Asuka shiryōkan, ed., *Asuka ike iseki* (Remains from Asuka Pond) (Nara, 2000), 40–41, plate 24.

21 A recent study of the iconography of this image type is Eileen Hsiang-ling Hsu, "Visualization Meditation and the *Siwei* Icon in Chinese Buddhist Sculpture," *Artibus Asiae* 62, no. 1 (2002): 5–32.

22 Two examples of an imported image are meditating bodhisattva no. 158 and the Kanshōin meditating bodhisattva in Nagano; see "Earliest Buddhist Statues," 158–60, 175–76, for detailed presentation of these. Curiously, one Soga-Tori style image, bodhisattva no. 155, displays the characteristic placement of the horizontal right leg resting on the left knee, but the right hand, instead of touching the cheek, is held up in the *abhaya mudra.*

23 See note 16 for a reference for the Nittenji meditating bodhisattva.

24 *TNM, Kondō butsu* I, fig. 22, 373 illustrates some of the standard side-belt forms.

25 The Nittenji figure, an example of the first type, may have originally had some sort of base. The Yachūji Miroku has a round base.

26 Features that might be relevant include: similar general arrangement of the jewelry, especially the strings hanging from either side of the crown; the two strings of the necklace; and the long strings descending from the rosettes at either side of the necklace.

27 The most extensive analysis yet to appear is Asaki Shūhei, "Yamagata Enpukuji no dōzō Kannon bosatsu ritsuzō to sono 'kyōdai butsu' " (Bronze Standing Statue of Avalokitesvara in the Enpukuji of Yamagata Prefecture and its "Fellow Images"), *Bukkyō geijutsu* 175 (1987): 11–26. Also important is Kaneko Hiroaki's essay in *TNM, 1988,* 374–76. This exhibition provided an unparalled opportunity to study numerous examples of this category.

28 This is in contradistinction to pairs in the "Forty-eight Buddhist Deities" collection, including a meditating bodhisattva pair (nos. 163 and 164), and a standing bodhisattva pair (nos. 179 and 188), as well as Kannon nos. 1 and 2 in the Hōryūji Museum. Presumably, the members of these pairs have always existed in close proximity.

29 The English language requires a writer to specify "one" or "more than one," even where he intends no such specificity. Generally, I will use the singular, with the possibility of the plural implied, allowing for two distinct artists.

30 An image very similar to Kannon no. 182 is in the collection of the Nara National Museum; see *Transmitting Divinity,* no. 38: 266–67. That sculpture requires further study.

31 Considerable surface damage on the Kaizōji Kannon makes it difficult to discern certain features; for example, one cannot see if the thumb of the right hand actually passes under the string, as it does in Kannon no. 182

32 Careful inspection reveals some differences in the treatment of the lotus petals.

33 Ultimately, these designs refer back to the openwork elements that occur so frequently on the pedestals of Korean Buddhist statues. See Matsubara Saburō, *Kankoku kondō butsu kenkyū* (Tokyo: Yoshikawa Kōbunkan, 1985), plates 15, 64c, 80b. 90a, d, 91, 93, 94a, 95, 96, 99a, l03–5, 110–15, 131–33, 135c, 141d, 143, 152, 154, 156, 157, 161, 163, 164, 168b,c, 169, 170.

34 The Kongōchōji Kannon, Kōchi Prefecture, has a related pedestal and can be seen as a fifth member of the group; see *TNM, 1988*, no. 116: 220 and 433–34.

35 For detailed analysis, see *NRT* 8 (Kōfukuji 2) (Tokyo, 1970), plates 1–3, 15–17, 66–67. The author of that account, Nishikawa Shinji, has included a few new details in "Kōfukuji no buttō" (The Head of a Buddha at Kōfukuji), in *Nihon chōkokushi ronshū* (Tokyo: Chūō Kōron Bijutsu Shuppan, 1991), 45–50. A general account is Kuno Takeshi, "Kōfukuji no buttō" (The Head of a Buddha at Kōfukuji), in his *Hakuhō no bijutsu*, 65–80. A recent publication with superb illustrations and a good text by Kaneko Hiroaki is Tokyo Kokuritsu Hakubutsukan, ed., *Kōfukuji kokuhō buttō* (The National Treasure Head of a Buddha at Kōfukuji) (Tokyo, 2005).

36 There is a possibility that the flanking bodhisattvas of the present main icon incorporate, to some degree, remains of the Yamadadera triad, but this is a problem too complicated to deal with here.

37 For a full account of the historical circumstances, see *NRT* 8, 7–8.

38 The relevant sections of *Gyokuyō* are in *NRT* 8, 85–91.

39 Significantly, the twenty-fifth day of the third month is the exact date of the suicides of Yamada Ishikawa Maro and his family, obviously implying the dedication of the triad to the memory of these martrys. For detailed coverage of this history, see Nabunken, ed., *Yamato Yamadadera ato*, 2 vols. (Tokyo: Yoshikawa Kōbunkan, 2002).

40 Ōhashi Katsuaki has a lot to say about the importance of the Kōfukuji Buddha head for seventh-century sculpture; since his position differs substantially from mine, I propose to deal with the broader implications of this in chapter 5, including the relationship with the Yakushiji Yakushi Triad.

4. LATER HAKUHŌ SCULPTURE

1 Noma Seiroku, "Shijūhattai butsu chū no ichizōke ni tsuite" (On a Style of Buddhist Image Found among the "Forty-eight Buddhist Statues"), *Kokka* 800 (1958): 350-55.

2 Because of their close relationship, the Kongōji Kannon is discussed together with Kannon no. 180 in my "Studio Practice in Hakuhō Sculpture."

3 This motif occurs in a slightly different configuration in the Sanzenji Kannon

(plate 22) and also in meditating bodhi-sattva no. 163 (plate 37).

4 Similar incised patterns on the petals can be seen in the flanking bodhisatt-vas of the Tachibana Shrine Amida triad, to be discussed below, and on the Daisenji bodhisattva, considered in the previous chapter.

5 McCallum, "A Standing Kannon in the Tokyo National Museum," 7-25.

6 Ibid. Figs. 11-12 illustrate a Sui-dynasty image that in this respect, and others as well, is close to no. 178.

7 For a discussion of the shrine box, see Im Namsu, "Den Tachibana fujin nenji butsu zushi" (The Shrine of the So-called Lady Tachibana Devotional Image), in Ōhashi Katsuaki, ed., *Hōryūji bijutsu: ronsō no shiten* (The Art of Hōryūji: Perspectives on Controversies) (Tokyo: Gurafusha, 1998), 285-306.

8 *NS Jitō* 4 (689).3.20 records the gift of an Amida, Kannon, and Seishi from Silla. Many of the stylistic features of our Amida triad are closely related to Silla monuments, so it is even possible that the 689 gift had a specific impact on the developments seen in the Tachibana Amida triad. I deal with these issues in an unpublished article, "The Amida triad of the Tachibana shrine."

9 It will be recalled that the designation "no. 4" is one I devised; see n. 41, chap. 2.

10 In my longer, unpublished analysis of the image in "Studio Practice in Hakuhō Sculpture," I undertake a

detailed comparison with the closely related Kannon no. 172.

11 Most relevant, perhaps, is a comparison with the flanking bodhisattvas of the Yakushiji Yakushi triad. This monu-ment will be discussed later, but here it should be noted that I am attributing it to the Nara rather than Hakuhō period.

12 In pose and several other details of the Kakurinji Kannon can be compared with the Kannon and Seishi pair no. 185.

13 Another possible sash representation was noted above in the discussion of Kannon no. 178. One of the earliest unequivocal depictions of the sash is seen in the Genshōji Kannon, Iwate Prefecture; see *TNM 1988*, no. 146 (p. 260) and p. 446. For a detailed discus-sion of this image, see Tanaka Megumi, "Genshōji dōzō Kannon ritsuzō ni tsuite" (Concerning a Gilt-bronze Standing Kannon at Genshōji), *Iwate daigaku kyōiku gakubu kenkyū nenpō* 44.2 (1984): 1-12.

14 I discuss this motif in my previous article on Kannon no. 178.

15 Detailed discussion of the inscription will be found in *Asuka-Hakuhō zaimei kondō butsu*, no. 8, 159-60, 187-88, plates 103-8.

16 For a recent survey of Izumo, see Katsube Shō, *Izumo no kuni fudoki to kodai iseki* (The Topography of Izumo and Ancient Remains) (Tokyo: Yamak-awa Shuppansha, 2002), especially 74-75. For an English account, see Joan R. Piggott, "Sacral Kingship and Con-

federacy in Early Izumo," *Monumenta Nipponica* 44, no. 1 (1989): 45-74. (The Gakuenji Kannon is identified by date, but not named [72-73]. There it is called "a small statue.")

17 See "Silla Symposium," 26-30.

18 See Asanuma Takeshi, "Yumechigai Kannon zō" (The Yumechigai Kannon Image), in Ōhashi, *Hōryūji bijutsu ronsō*, 171-91; Machida Kōichi, "Shō Kannon bosatsu zō" (The Yumechigai Kannon Image), in *Jōdai chōkoku shi*, 285-91.

19 See *Asuka-Hakuhō zaimei kondō butsu*, no. 10, 162, 189-90, plates 117-24.

20 Matsuyama Tetsuo, "Jindaiji dōzō Shaka nyorai zō ni tsuite" (Concerning the Bronze Image of Shaka Buddha at Jindaiji), *Bukkyō geijutsu* 133 (1980), 63-70; Kaneko Hiroaki, "Nyorai zō" (Buddha Image [Jindaiji]), *Kokka* 1100 (1987). According to Kaneko, similarities with the so-called Kō Yakushi at Shin Yakushiji (stolen) might suggest that the two images emerged from the same Yamato studio. For the Kō Yakushi, see Paine and Soper, plate 11.

21 I have discussed this matter in detail in *The Four Great Temples*, especially in chapter 3, 177-82.

22 Also, in the Kantō region, is a large Buddha Head at Ryūkakuji, Chiba, that undoubtedly was the main icon of the temple, where Hakuhō-period tiles were found; see Mizuno Keisaburō, *Hōryūji kara Yakushiji e*, 214, plate 75.

5. CONCLUSION

1 Donald F. McCallum, "The Evolution of the Buddha and Bodhisattva Figures in Japanese Sculpture of the Ninth and Tenth Centuries," PhD diss., New York University, 1973.

2 A brief discussion of these topics will be found in Donald F. McCallum, "Heian Sculpture at the Tokyo National Museum: A Review Article," Part 1, *Artibus Asiae* 35, no. 3 (1973): 278–92, especially 283–92.

3 Although beyond the scope of the present study, perhaps it is worth pointing out that the principal style of the eleventh century, the beautiful Jōchō lineage, tended toward schematic, formulaic expression during the twelfth century; see Donald F. McCallum, "Heian Sculpture at the Tokyo National Museum: A Review Article," Part 2, *Artibus Asiae* 36, no. 1/2 (1974): 147–60, particularly 150–53, 158–60.

4 In McCallum, "Tori-busshi and the Production of Buddhist Icons in Asuka-period Japan," 34-37, I analyzed in some depth the status of Tori, concluding that he was not a "hands-on" sculptor, but rather a high-ranking retainer of the powerful Soga clan, who exercised a supervisory role over the principal studio during the Asuka period.

5 Considerable information is available for the production processes that went into the making of roof tiles for temples; see Uehara Mahito, *Kawara o yomu* (Learning from Roof Tiles) (Tokyo: Kōdansha,

1997), 132–41, and Mori Ikuo, *Kawara* (Roof Tiles) (Tokyo: Hōsei Daigaku Shuppankyoku, 2001), 133–65.

6   Gina Barnes, "Role of the *Be* in State Formation," in *Production, Exchange and Complex Societies,* ed. E. Brumfiel and T. Earle (Cambridge: Cambridge University Press, 1987), 86–101.

7   For good examples, see the backs of the Daisenji bodhisattva (plate 115) and bodhisattva no. 190 (plate 114) illustrated in TNM, *Kondō butsu.*

8   Numerous books deal with the topic of fakes. I recommend Kenneth Lapatin, *Mysteries of the Snake Goddess: Art, Desire, and the Forging of History* (Cambridge, MA: Da Capo Press, 2002). Despite the somewhat sensationalist title, this is a scholarly book dealing with a famous sculpture in the Museum of Fine Arts, Boston, as well as with a number of other images, all of which have been attributed to the Minoan culture. Lapatin has serious reservations about these figures and suggests persuasively that most of them were made for the art market.

9   The copy is illustrated in National Palace Museum, Taiwan, *The Crucible of Compassion and Wisdom: Special Exhibition Catalog of the Buddhist Bronzes from the Nitta Group Collection at the National Palace Museum* (Taipei, 1987), plate 142. It is rumored that the Nitta collection was offered to Japanese museums, but none were willing to take it because of the number of spurious images. Many of the sculptures come from cultures about which I have no expertise, but I assume that at least some of the pieces must be genuine. Of the thirty or so Japanese images, practically all seem to me to be doubtful. (Readers may be interested to learn that a gilt-bronze meditating bodhisattva attributed to the Korean Three Kingdoms period, recently purchased by the Metropolitan Museum of Art, New York, is illustrated on plate 128.)

10 As noted in chapter 3, the same arrangement of belt ends is also seen in the tiny Buddha image (18.2 cm) housed at Iōji in Niigata, cited there in the discussion of no. 147. A related image is in a private collection, Tokyo; see Kuno Takeshi, *Zoku Nihon no chōkoku,* 5: *Chūgoku* (Continuation, Japanese Sculpture: Chūgoku [Region]) (Tokyo: Bijutsu Shuppansha, 1956), 44, plate 5; also illustrated in Matsubara and Tanabe, *Shō kondō butsu,* no. 32 and p. 340. This image requires further study.

11 William Watson, "*Verb. Sap.* on Asuka Bronze or, Who Would Be a Museum Curator," *Artibus Asiae* 53, no. 1–2 (1993): 89–97. This article has many illustrations.

12 Mark Jones, ed., *Fake? The Art of Deception* (Berkeley and Los Angeles: University of California Press, 1990), 299–301.

13 Yomiuri Shimbunsha, ed., *Dai Tōyō bijutsuten* (Great Oriental Art Exhibition) (Kyoto: Kyotoshi Bijutsukan, 1977), no. 104, 52.

14 Raymond Johnes, *Japanese Art* (London: Spring Books, 1971), plate 2.

15 Since I am speculating here, perhaps worthy of mention is the image's appearance in Kuno, *Kodai shō kondō butsu*, with full photographic coverage on pages 172–73. Possibly Kuno was involved at some stage in the transaction.

16 In the previously mentioned unpublished "Studio Practice in Hakuhō Sculpture," I provide a very detailed exegesis of all the pertinent questions.

17 Langdon Warner, *Japanese Sculpture of the Suiko Period* (New Haven: Yale University Press, 1923), plate 76 for the standing bodhisattva. A very doubtful meditating bodhisattva is illustrated on plate 59.

18 By far the most puzzling image in the Geidai collection is another standing bodhisattva that is perhaps the most complex of all known small gilt-bronze image; see Matsubara and Tanabe, *Shō kondō butsu*, no. 66, for excellent illustrations. A comprehensive analysis of this sculpture is Maria del Rosario ("Chari") Pradel's master's thesis, "A Standing Bodhisattva of the Tokyo University of Fine Arts" (Dept. of Art History, UCLA, 1990).

19 All four can be seen in postage-stamp-size illustrations in TNM, *Kondō butsu* vol. 1, 534, figs. 40–43. The Rakanji figure is illustrated in color in Nara Kokuritsu Hakubutsukan, ed., *Tokubetsuten: Bosatsu* (Special Exhibition: the Bodhisattva) (Nara, 1987), 198–99 and plate 57. Somewhat surprisingly, a large number of the Nitta Collection sculp-

tures, mentioned above, were shown in this exhibition (nos. 17, 29, 31, 32, 48–50, 58, 60, 65, and 102).

20 Enshrinement in a temple is not a total guarantee of authenticity, although by and large it is a reliable indicator.

21 Tokyo National Museum, ed., *Nachi kyōzuka ihō* (Recovered Treasures from the Nachi Sutra Mound) (Tokyo: Tokyo Bijutsu, 1985), figs. 96.1–4.

22 Ibid, 231. Although the names of several sculpture specialists at the museum are listed in the preface, individual entries are not signed, and so one cannot be sure who wrote this entry. Hasedera in Shiga Prefecture houses what is claimed to be a Kamakura-period archaistic copy of a seventh-century Shō Kannon; see Shiga Kenritsu Biwako Bunkakan, ed., *Tokubetsuten: Kosai no shaji* (Special Exhibition: Shrines and Temples on the West Side of the Lake) (Shiga, 1985), no. 38.

23 *NRT* 8, *Kōfukuji* II, fig. 3 (after p. 24); cited on 55 and in note 11 (p. 57). Better illustrations are in Kuno, *Kodai shō kondō butsu*, plate 16, figs. 120 a,b,c (p. 185), and in Yamato Bunkakan, ed., *Higashi Ajia no kondō butsu*, 140 and no. 56. See also Murata Seiko, *Shō kondō butsu no miryoku: Chūgoku, Kan hantō, Nihon* (The Charm of Small Gilt-bronze Images: China, the Korean Peninsula, and Japan) (Tokyo: Ribun Shuppan, 2004), 189, 243, and plate 36.

24 The standard source for Japanese Buddhist sculpture in foreign collections, *Zaigai Nihon no shihō*, vol. 8, *Chōkoku*

(Hidden Treasures Abroad, vol. 8, Sculpture) (Tokyo: Mainichi Shinbun, 1980), contains no illustrations of early gilt-bronze sculptures. I leave it to the reader to suppose the import of this omission.

25 Ōhashi, "Hakuhō chōkoku ron," 37–56. I have presented a preliminary critique of this article in McCallum, "Sanzenji Kannon bosatsu zō to Hakuhō dōgyō chōkoku no mondai," 20–23.

26 To be fair, in his "Chokuganji to kokka kanji no zōei soshiki" (Construction Organization for Imperially Vowed Temples and Nationally Administered Temples), *Bukkyō geijutsu* 222 (1996): 41–61, Ōhashi provides two illustrations, one each of the faces of the Kōfukuji Buddha head and the Yakushiji Yakushi Buddha, the images most directly related to his argument.

27 In this old system, Suiko is equivalent to my Asuka, Tenji to Hakuhō, and Tenpyō to Nara. Clearly, it was not a very precise system.

28 Mizuno, "Asuka-Hakuhō butsu no keifu," 51.

29 Ōhashi cites Matsubara Saburō, "Shiragi butsu ni okeru Tō yoshiki no juyō: futatsu no mondai ni tsuite" (Integration of the Tang Style into Buddhist Images of the Kingdom of Silla: On the Two Main Problems), *Bukkyō geijutsu* 83 (1972), 41–52; and Mōri Hisashi, "Hakuhō chōkoku no Shiragi-teki yōso," in Tamura and Hong, *Shiragi to Asuka-Hakuhō bukkyō*, 113–45. Both of these authors published numerous

other studies demonstrating the importance of the Korean peninsula for an understanding of Asuka and Hakuhō sculpture, as did Kuno Takeshi.

30 Ōhashi, "Hakuhō chōkoku ron," 44.

31 Ōhashi Katsuaki, "Hakuhō butsu to shō Tō bunka" (Hakuhō Sculpture and Early Tang Culture), *Rekishi kōron* 116 (1985): 39–46, offers a general account of his "Period I" and "Period II."

32 McCallum, *The Four Great Temples*, chap. 2.

33 Ōhashi Katsuaki, "Kawaradera no zōbutsu to Hakuhō chōkoku no jōgen ni tsuite" (Production of Buddhist Sculpture at Kawaradera and the Earliest Date of Buddhist Images Made in the Hakuhō Era), *Bukkyo geijutsu* 128 (1980): 11–25.

34 In addition to "Chokuganji to kokka kanji no zōei soshiki," cited in n. 26, these issues are also explored in "Ōdera ko" (A Theory on the 'Great Temples'), *Waseda Daigaku Daigakuin Bungaku Kenkyūka Kiyō* 41 (1997): 105–21.

35 McCallum, "Silla Symposium," 28–29.

36 Warner, *Japanese Sculpture of the Suiko Period*. See Alexander C. Soper, "Notes on Hōryūji and the Sculpture of the 'Suikō Period'," *Art Bulletin* 33, no. 2 (1951): 77–94, for a crushingly harsh, albeit generally accurate, assessment of Warner's results. He is similarly critical of Karl With's *Buddhistische Plastik in Japan* (Vienna: Kunstverlag Anton Ashroll and Co., 1920), although in fairness to his predecessors it must be said that Professor Soper makes a few

errors himself, as I assume I myself am making!

37 Langdon Warner, *The Craft of the Japanese Sculptor* (New York: McFarlane, Warde, McFarlane, and Japan Society of New York, 1936), 13–16, plates 13–15.

38 Robert T. Paine and Alexander C. Soper, *The Art and Architecture of Japan* (Harmondsworth and Baltimore: Penguin Books, 1955); discussion, 17–18, plates 8–9.

39 William Watson, *Sculpture of Japan; From the Fifth to the Fifteenth Century* (New York: Viking, 1959), 22, plate 21.

40 Penelope Mason, *History of Japanese Art* (New York: Prentice Hall, 1993).

41 Actually, inaccuracies abound in Mason, *History of Japanese Art*. The Hōryūji Kondō Yakushi is dated to "1st half 7th century" in the caption, but in the text (43–44, 55) Mason correctly opts for a Hakuhō date; similarly, the Chūgūji Miroku is labeled "7th century" (plates 66–67), but the text (p. 54) narrows that down to "the statue is clearly a work of the Hakuhō period."

42 Penelope Mason, *History of Japanese Art*, 2d ed., revised by Donald Dinwiddie (Upper Saddle River, N.J.: Prentice Hall, 2005).

43 Joan Stanley-Baker, *Japanese Art* (London: Thames and Hudson, 2000), 40–44.

44 Donald F. McCallum, *Zenkōji and Its Icon: A Study in Medieval Japanese Religious Art* (Princeton: Princeton University Press, 1994), chap. 7, "Later Kamakura Copies of the Zenkōji Amida Triad," 125–54. Although not specifically relevant to the present study, two recent exhibition catalogues present excellent illustrations and new data on the Zenkōji tradition: Nagano ken Shinano bijutsukan, ed., *Zenkōji gokaicho kinen: "Inori" no katachi, Zenkōji shinko ten* (Anniversary of the Zenkōji *gokaicho*: Forms of "worship," Zenkōji belief) (Nagano, 2009); and Nagano kenritsu rekishikan, ed., *Kaikan 15 shunen shunki kikaku ten: Zenkōji shinko, ruten to henreki no kange* (Fifteenth Anniversary Special Exhibition: Zenkōji Belief: Teachings of Itinerancy) (Nagano, 2009).

45 See McCallum, *Zenkōji and Its Icon*, "A Group of Undated Images," 146–49, plates 34–39.

46 Ibid., 179–94.

47 See McCallum, *The Four Great Temples*, chap. 4, "Yakushiji," for information and citations relevant to the next three paragraphs.

48 Presumably "early 8th century" refers to the years 700–710, since the authors who use it almost invariably attribute the Yakushi triad to Hakuhō.

49 The situation with secular buildings is different, as many of the structures of the Fujiwarakyō palace were deconstructed, moved to the new site, and reconstructed there. Because this seems not to have happened with temples, it is possible that "transfer" in their cases may refer to some sort of transfer of charter rather than to a physical move.

50 For recent studies of the Golden Hall

Yakushi triad, see Im Namsu, "Kondō Yakushi sanzon zō" (The Yakushi Triad of the Golden Hall) in Ōhashi Katsuaki, ed., *Yakushiji sensanbyakunen no seika* (The Flowering of Yakushiji through Thirteen Hundred Years) (Tokyo: Ribun Shuppan, 2000), 89–110; and Shimono Akiko, "Kondō Yakushi nyorai zō; daiza" (The Pedestal of the Yakushi Buddha), ibid., 111–30. Scholars today no longer accept Sekino's Hakuhō date for the Lecture Hall Yakushi triad; see Koizumi Yoshihide, "Kōdō Yakushi sanzon zō," (The Yakushi triad in the Lecture Hall), ibid., 148–85; excellent colorplates can be found in Nara Kokuritsu Hakubutsukan, ed., *Tenpyō* (Nara, 1998), 229, plate 68 (pp. 80–81).

51 Further discussion of the dating of the Heijōkyō Yakushiji Yakushi triad will be found in McCallum, *The Four Great Temples*, 232–34.

52 Meyer Schapiro, *The Language of Forms: Lectures on Insular Manuscript Art* (New York: The Pierpont Morgan Library, 2005).

53 "Style" originally appeared in A. L. Kroeber, ed., *Anthropology Today: An Encyclopedic Inventory* (Chicago: University of Chicago Press, 1953), 287–312, and has been frequently anthologized, but is currently most readily available in Meyer Schapiro, "Style (with bibliography)," in *Selected Papers, Theory and Philosophy of Art: Style, Artist, and Society* (New York: George Braziller, 1994), 51–102.

54 This effort was facilitated by one of Schapiro's students, Jane E. Rosenthal. See her "Introduction" to Schapiro, *Language of Forms*, 1–5, for an informative account of the process whereby the lectures were transformed into a book.

55 I say "relatively" here because the Lion symbol is usually that of St. Mark. This variation, however, does not affect the present discussion.

56 I am not the first to compare these manuscript illuminations with totally unrelated Asian art; see Robert W. Bagley, "Meaning and Explanation," *Archives of Asian Art* 46 (1993): 6–26, where pages from the *Book of Kells*, the *Lindisfarne Gospels*, and the *Gospels of St. Chad* are illustrated in full color prior to a discussion of Shang and Zhou bronze vessels. Bagley's discussion is related to Max Loehr's famous analysis of the meaning, or lack thereof, of Shang imagery. Although I have never been convinced by Loehr's conclusions, I certainly sympathize with his intense visual analysis of the bronzes.

57 Schapiro's concluding comments are worth quoting in full: "In this lecture I have tried to show that Insular book painting is far from being an art of ornament in which figures are submitted to rigorous rules of geometrical construction and follow the principles of repetition and symmetry characteristic of other types of ornament. Rather, the drawing of the figures and accompanying details, such as those in the frames, have qualities that we associate with reality, nature, and the empirical

world: articulation, organic continuity, and subdivision, response of objects to their surroundings—the interplay of neighboring parts. (In these respects, this art hardly warrants Ruskin's contemptuous judgement.)" See Schapiro, *Language of Forms,* 27.

58 For the production of Buddhist sculptures, see Nedachi Kensuke, "Busshi no sekai" (The World of Sculptors), in *Semon ginō to gijutsu* (Specialized Skills and Techniques), vol. 5 *of Rettō no kodaishi: hito, mono, koto* (Ancient History of the [Japanese] Archipelago: People, Things, Circumstances), ed. Uehara Mahito et al. (Tokyo: Iwanami Shoten, 2006), 133–65. Beyond the topic of sculpture, this volume offers excellent up-to-date accounts of various specializations such as painting, stonework, metalwork, architecture, etc.

GLOSSARY

Abe　阿部

Asuka　飛鳥

Asukadera　飛鳥寺

bakufu　幕府

bussha　仏舎

butsuden　仏殿

chihō gōzoku　地方豪族

Chūgūji　中宮寺

Daikandaiji　代官大寺

Daisenji　大山寺

dakō kyokusen　蛇行曲線

dōgan　童顔

dōgyō　童形

Fujiwarakyō　藤原京

Fukuoka Art Museum　福岡美術館

Fusō ryakki　扶桑略記

Gakkō　月光

Gakuenji　鰐淵寺

Genmei　元明

gōzoku　豪族

Gyokuyō　玉葉

Hakuchi　白雉

Hakuhō　白鳳

hansetsu kuyō　半截九曜

Hasedera　長谷寺

Heian　平安

Heijōkyō　平城京

henzan　偏衫

Hōonji　報恩寺

Hōrinji　法輪寺

Hōryūji　法隆寺

Ichijōji　一乗寺

Idemitsu　出光

ie goto　家毎

Ienaga Saburō　家永三郎

Izumo fudoki　出雲風土記

Jindaiji　深大寺

Jitō　持統

jōhaku　条帛

jōroku　丈六

Kaizōji　海蔵寺

Kakurinji　鶴林寺

Kamakura　鎌倉

Kannon　観音

Kanshinji　観心寺

Karu no miko　軽皇子

Kawaradera　川原寺

kebutsu　化仏

kikajin　帰化人

Kim Lina　金理那

Kōfukuji　興福寺

Koguryo　高句麗

kokka bukkyō　国家仏教

Kōmyōji　光明寺

Kongōji　金剛寺

Kōtoku　孝徳

Kō Yakushi　香薬師

Kudara Kannon　百済観音

Kudara Ōdera　百済大寺

Kujō Kanezane　九条兼実

kuniguni　諸国

Kuno Takeshi　久野健

Kuratsukuri be　鞍作部

Kura Yamada Ishikawa Maro
　　倉山田石川麻呂

Kusakabe　草部

Liang　梁

maetsukimi　公卿

Matsuura Masaaki　松浦正昭

Mei no iratsume　姪娘

Miroku　弥勒

Mizuno Seiichi　水野清一

Monmu　文武

Motoori Norinaga　本居宣長

Nachi　那智

Nara　奈良

Nezu bijutsukan　根津美術館

Nihon no bijutsu　日本の美術

Nihon ryōiki　日本霊異記

Nihon shoki　日本書紀

Ōama no ōji　大海人皇子

Ōhashi Katsuaki　大橋一章

Ōtomo　大伴

ōtoneri　大舎人

Ōtsu　大津

Paekche　百済

Qi　斉

Rakanji　羅漢寺

Saimei　斉明

Sanzenji　山千寺

Seishi　勢至

Sekino Tadashi　関野貞

senbutsu　塼仏

Shaka　釈迦

Shang　商

Silla　新羅

Shitennō　四天王

shizoku bukkyō　氏族仏教

shō kondō butsu　小金銅仏

Shōtoku　聖徳

Soga　蘇我

　　Himuka　日向

　　Iname　稲目

　　Iruka　入鹿

　　Umako　馬子

sōgishi　僧祇支

Song, King　聖王

Suiko　推古

Sushun　崇峻

Tachibana Shrine　橘厨子

Taika kaishin　大化改新

Taimadera　当麻寺

Taira no Shigemori　平重盛

Takara　宝

Takechi Ōdera　高市大寺

Tamura Enchō　田村圓澄

Tenji　天智

Tenmu　天武

tennō　天皇

Tenpyō　天平

toraijin　渡来人

Tori busshi　鳥仏師

Uehara Shōichi　上原昭一

ujidera　氏寺

Uno　鸕

Wakayamatobe no Omi Tokotari
　　若倭部臣徳太理

Wei　魏

Yachūji　野中寺

Yakushiji　薬師寺

Yamadaden　山田殿

Yamadadera　山田寺

Yumechigai Kannon　夢違観音

Yumedono Kannon　夢殿観音

Yoshida Kazuhiko　吉田一彦

Yoshimura Rei　吉村怜

Zen　禅

Zenkōji　善光寺

Zhou　周

zushi　厨子

Chen, dynasty, 5

chihō gōzoku, 12

Chinese sculpture, 4–5

chokuganji, 87

chronology, 6, 23, 38, 60, 82, 85, 91. *See also* cyclical characters

Chūgūji Miroku, 10

"closely related images," 54–57

commissions, 87, 90. *See also* patrons

"complex variables," 49, 50

copies, 4, 54, 83, 85

costume: of bodhisattva, 7, 54, 60; of Buddha, 25, 29, 40, 41, 78; of Kannon, 21, 28, 41, 43, 44, 51, 70, 73, 77; of meditating bodhisattva, 34, 46, 49. *See also* belt; crown; necklace; ribbons; tassel

crown, 7, 19, 34, 44, 49, 51, 77, 84; with *kebutsu,* 17, 55; mountain-shaped, 7, 107n6; of Seishi, 25; three-plaque, 17, 21, 65; three-plaque with *kebutsu,* 25, 70, 72, 74, 76

cyclical characters, 17, 47, 101n8

Daikandaiji, 11

Daisenji bodhisattva, 54–57, **55**

dhoti, 7, 60. *See also* skirt (*kun*)

diadem bands, 44, 70

dōgan, 28

dōgyō, 28

drapery elements, bodhisattva. See *dhoti; henzan;* sash (*jōhaku*); scarf (*tenne*); skirt (*kun*)

earrings, 65

edict: of 594, 12; of 680, 11; of 685, 11–14; of 691, 14, 100n48

elite: provincial, 12; style, 28, 77, 78, 104n32, 108n14; studio, 46; temples, 13

eyebrows, 70, 73

eyelids, 34

face. *See* eyebrows; eyelids

fakes, 82–84, 113n9

"Forty-eight Buddhist Deities," xiii, 6, 17, 23, 54, 57, 99n45. *See also* bodhisattva, meditating; bodhisattva, standing; Buddha

Four Great Temples, 11, 87, 90, 91. *See also* Asukadera; Fujiwarakyō Yakushiji; Kawaradera; Kudara Ōdera

Fujiwarakyō, 11

Fujiwarakyō Yakushiji, 91

Fukuoka Art Museum meditating bodhisattva, 47–50, **48**

Fusō ryakki, 12

Gakkō bodhisattva, 88

Gakuenji Kannon, 70, 73–75, **74**, 87, 88

"gap theory," 4–5

Genmei, Empress, 14

gōzoku, 12

Gyokuyō, 57

hair, 34, 43, 73, 77. *See also* topknot

Hakuchi, ix, x

Hakuhō, defined, ix. *See also* historiography

hansetsu kuyō, 44, 47, 107n11

Harris, Victor, 83, 84

Hasedera Kannon, 76, **76**, 77

Heijōkyō, 14, 16, 91

Heijōkyō Yakushiji, 91, 92

henzan, 25, 30, 40, 68

hibutsu, 89

historiography: of Hakuhō period, 10, 15–17; Ōhashi's work on, 85–86; of Taika

Kōfukuji: Buddha head, 23, **58**, 59, 78, 87, 88, 91; East Golden Hall, 57
Kōfukuji standing bodhisattva, 84, 85
Koguryo, 5, 10
Kōgyoku, Empress, 10
Kōkan Shiren, 12
kokka bukkyō, 12
Kōmyō, Empress, 66
Kongōji Kannon, 63–65, **64**
Kōryūji Miroku, 8
Kōtoku, Emperor, 10
Kudara Kannon, 8, 30, 87
Kudara Ōdera, 10, 11, 87
Kujō Kanezane, 57
kuniguni, 11, 12
Kuno Takeshi, xiii, 13, 14, 30, 40, 114n15
Kura Yamada Ishikawa Maro, 23, 59
Kuratsukuri be, 6
Kusakabe, Prince, 14

Levine, Gregory, x
Liang dynasty, 4

maetsukimi, 14
Mason, Penelope, 88
Matsubara Saburō, 86
Matsuura Masaaki, ix
meditating bodhisattvas. *See* bodhisattvas, meditating

Mei no iratsume, 14
methodology of book, 3, 4, 54
Miroku: as bodhisattva, x, 8, 47; as Buddha, x; identification of, 49, 108n19
Mizuno Seiichi, 16, 86, 87
Monmu, Emperor, 14
Mōri Hisashi, 86
Motoori Norinaga, 12

Nachi standing bodhisattva, 84, 85
Naka, Prince, 10, 11
Naniwa, 10, 11
necklace: of Kannon, 25, 41, 44, 65, 73, 76; of meditating bodhisattva, 47, 49; pectoral, 17; of standing bodhisattva, 7
Nezu Museum halo, 21, 23, 103n20
Nihon no bijutsu, ix
Nihon reiiki, 13
Nihon shoki, ix, 5, 10, 14, 91
Nittenji meditating bodhisattva, 49, 108n16, 109n25
Northern Qi dynasty. *See* Qi, Northern, dynasty
Northern Zhou dynasty. *See* Zhou, Northern, dynasty

Ōama, Prince, 11
Ōhashi Kazuaki, 85–87, 115n26
Ōkimi, 23
Ōtomo, Prince 14
ōtoneri, 14
Ōtsu, 11

Paekche, 5, 10
Paine, Robert, 88
patrons, 4, 47, 80–82, 90
pedestals: for bodhisattvas, 21, 28, 34, 44, 46, 51, 52, 65, 70, 74; for Buddhas, 30; for "closely related images," 56, 57; inscriptions on, 47, 49, 73; for meditating bodhisattvas, 34, 35, 46, 47; octagonal, 47, 49, 51, 56, 74; spurious examples of, 84, 85; for triads, 23, 25–27, 67, 69
periodization, 16, 86
prototypes, Chinese and Korean, x, 4, 5, 7, 49, 80; of bodhisattvas, 18, 33; of Bud-